Improving Service-Learning Practice

Research on Models to Enhance Impacts

A Volume in
Advances in Service-Learning Research

Improving Service-Learning Practice

Research on Models to Enhance Impacts

Edited by

Susan Root
RMC Research Corporation

Jane Callahan
Providence College

Shelley H. Billig
RMC Research Corporation

INFORMATION AGE
PUBLISHING

Greenwich, Connecticut • www.infoagepub.com

Library of Congress Cataloging-in-Publication Data

Improving service-learning practice : research on models to enhance impacts
/ edited by Susan Root, Jane Callahan, Shelley H. Billig.
    p. cm. – (Advances in sevice-learning research)
  Includes bibliographical references and index.
  ISBN 1-59311-457-5 (pbk.) – ISBN 1-59311-458-3
  1. Student service–Congresses. 2. Student service–Research–Congresses.
I. Root, Susan, 1948- II. Callahan, Jane. III. Billig, Shelley. IV. Advances
in service-learning
  LC220.5.R66 2005
  361.3'7–dc22
                                                                    2005026058

Printed in the United States of America

ACKNOWLEDGMENTS

We gratefully acknowledge the painstaking work of our editor, Mary Ann Strassner, and all of the scholars who wrote for this book and presented at the 4th Annual International K–H Service-Learning Research Conference. This book could not have been finished without the generous funding of the W.K. Kellogg Foundation. Special thanks to the continuing support of Chris Kwak, Robert Long, and Anne Petersen.

CONTENTS

Section III
Methodological Models and Issues

Section IV
Future Directions

INTRODUCTION

Over the past decade, research in service-learning in P–12 schools, higher education, and teacher education has come of age. A field initially limited to program evaluations and examination of student impacts has expanded to include studies of factors that influence the quality of service-learning, impacts on faculty and communities, and institutionalization in various settings. In addition, researchers are increasingly developing comprehensive models that incorporate combinations of these variables and provide information about the ways in which service-learning is implemented, monitored, and sustained at all levels of schooling.

This fifth book in the *Advances in Service-Learning Research* series continues to expand the discussion of service-learning research and practice. The chapters were selected through a refereed, blind-review process from papers presented at the 4th Annual International K–H Service-Learning Research Conference held October 2004 in Greenville, South Carolina. The chapters focus on topics that address a variety of issues in higher education and teacher education and are organized into four sections.

The first section includes studies of service-learning in teacher education and begins with a chapter by Root that revisits studies carried out by the National Service-Learning and Teacher Education Partnership during its 6-year history. These studies addressed questions about the status of service-learning in teacher education, factors that affected adoption, principles of good practice, and impacts of service-learning on teacher candidates, and sets the stage for future research directions. In the second chapter, Anderson and Callahan use a modified version of Furco's (1999)

Improving Service-Learning Practice: Research on Models to Enhance Impacts, pages ix–xii
Copyright © 2005 by Information Age Publishing

Self-Assessment Rubric for the Institutionalization of Service-Learning in Higher Education to examine the adoption of service-learning in teacher education programs and variables that affect success. Their study concludes that as in the rest of higher education, there are critical elements that promote adoption, including an influential champion and an institutional mission that is committed to working with the community. In chapter 3, Gonsier-Gerdin and Royce-Davis examine the ways in which service-learning strengthened the critical teaching competencies of advocacy and leadership in two collaboratively taught special education courses. They determine that these opportunities to reach the community in less traditionally defined ways resulted in significant student and instructor outcomes as well as reciprocal benefits to a broader community membership. The authors proceed to suggest that service-learning projects and processes may serve as productive vehicles for the teaching and learning of advocacy and leadership dispositions, knowledge, and skills in support of social justice for new teachers.

Section II of the volume focuses on implementation and suggests new links between theory and practice that can inform and improve service-learning. In chapter 4, Moely and Miron use Morton's (1995) paradigms of service to assess students' orientations toward service and preferences for different types of community service activities. Their study suggests that students showed a strong and consistent preference for the Charity orientation and that they appear to be more comfortable with the activities involved in "helping" than with activities that attempt societal change. In chapter 5, Schnitzer suggests that a motivational theory of work environments can be used to diagnose the quality of service placements and links the theory to indicators utilized by Eyler and Giles (1999). The chapter closes by suggesting that service-learning project design, with an eye to skill variety, task identity, task significance, autonomy, and feedback, could lead to greater learning for students. Concluding this section, Billig, Root, and Jesse discuss their study of the impacts of K–12 service-learning program quality on civic development and school engagement. Examining program components such as reflection, linkage to standards, direct contact with those being served, and the role of the teacher, they provide results that are worthy of consideration, but suggest that more data are needed to understand how impact can be maximized.

Section III includes discussions of a variety of new research models for examining complex issues in service-learning. The section begins with chapter 7 in which Welch, Miller, and Davies describe a new approach to studying civic engagement and service-learning involving triangulation between theoretical and practitioner perspectives. The authors present an illustration of how this method was employed in the analysis of civic engagement skills and demonstrate some clear discrepancies in terms of how specific groups view skills for civic education or engagement. They go on to present some implications of these findings and suggest that scholars and instructors carefully consider not only what is taught in terms of civic engagement, but how it is taught. Chapter 8 provides a rationale for the use of randomized control field trials (RCFT) in service-learning research.. Aronson and colleagues suggest that service-learning research can be appreciably enhanced by creating theoretical models of service-learning and evaluating them using rigorous methods. Challenges associated with conducting RCFTs, as well as strategies for overcoming those challenges are presented. The focus of chapter 9 is on a civic engagement audit system and the information it can provide. The Shumers describe a project that conceptualized and measured civic connections at a large, urban university. They developed a survey, audit, and taxonomy of terms for analyzing the relationships between an institution of higher education and its faculty, staff, students, and community that offer new promise in efforts to define the "engaged" university. In chapter 10, the final chapter in this section, Fitch uses a mixed methods approach of both quantitative and qualitative measures based on "contact theory" to examine the intercultural service-learning experiences of college students. The discussion provides both strengths and limitations of this method and suggests ways that experiences might be made more significant. Implications for best practices for designing intercultural service-learning experiences are suggested.

The volume closes with Chapter 11 in which authors Billig, Root, and Callahan address the prospect of forming a professional association for the service-learning research community. The etiology of the idea, benefits of forming an association, the need for incorporation into a nonprofit organization, ways to get started, board composition and regeneration plan, bylaws and a code of ethics, and a strategic plan for growth and sustainability are discussed. The chapter concludes with a call to action.

Although more established than it was a decade ago, service-learning continues to be a peripheral element in discussions of education reform and in many P–12, postsecondary, and teacher education programs. This fifth volume in the *Advances* series presents new paradigms that can lead practitioners to create more powerful experiences, and lead researchers to a better understanding of the relationships between service-learning, participants, context, and outcomes. If implemented, the models in this volume can do much to help us better understand the essence of service-learning and add to its value to education and the development of engaged citizens.

REFERENCES

Eyler, J., & Giles, D. (1999). *Where's the learning in service-learning*, San Francisco: Jossey-Bass.

Furco, A. (1999). *Self-assessment rubric for the institutionalization of service-learning in higher education.* Berkeley, CA: University of California, Berkeley.

Morton, K. (1995). The irony of service: Charity, Project Development, and social change in service learning. *Michigan Journal of Community Service Learning, 2,* 19–32.

Section I

TEACHER EDUCATION MODELS, IMPACTS, AND ISSUES

CHAPTER 1

THE NATIONAL SERVICE-LEARNING IN TEACHER EDUCATION PARTNERSHIP

A Research Retrospective

Susan Root

ABSTRACT

The National Service-Learning in Teacher Education Partnership (NSLTEP) was a 6-year collaborative project funded by the Corporation for National and Community Service to advance the integration of service-learning in teacher preparation. Throughout NSLTEP's history, expanding the knowledge base on service-learning in teacher education was a vital goal. This chapter reports on the two strands of research conducted as part of the collaborative: studies of practice (e.g., the current status of service-learning, challenges associated with implementation, and good practice) and studies of impacts (e.g., impacts on preservice teacher dispositions, prosocial reasoning, and beliefs about teaching and learning).

Improving Service-Learning Practice: Research on Models to Enhance Impacts, pages 3–16

INTRODUCTION

In the 1990s, data began to accumulate from a few studies showing that service-learning could play a positive role in meeting the goals of teacher education programs and fostering the skills and dispositions needed for competent, caring teaching. For example, in studies by Flippo, Hetzel, Gribonski, and Armstrong (1993) and Green, Dalton, and Wilson (1994) on the impact of tutoring projects, education student tutors either gained in commitment to teaching or were more likely to maintain their commitment to teaching than comparison students. Other studies emerged indicating that preservice teachers who participate in service-learning demonstrate increased awareness of diversity issues, reduced stereotyping, and greater sensitivity to the need to adapt curricula and instruction to the needs of diverse youth (Boyle-Baise, 1998; McKenna & Ward, 1996; Tellez, Hlebowitsh, Cohen, & Norwood, 1995; Vadeboncoeur, Rahm, Aguilera, & LeCompte, 1994). Finally, a few studies appeared that linked involvement in service-learning to growth in moral development, particularly attitudes of compassion and concern toward students (Flippo et al., 1993; Potthoff et al., 2000; Root & Batchelder, 1994).

In 1997, Dr. Rahima Wade of the University of Iowa obtained a grant from the Corporation for National Service to form the National Service-Learning in Teacher Education Partnership (NSLTEP). The "overall goal for the 3-year grant was to build a national network of service-learning teacher educators." The partnership included seven regional directors, who provided training and technical assistance to over 48 teacher education programs involving hundreds of teacher educators over the course of the grant. In 2001, NSLTEP regional directors in cooperation with the American Association of Colleges for Teacher Education (AACTE) applied for and received funding from the corporation for an additional 3 years of operation.

Throughout NSLTEP's existence, strengthening the knowledge base on the status and consequences of efforts to include service-learning in teacher preparation was a major goal. Partnership directors concentrated their investigations on two areas of inquiry. One concerned the dispersion of service-learning throughout teacher education, its current state, facilitators and barriers to adoption and institutionalization, and characteristics of quality service-learning practice. In 1997, the NSLTEP conducted the first survey on the status of service-learning in U.S. teacher education programs. Results showed that 225 programs had adopted service-learning at that point, and another 200 intended to implement it in the future.

In 2001, Anderson and Erickson (2003) launched an extensive follow-up investigation of the status of service-learning in teacher preparation. They surveyed administrators or faculty members at 528 institutions, 499 that were affiliated with AACTE and 29 that were not. Respondents were surveyed about the position of service-learning in their programs, the extent of faculty and student involvement in programs that had adopted service-learning, the types of service-learning activities in which students engaged, and their rationales for using service-learning. Fifty-nine percent of respondents indicated that students were introduced to service-learning in their teacher education programs. However, the breadth and depth of faculty and student participation was limited. At the majority (51%) of institutions, less than a third of full-time faculty had adopted service-learning, and 19% reported no involvement. Very few programs (4%) described an institutionalized program in which service-learning was taught by all faculty. Twenty-three percent of institutions reported that none of their preservice teachers participated in service-learning, At 26% of the institutions, the participation in service-learning rate was less than one-third; at 12% of the institutions, the participation was between one-third and two-thirds; and at 15% of the institutions, the participation rate was more than two-thirds, but less than 100%. Only 24% of institutions reported full participation by all preservice teachers.

Participants' replies to the question of where service-learning was housed in their programs indicated that by far the most common "home" was in student teaching (86%); followed by English as a second language; foundations courses, such as Introduction to Teaching and Foundations of Education; and methods courses, such as language arts and social studies methods. The authors noted the discrepancy between their finding that 86% of the 294 adopting programs included service-learning in student teaching, but that only 195 programs prepared candidates to use service-learning as a pedagogy.

Teacher educators offered a number of reasons for including service-learning in their programs. The rationales most frequently cited were familiarizing and connecting candidates with the community (60%); increasing candidate sensitivity to diversity (58%); and contributing to candidates' personal and social development (53%). Other less frequently cited rationales included a desire to prepare candidates to use service-learning as a teaching method, to develop habits of critical inquiry and reflection, and to gain career awareness.

In addition to exploring the status of service-learning in teacher education, NSLTEP researchers have also sought to uncover the challenges encountered by faculty that adopt it. Anderson and Pickeral (2000) surveyed 123 individuals in various roles in teacher preparation, including 72 education faculty members experienced in using service-learning, 22 education faculty with no experience, 13 deans of education, and 16 service-learning coordinators at state departments of education regarding perceived barriers to service-learning implementation. Obstacles to implementation were categorized into four types:

1. Institutional (e.g., lack of funding);
2. Curricular (e.g., lack of time in preservice curriculum);
3. K–12 and community (e.g., difficulty communicating with K–12 teachers and/or community agency staff); and
4. Faculty and student issues (e.g., lack of faculty time for planning and implementation, lack of student interest in this approach).

Results showed few differences in the types of challenges identified by various groups in their sample. The impediment most often cited across all groups was lack of faculty time to implement service-learning, followed by the overcrowded preservice curriculum and lack of faculty time for planning. Other significant challenges included the discrepancies between service-learning practice and faculty roles and rewards, and between service-learning and departmental or institutional priorities. The authors followed their survey of challenges with a phone interview with 30 participants to elicit their strategies for overcoming obstacles to service-learning implementation. Respondents generated 155 strategies that were subsumed by the authors under five themes:

1. "Teacher educators can implement most of the strategies without . . . external funds or even additional internal resources;
2. Initial use of service-learning should be on a small scale;
3. Teachers educators should have "a clear understanding of the philosophy and practice of service-learning,
4. Collaboration is essential for success with service-learning; and
5. Policies and infrastructure that align to support effective practice is necessary for success with service-learning" (pp. 18–20).

As well as studying the status of and factors surrounding the implementation of service-learning in teacher preparation, Anderson and Hill (2001) completed a Delphi study to surface principles for good practice using this approach. Expert service-learning practitioners completed a succession of surveys regarding the elements of high-quality practice. The results revealed 10 principles on which they agreed, including, for example, that preservice teachers should be prepared to utilize service-learning as a pedagogy, both through being participants in service-learning themselves and through instruction in the pedagogy of high-quality service-learning, and that teacher educators should align outcomes of service-learning in teacher education with national and state program standards for accreditation and certification.

In addition to research on the status of service-learning in teacher education, a second area of inquiry throughout NSLTEP's history concerned the impacts of this approach on teaching candidates. Although early studies had shown benefits for service-learning, they had been marred by a number of methodological limitations. For example, investigators demonstrated little agreement about the most significant outcomes of service-learning in teacher preparation or measures for assessing these outcomes. In many studies, the primary sources of data comprised course evaluations and assignments, with supplementary data provided in some cases by qualitative measures such as interviews. In many studies, the course instructor(s) served as the sole or one of the evaluators, making it impossible to discount the possibility of bias. Finally, several studies that used objective measures failed to include a comparison group and adhered to a simple pre/post design, neglecting the potential contributions of moderating variables such as candidate and service experience characteristics.

NSLTEP researchers sought to strengthen the knowledge base on service-learning impacts on preservice teachers by addressing some of these methodological limitations. The first impacts study, launched in 1999 (Root, Callahan, & Sepanski, 2002a, 2002b) examined the relationships between participating in service-learning and the development in preservice teachers of teaching efficacy (Armor et al., 1976; Ashton & Webb, 1986; Guskey & Passaro, 1994); commitment to teaching (Colardarci, 1992; Schlecty & Vance, 1983); a service ethic of teaching (Serow, Eaker, & Ciechalski, 1992; Serow, Eaker, & Forrest, 1994); and acceptance of diversity (Sleeter, 2001), self-reported changes in attitudes toward pupils and teaching, and intent to utilize service learning in future teaching. An additional goal of this study was to explore the moderating influences of characteristics of the service-learning experience and candidates on the dependent variables.

Participants included 442 education students enrolled in service-learning courses in nine teacher education programs who were members of the National Service Learning in Teacher Education Partnership. Participating institutions ranged from a major national research university to regional universities and small liberal arts colleges. Participants completed pre- and post-surveys at the beginning and conclusion of their service-learning courses. In addition to outcome scales, the pre-test included measures of demographic characteristics, and the post-test, a measure of candidates' perceptions of their service-learning experience. Factor analysis of the characteristics of the service-learning experience scale yielded four factors:

1. Quality experience;
2. Instructor support;
3. Peer collaboration; and
4. Responsibility.

Multivariate analyses of variance (MANOVAs), controlling for repeated measures, were conducted to determine overall pre/post differences on the outcome measures. Regression analyses tested for the contribution of student characteristics and characteristics of the service-learning experience to the outcomes.

Results indicated that preservice teachers who participated in service-learning made significant gains in their attitudes toward diversity, desire to teach because of teachers' ability to bring about social change, and intent to incorporate service-learning in their future teaching. Two sets of characteristics of the service-learning experience emerged as correlates of performance on the outcome measures. Quality experience, a factor that included aspects of the service-learning experience, such as perceived challenge, relevance to teaching, and exposure to diversity, was positively associated with post-test scores on commitment to teaching, when controlling for pre-test scores. A second factor, instructional support, comprised of instructor and placement staff support for the candidate, training to perform service-learning tasks, and instruction in using service-learning as a teaching method, was positively linked to teaching efficacy. In addition to these factors, individual features of the service-learning experience were also linked to post-test performance. For example, having an instructor who helped one adjust to the service-learning experience was associated with greater commitment to teaching and desire to enter teaching because of the teachers' ability to address social problems. Assisting a K–12 teacher with a service-learning project was correlated with greater commitment to teaching and acceptance of diversity.

Although this initial study added to the knowledge base on the impacts of service-learning on preservice teachers, it was characterized by a key flaw: a failure to distinguish between the divergent purposes for and approaches to using service-learning within teacher education and the different outcomes that might be expected for each. Teacher educators have identified various rationales for integrating service-learning into courses and programs, such as career exploration, socializing future teachers in the civic and ethical resonsibilities of the profession, and preparing new teachers to use this method. Just as the rationales for adopting service-learning have diverged, so too have the contexts in which it is offered. In some programs, service-learning is embedded in foundations courses in order to strengthen prerequisite dispositions for teaching, such as sensitivity to diversity; in others, its home is a methods course and/or practicum or student teaching where candidates learn how to design and implement it with K–12 students; in still others, service-learning is a crucial program strategy that is integrated throughout courses. In the second 3 years of NSLTEP, differentiating between the outcomes that might be expected from these different purposes and contexts for service-learning in teacher education was a major research goal.

Two impact studies were designed and implemented during AACTE/ NSLTEP. The goal of the first (Root, Howard, & Daniels, 2004) was to explore the effects of using service-learning to strengthen preservice teachers' ethic of care or prosocial moral development. This study examined the associations between service-learning participation and candidates' values, prosocial moral reasoning in response to hypothetical classroom dilemmas, and affective responses to hypothetical situations involving student distress. In addition, the study sought to determine the role of characteristics of the service-learning experience and attributes of participants in moderating service-learning outcomes.

Potential participants were identified by securing nominations from NSLTEP directors of courses and faculty in which service-learning was being used to foster the development of an ethic of care. Nominees were contacted, and descriptions of their courses sought to determine the fit between their courses and the goals of the study, as well as their willingness to participate. The final sample included 19 students from a small Midwestern college enrolled in a service-learning course on human relations in education, and 45 students enrolled in an Introduction to Education course at a Midwestern regional university that included service-learning.

Candidates completed surveys at the beginning and end of their courses. The surveys included a measure of values adapted from the Cooperative Institutional Research Program (CIRP) Freshman Survey. A second section comprised three care-based dilemmas involving a conflict between a teacher need and a student's need for care in which respondents were asked to recommend a course of action and rate the importance of various considerations in the teacher's decision making. Each consideration represented a particular stage of prosocial/moral reasoning, as shown in Figure 1.1. One M (meaningless) item was included in each set of considerations as a check on subjects' tendency to choose a pretentious- sounding item (Carlo, Eisenberg, & Knight, 1993).

In the third section of the survey, respondents recalled and analyzed a care-related dilemma from their own classroom experience, including the student need involved, emotions the candidate felt in response to the

```
1. Hedonistic Reasoning
2. Concrete Needs
3. a. Approval Orientation
   b. Stereotyped Reasoning
4. a. Empathy
   b. Self-Reflective Thinking
5. Principled Thinking
```

Figure 1.1.   Stages of Prosocial/Moral Reasoning

need, actions the candidate considered taking, the action that was finally taken, and an evaluation of the action with supportive reasoning. The final two sections of the survey were intended to assess participants' affective responses to hypothetical instances of student distress and classroom situations likely to provoke such distress. In one, participants were presented with two hypothetical scenarios involving individual children (one of whom internalized distress and the second who externalized distress) and asked to rate the degree to which they felt various prosocial emotions (empathy, guilt, sadness, or personal distress [reverse scored]) after reading each scenario. Candidates also rated their self-perceived skill in handling the situation and the degree of control they anticipated having over themselves and others. The final section of the survey provided respondents with short statements describing typical teaching situations likely to produce student distress (e.g., "When a student gives the wrong answer to a question in class") followed by a prosocial response (e.g., "I tend to feel protective of them"). Participants then rated the degree to which each statement applied to them.

Because of their different objectives, results for each course were analyzed separately. Participants in both courses showed significant pre/post changes in values during the service-learning course. Those from the human relations course showed significant gains in the average rank assigned to the values of "promoting racial understanding" and "developing a meaningful philosophy of life." First-year candidates at the university, on the other hand, showed a significant increase in the importance assigned to "expressing my individual talents and creativity."

Results for the care-based dilemmas were complex and provided only partial support for the hypothesis of a positive effect for service-learning on candidates' prosocial moral reasoning. For example, candidates from the small college demonstrated a significant increase in their tendency to select the principled reasoning consideration as most important on the first and third dilemmas, and a decline in hedonistic reasoning on the second dilemma. However, the second dilemma also elicited a decline in higher stage self-reflective reasoning. The university students showed an increased tendency to identify the principled consideration as most important on the first dilemma and an increase in the number of student-centered actions recommended on the third. However, across dilemmas, there was a decrease in the importance attached by these students to several prosocial reasoning considerations.

Very few significant changes occurred over time in the care-based dilemmas generated by candidates themselves. In response to the measure of affective responses to scenarios about hypothetical students in distress, candidates from the small college showed significant gains in the level of guilt-related affect (e.g., feelings of regret, remorse) reported in response to a scenario about a student who acted out (instead of internalizing) distress. Additionally, these participants demonstrated an increase in their self-perceived skill at handling the scenario. University preservice teachers showed significant gains in their empathy and sadness scores in response to both scenarios. On the final measure of responses to classroom situations likely to elicit negative student affect, university students demonstrated a significant decline in personal distress (an affective response negatively associated with prosocial behavior).

A second impacts study conducted as part of AACTE/NSLTEP (Root et al., 2004) investigated the effects of using service-learning for a different purpose and in a different context in teacher preparation than the first. Specifically, this investigation sought to explore the impacts of learning service-learning as pedagogy on preservice teachers' beliefs about teaching and learning. Previous studies had shown that exposure to service-learning in an education course or practicum positively impacted candidates' intent to use this approach (Root, Callahan, & Sepanski, 2001a; Wade et al., 1999). However, despite extensive literature demonstrating that teachers' thinking contributes to their comprehension of educational concepts and skills and classroom practice, only one study of service-learning in teacher education has targeted candidates' cognition as an outcome. Wade, Harwood, Carlson, and Ryan (2001) assessed the influence of pre-service teachers' characteristics (e.g., age, gender, certification program) and experiences with service-learning and community service on the quality of their thinking about service-learning. One hundred ninety candidates from seven teacher education programs were asked to design service-learning activities in response to a hypothetical teaching scenario. Results showed that approximately half the participants generated good- to high-quality service-learning experiences. Further analyses indicated that candidates who had taken at least one education course that included service-learning were more apt to produce quality activities than candidates who had not.

The second impacts study extended these findings by examining the effects of exposure to the pedagogy of service-learning on preservice teachers' beliefs about instruction. The types of beliefs identified for inclusion in the second study were thought to be susceptible to change as a result of instruction in service-learning as a method. These beliefs included:

- Epistemological beliefs (beliefs about what knowledge is and how it is acquired);
- Curricular goals (beliefs about the most important goals of instruction); and
- Candidates' orientation toward instruction (tendency to endorse constructivist vs. transmission-oriented teaching strategies).

In addition, the study also sought to determine the consequences of learning the pedagogy of service-learning on candidates' intent to use this approach in their future teaching, and the links between changes in beliefs and intent to use service-learning in one's own teaching.

Faculty involved in the second study included two NSLTEP regional directors and two teacher educators who had received training and technical assistance during the first NSLTEP project. All taught methods courses that included instruction in the pedagogy of service-learning. Final participants for the study were 38 education students from three institutions: a small liberal arts college in the Midwest, a religious university in the Midwest, and a religious university in the Northwest. Participants completed pre- and post-surveys at the beginning and end of their methods classes.

Surveys included a scale intended to measure beliefs in simple and certain knowledge adapted from Schommer-Aikins (2002) and Schommer (1993), and a measure of curricular goals adapted from Ennis's Value Orientation Inventory (Ennis & Chen, 1993; Ennis & Hooper, 1988). Belief in constructivist-oriented versus transmission-oriented teaching was assessed by asking respondents to endorse either alternative from a scale with nine sets of options for teaching practices. Intention to use service-learning was measured by asking participants to estimate the likelihood that they would include a project to address human needs, environmental issues, or political issues in their future teaching. In addition to the outcome measures, the pre-survey included measures of candidate characteristics and the post-survey included several measures of perceptions of the service-learning experience.

Data were analyzed for the entire sample and for each institution. Results showed that candidates made marginally significant gains in their tendency to reject an epistemological belief in certain knowledge. No significant changes occurred in curricular goals for the entire sample; however, candidates at one institution demonstrated a significant increase in the emphasis placed on Self-Actualization as a curricular goal. Overall, participants showed a significant increase in their tendency to agree with the constructivist-oriented statement, "I will give students complex, real-life problems to solve...." Additionally, candidates at two institutions showed significant gains in their commitment to authentic assessment, and those at one institution increasingly endorsed small group learning.

Several characteristics of the service-learning experience predicted participants' post-test beliefs about teaching and learning. For example, those who perceived that their service-learning experience had been more challenging showed greater gains in their tendency to reject a view of knowledge as simple. The amount of responsibility participants had for planning and implementing service-learning in a K–12 classroom was associated with a stronger tendency to endorse promoting social responsibility as a curricular goal. Finally, while the strongest correlate of intent to use service-learning was the participant's pre-test score on this measure, preservice teachers who showed greater increases in their tendency to reject views of knowledge as simple and as certain showed greater gains in their intent to use service-learning.

As funding for NSLTEP ended in 2003, regional directors, their teacher education partners, and affiliated organizations planned ways to continue the collaboration that began in 1997. Their conversations led to the establishment of an International Center for Service-Learning in Teacher Education (ICSLTE) at Clemson University in 2003. The mission of ICSLTE is to promote the sustained and widespread use of high-quality service-learning in K–12 and teacher preparation settings through several strategies, including "promoting excellence in service-learning by supporting, conducting, and disseminating current [and future] research on service-learning in teacher education" (www.clemson.edu/ICSLTE/about/whoWeAre.htm ¶3, goal 2).

Tactics planned by ICSLTE for advancing research on service-learning in teacher education include:

- Critically synthesizing current research in the field and producing an annual summary and annotated bibliography to be shared in publications, on Internet sites, and on listservs.
- Supporting conceptual work and suggestions for research questions by commissioning annual white papers by teams of service-learning researchers and deans, directors or chairs in teacher education that examine the links between service-learning and critical issues in teacher preparation and Pre-K–12 reform, such as highly qualified teaching and teacher retention.
- Providing professional development and technical assistance to support research and evaluation activities on service-learning and teacher education to teacher educators and programs seeking research and evaluation assistance.

- Expanding C.A.R.T. (the Compendium of Assessment and Research Tools) created by RMC Research Corporation to include guidelines and instruments appropriate to teacher education, including measures of program quality, context, and outcomes.
- Coordinating communication among a network of researchers and other professionals interested in research on service-learning in teacher education (e.g., teacher education and liberal arts faculty, providers of inservice professional development, and representatives of professional and accreditation organizations) to facilitate an exchange of research strategies, instruments, and data.
- Pursuing funding for collaborative national research projects that would address the most essential questions on service-learning in teacher preparation.

REFERENCES

Anderson, J. B., & Erickson, J. A. (2003, Summer). Service-learning in teacher education. *Academic Exchange Quarterly, 7*(2), 111–115.

Anderson, J., & Hill, D. (2001). Principles of good practice for service-learning in pre-service teacher education. In J. Anderson, K. Swick, & J. Yff (Eds.), *Service-learning in teacher education: Enhancing the growth of new teachers, their students, and communities.* Washington, DC: American Association of Colleges for Teacher Education.

Anderson, J., & Pickeral, T. (2000). Challenges and strategies for success with service-learning in preservice teacher education. *National Society for Experiential Education Quarterly, 25*(3), 7–22.

Armor, D., Conroy-Oseguera, P., Cox, M., King, N., McDonnell, L., Pascal, A., Pauly, E., & Zellman, G. (1976). *Analysis of the school preferred reading programs in selected Los Angeles minority schools* (Rep. No. R-2007-LAUSD). Santa Monica, CA: Rand Corporation. (ERIC Document Reproduction Service No. ED130243)

Ashton, P., & Webb, R. (1986). *Making a difference: Teachers' sense of efficacy and student achievement.* New York: Longman.

Boyle-Baise, M. S. (1998). Community service learning for multicultural teacher education: An exploratory study with preservice teachers. *Equity & Excellence in Teacher Education, 31*(2), 52–60. (ERIC Document Reproduction Service No. EJ574639)

Carlo, G., Eisenberg, N., & Knight, G. P. (1992).An objective measure of prosocial moral reasoning. *Journal of Research on Adolescence, 2,* 331–349.

Colardarci, T. (1992). Teachers' sense of efficacy and commitment to teaching. *Journal of Experimental Education, 60,* 323–337.

Ennis, C., & Chen, A. (1993). .Domain specifications and content representativeness of the revised Value Orientation Inventory. *Research Quarterly Exercise Sport, 64*(4), 436–446.

Ennis, C., & Hooper, L. (1988). Development of an instrument for assessing educational value orientations. *Journal of Curriculum Studies, 20*(3), 277–280.

Flippo, R., Hetzel, C., Gribonski, D., & Armstrong, L. (1993). *Literacy, multicultural, sociocultural considerations: Student literacy corps and the community.* Paper presented at the annual meeting of the International Reading Association, San Antonio, TX. (ERIC Document Reproduction Service No. ED356466)

Green, J., Dalton, R., & Wilson, B. (1994). *Implementation and evaluation of TEACH: A service-learning program for teacher education.* Paper presented at the annual meeting of the Association of Teacher Educators, Atlanta, GA.

Guskey, T., & Passaro, P. (1994). Teacher efficacy: A study of construct dimensions. *American Educational Research Journal, 31*(3), 627–643.

International Center for Service-Learning in Teacher Education goals. (n.d.) Retrieved September 20, 2005, from http://www.clemson.edu/ICSLTE/about/whoWeAre.htm

McKenna, M., & Ward, K. (1996). Service-learning: A culturally relevant pedagogy. *Thresholds in Education, 22*(2), 18–21.

Potthoff, D., Dinsmore, J., Stirtz, G., Walsh, T., Ziebarth, J., & Eifler, K. (2000). Preparing for democracy and diversity: The impact of a community-based field experience on preservice teachers, knowledge, skills, and attitudes. *Action in Teacher Education, 22*(1), 79–92.

Root, S., & Batchelder, T. (1994*). The impact of service-learning on preservice teachers' development.* Paper presented at the annual meeting of American Educational Research Association, San Francisco.

Root, S., Callahan, J., & Sepanski, J. (2002a). Building teaching dispositions and service-learning practice. *Michigan Journal of Community Service Learning, 8*(2), 50–60.

Root, S., Callahan, J., & Sepanski, J. (2002b). Service-learning in teacher education: a consideration of qualitative and quantitative outcomes. In A. Furco & S. H. Billig (Eds.), *Advances in service-learning research: Vol. 1. Service-learning: The essence of the pedagogy* (pp. 223–244). Greenwich, CT: Information Age Publishing.

Root, S., Howard, R., & Daniels, J (2004).*The impact of a service-learning experience in teacher preparation on preservice teachers' prosocial moral development* Paper presented at the annual conference of the Association for Moral Education, Dana Point, CA.

Schlechty, P., & Vance, V. (1983). Recruitment, selection, and retention: The shape of the teaching force. *Elementary School Journal, 84*(4), 469–487.

Schommer, M. (1993), The influence of age and education on epistemological beliefs. *British Journal of Educational Psychology, 68,* 551–562.

Schommer-Aikins, M. (2002). An evolving theoretical framework for an epistemological belief system. In B. Hofer & P. Pintrich (Eds.), *Personal epistemology: The psychology of belief about knowledge and knowing* (pp. 103–118). Hillsdale, NJ: Lawrence Erlbaum Associates.

Serow, R., Eaker, D., & Ciechalski, J. (1992). Calling, service, and legitimacy: Professional orientations and career commitment among prospective teachers. *Journal of Research and Development in Education, 25*(3), 136–141.

Serow, R., Eaker, D., & Forrest, K. (1994). "I want to see some kind of growth out of them": What the service ethic means to teacher-education students. *American Educational Research Journal, 31*(1), 27–48.

Sleeter. C. (2001). Preparing teachers for culturally diverse schools: Research and the overwhelming presence of Whiteness. *Journal of Teacher Education, 52*(2), 94–106.

Tellez, K., Hlebowitsh, P., Cohen, M., & Norwood, P. (1995). Social service field experiences and teacher education. In J. Larkin & C. Sleeter (Eds.), *Developing multicultural teacher education curricula* (pp. 65–78). Albany: State University of New York Press.

Vadeboncoeur, J., Rahm, J., Aguilera, D., & LeCompte, M. (1995, April). *Learning in the service of citizenship: The limitations of service learning.* Paper presented at the annual meeting of the American Educational Research Association, San Francisco.

Wade, R., Anderson, J., Yarbrough, D., Pickeral, T., Erickson, J., & Kromer, T. (1999). Novice teachers' experiences of community service-learning. *Teaching and Teacher Education, 15*, 667–684.

Wade, R., Carlson, H., Harwood, A., & Ryan, L. (2001, April). Impacts on preservice teachers' thinking about community service-learning. Paper presented at the annual meeting of the American Educational Research Association, Seattle, WA.

CHAPTER 2

THE INSTITUTIONALIZATION OF SERVICE-LEARNING IN PRESERVICE TEACHER EDUCATION

Jeffrey B. Anderson and Jane Callahan

ABSTRACT

Although the integration of service-learning into preservice teacher education programs has grown rapidly in recent years, serious challenges to its use and institutionalization exist. This study involved an in-depth examination of the policies and practices that five select teacher education programs applied to achieve their current degree of institutionalization. The study used a modified version of Furco's (1999) "Self-Assessment Rubric for the Institutionalization of Service-Learning in Higher Education." Results indicate that most institutions institutionalized service-learning by building on their unique history, mission, and culture; relying on a service-learning faculty champion; establishing a positive relationship with K–12 and other community partners; and finding external and/or internal funding support for service-learning.

Improving Service-Learning Practice: Research on Models to Enhance Impacts, pages 17–36

INTRODUCTION

Teacher education programs across the nation are addressing the challenge of integrating service-learning into their curricula. Anderson and Erickson (2003) reported that, in a national study, 59% of teacher education programs indicated they include service-learning as a component of teacher candidate preparation. However, serious challenges to the use and institutionalization of service-learning in preservice teacher education exist, including the already overcrowded curriculum, demands placed on teacher preparation programs by state departments of education and national accreditation organizations, and the need for faculty to understand the theory and practice of service-learning in order to prepare new teachers to use it as a pedagogy. These pressures, along with challenges common to service-learning use in all higher education disciplines, make the institutionalization of service-learning in teacher education a complex endeavor both to conduct and to study. This study was designed to contribute to our knowledge in this area by drawing conclusions and making recommendations for practice from the indepth examination of five select teacher education programs' efforts to institutionalize service-learning. More specifically, the study addresses the following questions:

- What policies, practices, and infrastructure are in place in each school, college, or department of education (SCDE) that have helped or hindered the institutionalization of service-learning?
- What processes and activities did SCDE faculty, administrators, and others engage in to achieve the current status of service-learning institutionalization?
- Was there a linear sequence in which these activities were conducted? Or did issues reemerge in a spiral-like process? How long did institutionalization take?

LITERATURE REVIEW

A review of the literature on the integration of service-learning into both K–12 schools and institutions of higher learning suggests that the process involves both individual and organizational development and implementation (Billig, 2002). Holland (2000), in her study of institutionalizing service-learning into higher education, suggested that we must engage in research that examines all components of the institutionalization process and noted that it is important to understand both institutional and individual faculty motivation for undertaking service-learning.

Billig (2002) described four stages in the institutionalization process: adoption, implementation, institutionalization, and sustainability. Adoption refers to the awareness of and experimentation with an innovation. Implementation makes use of the innovation routine in adherence to elements of best practice. Institutionalization makes the innovation no longer separate but "a normative part of the organization and its culture" (p. 246). Finally, sustainability "involves the ability to maintain or increase program efforts by building constituencies, creating strong and enduring partnerships, generating and leveraging resources, and identifying and securing funding sources that are available over time" (p. 247).

Case studies of the institutionalization of service-learning have also been conducted in institutions of higher education. Holland (1997) examined four institutions that had identified service-learning or community-based scholarship as central to their mission. A second project examined the institutionalization of service-learning at 19 institutions that had received grants to support its adoption. Using data from both studies, the authors developed a matrix for coding the degree to which service and service-learning were accepted as a priority at the institutions. One axis of the matrix lists potential institutional loci for the expression of institutional commitment to service-learning such as mission, promotion, tenure and hiring policies, and faculty involvement. The other expresses a continuum of levels of commitment ranging from low relevance to full integration.

Drawing on the work of Kecskes and Muyllaert (1997), Furco (2002), in a study of 43 campuses, developed a self-assessment matrix to focus on five dimensions of service-learning institutionalization in higher education. Using this matrix, his research demonstrated that the institutionalization of service-learning was related to an institution's (1) mission and philosophy, (2) faculty support for and involvement in service-learning, (3) institutional support for service-learning, (4) student support and involvement in service-learning, and (5) community participation and partnerships. He rated these dimensions on the degree to which service-learning was integrated into the institution and noted three stages:

1. Critical Mass Building, characterized by a lack of agreement about the definition of service-learning;

2. Quality Building, characterized by a common institutional definition and a growing operationalization of service-learning; and stage three,

3. Sustained Institutionalization, in which a formal, universally accepted definition for service-learning is accepted and systemically operationalized among all stakeholders at the institution (p. 48).

Furco concluded that the nature and tenor of each institution shapes the degree to which service-learning is institutionalized. The purpose for integrating and using service-learning differs depending on a number of factors and needs to be tied to an institution's public or civic mission.

Callahan and Root (2003) conducted a study of the institutionalization of service-learning in the teacher education programs at four large state institutions in Michigan. Their research examined the effects of using a "Faculty Fellow" model of training and technical assistance developed at Eastern Michigan University. They found that the integration of service-learning was impacted by factors, such as leaders with more extensive knowledge of and commitment to service-learning and the importance of compatibility of service-learning with individual and organizational goals, responsibilities, and histories. In addition, although many models of change discuss the importance of administrative backing (Bringle & Hatcher, 2000; Holland, 1997), this factor appeared to have had marginal influence in the institutions studied. Moreover, program approval issues, which had been hypothesized as being an important factor for institutionalizing service-learning in teacher education, appeared to have little if any influence in any of the programs in the study.

Although limited, the research on the institutionalization of service-learning in teacher education provides a platform for beginning to understand the process of how and why schools, departments, and programs dedicated to preparing teachers can successfully assimilate service-learning. Existing studies provide information and tools to examine the institutional process, but more research needs to be conducted on the actual process through which institutionalization takes place and on the factors that support or inhibit the institutionalization process.

METHODS

Participants

Participants in this study were faculty, administrators, students, and community partners at five SCDEs in higher education institutions (see Exhibit 2.1). SCDEs were selected for participation in the study based on the following five criteria:

1. Wide geographic distribution;
2. Diverse types of institutions;
3. Preliminary evidence of institutionalization of service-learning in the SCDE;
4. Existence of a willing, knowledgeable primary contact person; and
5. SCDE administrative approval to participate in the study.

Exhibit 2.1.   Characteristics of Participating SCDEs

Institution	Region	Location	Type	Public/Private
A	West Coast	Rural	Comprehensive	Public
B	New England	Rural	Small liberal arts	Private
C	Midwest	Urban	Small liberal arts	Private
D	New England	Rural	Comprehensive	Public
E	West	Rural	Research	Public

Schools, Colleges, and Departments of Education

Institution A is one campus in a large state university system, located in a town that serves a large agricultural area. The university enrolls approximately 15,000 students including 9,000 undergraduates and 6,000 students in 40 master's degree programs. The School of Education is divided into two distinct, independent departments, both of which offer initial teacher certification programs at the undergraduate and graduate levels. Department A includes 15 faculty that teach a total of 250 students in seven certification programs, while Department B houses 30 faculty who teach a total of 400 students in eight programs. A tenured faculty member experienced with the use of service-learning completed the institutionalization matrix.

Institution B is a small, private college located in a small town in rural New England. About 85% of the 1,000 students come from out of state, mainly from the Northeast. The college offers both a bachelor and a master's of science degree in education and has teacher certification programs in elementary/special, secondary, and physical education. Each year approximately 25 students graduate with degrees in education. The education department has 4 full-time faculty members and 10 adjunct faculty, many of whom hold full-time positions in local school districts. The director of the teacher preparation program completed the institutionalization matrix.

Institution C is a small liberal arts college located in the heart of a large Midwestern city. The college enrolls approximately 3,000 students, 2,500 undergraduates and 500 graduate students, in 12 master's degree programs. The Department of Education includes 14 full-time faculty members who teach 500 undergraduates in three undergraduate and two graduate teacher education programs. The college recommends for certification approximately 200 new teachers per year. A tenured faculty member with considerable experience with service-learning completed the institutionalization matrix.

Institution D is a land-grant college located in a small town in New England. It serves approximately 4,500 undergraduate and graduate students, primarily from within the state, but also from other New England states. The education department is housed in the College of Professional and Graduate Studies and offers majors in elementary, special, and early childhood education. In addition to the 18 faculty members on tenure tracks, it also includes three or four "associate" faculty who are local teachers rotating in for a year or two from nearby schools. The secondary education program employs eight faculty who hold joint appointments with academic disciplines and teach methods courses. The institutionalization matrix was completed by the chair of the elementary/special education and early childhood programs.

Institution E is a land-grant, public, research university in a western state. The university is located in a small town in an agricultural area. The university enrolls approximately 12,000 students in nine colleges, including 8,800 undergraduates, 500 master's degree students in 77 programs, and 1,000 doctoral students in 33 programs. The College of Education includes 15 full-time faculty who teach in one or more of the five undergraduate or three graduate-level teacher certification programs. A full-time, tenured faculty, experienced with the use of service-learning completed the institutionalization rubric.

Instrument Development

The institutionalization process was examined through a framework provided by Furco (2002) in his Self-Assessment Rubric for the Institutionalization of Service-Learning in Higher Education. The self-assessment rubric used in this study retained Furco's five dimensions and also added others, particularly four items to more specifically address conditions and issues in SCDEs.

1. Alignment with educational reform efforts;
2. Faculty use of service-learning pedagogy;
3. Teacher candidate learning and application of service-learning; and
4. Alignment with standards

The interview protocol consisted of 25 questions designed to gain deeper insights regarding each of the five dimensions included in the Self-Assessment Rubric. Follow-up questions were designed to assist the interviewers in obtaining a clear, detailed understanding of all aspects of service-learning institutionalization. These questions were asked as necessary and relevant for the individual being interviewed.

Data Collection

All data were collected during 2003 and 2004 using the self-assessment rubric developed for his study, individual and focus group interviews, and a variety of artifacts. The primary contact at each SCDE completed the six-page, 26-item rubric. The researchers visited campuses for 1 or 2 days to conduct a detailed, 2- to 3-hour interview with the individual serving as the primary contact for the study, and hour interviews with such individuals as the department chair, institutional administrators (i.e., a dean, a provost, or vice-president), the campus service-learning coordinator, and K–12 and community partners. One-hour focus group interviews were conducted with service-learning faculty, non-service-learning faculty, and students who were nearing completion of their program. A total of 39 interviews were completed. All interviews were conducted by one of the two researchers. With few exceptions, these interviews were conducted onsite.

Artifacts collected included SCDE and university or college mission statements, strategic plans, accreditation documents, catalogs and course descriptions, written agreements with K–12 and other community partners, and promotion and tenure guidelines. The researchers also examined SCDE and college or university Web sites.

Data Analysis

Self-Assessment Rubric Data

The researchers examined carefully all responses to the 26 items in the Self-Assessment Rubric and used these responses to guide the choice of questions asked in the various interviews. For example, if a respondent indicated that service-learning was included in the SCDE strategic plan, they were then asked to describe the process they engaged in to achieve this result.

Interview and Artifact Data

The researchers completed a qualitative analysis of the 39 interview transcripts and artifacts from the five SCDEs by using the three subprocesses of analysis recommended by Miles and Huberman (1984): data reduction, data display, and conclusion drawing and verification. First, reading and rereading the transcripts allowed for the emergence of several categories. Interviewees' responses were then placed into these initial categories. For example, responses related to enhancing faculty understanding and use of service-learning were grouped together and placed in the category "faculty support for and involvement in service-learning." Next, the data were reduced by summarizing key ideas for each category expressed by each interviewee. These key words and phrases were displayed in a chart for each category. During the process of drawing conclusions, special attention was paid to identifying discrepant evidence and rival explanations (Miles & Huberman, 1984).

FINDINGS

Findings developed from Self-Assessment Rubric responses, interviews, and artifact data are presented for each institution organized around the five dimensions of the Self-Assessment Rubric.

Institution A

The philosophy and mission of Institution A's SCDE was profoundly shaped by a decision made in the early 1990s by the dean, with the support of the provost and president, to split its faculty into two completely separate entities. Divided by philosophies of education, personal characteristics, and work preferences, the split resulted in productive, innovative faculty forming Department A and the semi-retired faculty establishing Department B. Department A has strongly institutionalized service-learning with the complete support of all 15 faculty members and the department chair; Department B has very limited administrative and faculty support for service-learning. The split allowed faculty supportive of service-learning to move relatively rapidly to integrate it throughout Department A with little resistance and eventually create a high-quality, sustainable service-learning presence.

Service-learning is included in the university and the statewide system's mission, and was reinforced by the provost's insistence in the 1990s that emphasis shift from teaching to student learning and from a long-term campuswide history of student involvement with the larger community through internships and field experiences. A service-learning initiative from the statewide system's Chancellor's office provided both philosophical support and grant funds. Service-learning will be included in the new mission and goals of Department A, its administrators and key service-learning faculty believing it most productive to make written policies arise from department consensus and successful practice.

All faculty in Department A understand and support service-learning as an essential component of preservice teacher education. Service-learning tacitly is recognized and soon will be formalized for all faculty in the promotion and tenure process. The entire department was initially sold on the value of service-learning by an enthusiastic K–12 teacher who involved all faculty in a service-learning project. Immediately afterward, a very influential and widely respected service-learning faculty "champion" emerged who has since been provided with release time over several years to mentor faculty new to service-learning and who has also obtained grant funds to help train faculty. In addition, the department chair and dean provided funds for faculty to attend service-learning conferences and workshops. It is now expected that all new faculty will understand and embrace service-learning. The strong advocacy and use of service-learning by a critical mass of Department A faculty has attracted new, like-minded faculty members.

All Department A students are introduced to service-learning through participation in a hands-on field experience in the beginning of their degree program. They all learn how to use service-learning as a pedagogy and almost all of them use it during their student teaching experience, depending on circumstances. Student interests and requests did not play an important role in bringing service-learning into Department A, although their positive response to it has allowed service-learning to remain. There has never been a "service-learning center" on campus to facilitate and support service-learning. A primarily student-run volunteer center does some of this work, but many see a major need for a professionally run, well-funded service-learning center.

Key Points

Institution A has been successful with its efforts to institutionalize service-learning due to a number of intentional strategies and some positive unintended consequences.

- A paradigm shift from teaching to learning and the opportunity for like-minded faculty to form their own department allowed service-learning to flourish.
- An influential, respected faculty member served as service-learning champion and an enthusiastic K–12 teacher promoted the value of service-learning.
- Faculty new to service-learning received mentoring and training support on service-learning and connections with like-minded faculty.
- Service-learning was initially advocated by a faculty member and a K–12 teacher rather than by an administrative champion, thus avoiding faculty resistance.
- Policies until after practice have changed.

Institution B

Initially envisioned as a place where returning veterans of World War II could get an education, the college has had a strong and lengthy relationship with the community. Since the college opened, service has been an important aspect of its mission, and faculty, students, and administrators agree that they are part of the community and that the college should contribute to the community. In addition, there has long been the belief that students "learn best by doing" and that learning by doing is a good pedagogy. This philosophy provided fertile ground in which service-learning could grow and develop.

Because of the small number of full-time faculty in the education program, each instructor teaches a number of courses, and some are taught by teachers and administrators from neighboring school districts. The chair of the education department, a graduate of the college herself, has taught there for many years and has been very influential in supporting and promoting service-learning. She included service-learning systematically into education core classes, which she taught. Developing partnerships with schools and community agencies, she provided workshops and training in service-learning and increased the number of faculty that could use the strategy effectively. At the same time, she prepared schools themselves to engage in service-learning. Service-learning is now a central feature of the program.

Over the past 10 years, service-learning has gradually become a collegewide strategy, driven by a number of grants and supporting a variety of other college initiatives. With the support of a new faculty dean who is committed to service and service-learning, the college applied for and was awarded several grants that it used to support service-learning. A civic engagement grant funded the coordination center for service-learning on campus. In addition, as the administration saw that service and service-learning could provide avenues to opportunities and grants that would further the mission of the college, they created a subcommittee of the Board of Trustees for Civic Engagement and Social Responsibility, which supports service across the college, and highlighted service-learning in the evidentiary report for accreditation by the New England Association of Schools and Colleges (NEASC).

Service has gradually become a factor in hiring practices for both faculty and administrators, and although the college does not grant tenure, service figures heavily in the promotion process. New faculty are hired with the expectation that they will use service-learning, and they are trained in the strategy and mentored into the process by chairs and other faculty. Service-learning is now at the center of praxis of all 65 faculty.

At present all teacher education candidates both participate in and learn to use service-learning in K–12 classrooms. There are ongoing service-learning activities in the community and opportunities for students to develop new projects. The program has developed a chain of practice from preservice to inservice. Graduate courses are provided for cooperating teachers to help them to understand and be able to use service-learning in their own classrooms. Partnerships with local schools and with teachers have been well established, and student assignments are well understood. Teacher candidates and teachers are provided with opportunities for mini-grants to fund their service-learning projects during student teaching, and a number of districts have written grants to support service and service-learning opportunities for college students. For a number of years, one local superintendent has included funds for service-learning supplies and projects in the yearly school budget.

Key Points

Institution B has institutionalized service-learning in the following ways:

- A strong and influential champion for service-learning at the institution has been on staff and in the community for a long time and knows and understands both cultures very well.
- The college and the community have a history of working collaboratively, and the mission of the college supports service.
- Strong connections have been made with local schools and agencies, and training and support have been provided to ensure that there is agreement on the value of service-learning and how it will be carried out.
- School administrators and teachers advise the program and meet regularly to discuss and develop service-learning projects and activities.
- The small size of the faculty makes it easier to effect significant change.
- New faculty were hired with the expectation that they would use service-learning and are supported in their efforts.

Institution C

Service-learning is strongly integrated into the SCDE at Institution C because it directly addresses the mission of the college and has been institutionalized campuswide. The college was founded in 1869 with a mission of "education for service to the church and community" and moved from a rural area to the inner city in order to more effectively serve European immigrants, eventually separating from its founding church.

The college moved from deep involvement in experiential education in the 1960s to a focus on service-learning in the late 1980s, due primarily to the efforts of a faculty champion outside the department of education. In about 1992, the school's education department began to seriously consider service-learning as a possible central focus to their mission. By 1999, the department felt service-learning had been securely institutionalized in the department through ongoing discussions of this approach and agreement on a definition that would help faculty intentionally focus on designing pertinent courses. Service-learning is now one of three central components of the teacher education program. Including service-learning in the department's strategic plan has helped faculty turn all field placements for teacher candidates into service-learning experiences and resulted in all students' and faculty members' regular use of service-learning terminology. This has clarified communication and made progress with service-learning more rapid.

All prospective faculty must now demonstrate support for service-learning during the interview process, and preferably come with considerable knowledge of and experience with service-learning as a pedagogy. The overall college commitment to service-learning implies that all faculty must use it to be retained and promoted, although this policy is not yet in writing. All 13 of the current education department faculty use service-learning in at least one course and 8 of the 13 are strong advocates for expanded and improved service-learning efforts. The most pressing need now is to provide follow-up training, especially for new faculty.

Faculty and administrators report that it was essential to have a respected, tenured faculty member as a service-learning champion, one who generated faculty support for service-learning and wrote a grant that provided intensive service-learning training for all department faculty. This faculty member supported appreciation dinners, stipends for service-learning use and syllabus revision, and service-learning awards, all very helpful in the beginning. The most pressing need at this stage is to provide follow-up training, especially for new faculty.

The faculty service-learning champion was on the board of directors for a nearby community school and facilitated the development of a strong partnership that resulted in the departments' teacher candidates providing all the science and physical education instruction for students at the community school. In addition, both the department and the community school have written several grants that provide funds for the others' service-learning activities.

There is now considerable support for service-learning from both the department and the college. All service-learning funding is from the regular college budget rather than being grant dependent. This includes the college recently funding the position of a full-time staff member in the Center for Service, Work, and Learning whose primary function is to support faculty and students from the education department in their service-learning classes. In addition, the last three deans hired at the college all used service-learning as a teaching method when they were faculty members either at Institution C or elsewhere. This helps ensure their understanding of the benefits and requirements of service-learning courses.

Key Points

At Institution C practices and strategies essential to service-learning institutionalization included:

- Connecting service-learning to the mission that drives the college.
- Hiring and then supporting faculty and staff who demonstrate that they are "called" to engage in service-learning and are given the freedom to creatively use service-learning.
- Having a well-respected, influential, and committed faculty champion.
- Having a campus center for service-learning for support and cheerleading, especially in the early years, as well as providing staff to work with department of education faculty and students to design and engage in service-learning.
- Rewarding successful use of service-learning in tenure and promotion decisions.

Institution D

As a land-grant institution, there has been a history of service in the university, but nothing specifically mentions service-learning in the college mission statement. Informally, however, there seems to be a common understanding across the institution that community work should be attached to curriculum and that there is a relationship between service and learning. In addition, the campus is unionized and follows a Boyer perspective of application of learning. Service fits well into this philosophy. There is an internally well-funded, campuswide office of service-learning with a full-time coordinator. However, over the past few years the administration of the college has changed a number of times, and many issues have taken a back seat, including service-learning. Currently, there are no real campuswide incentives to encourage faculty to use service-learning, although small grants raise interest in some disciplines.

Initially, a tenured faculty member formally introduced service-learning to the education department through the award of a grant from the National Service-Learning and Teacher Education Partnership. At that time it was perceived as something that fit well with the department conceptual framework and might support accreditation requirements of the National Council for Accreditation of Teacher Education (NCATE), and an effort was made to integrate the strategy into some courses. In no course, however, was or is service-learning pedagogy taught, and no teacher candidates carry out projects in K–12 classrooms.

Although there were no systematic activities to help faculty to understand service-learning, new hires learn about it through "course teams," which teach different sections of the introductory courses. Approximately 50% of the people in the department have a generic sense of what service-learning is, and how it differs from service, but there is no thought of purposefully increasing the percent or integrating service-learning more fully into any of the education programs.

Teaching candidates are informed about service-learning in the college catalogue and all must participate in the three courses that are part of the admission process for education programs. Students must reflect on how their service connects to teaching and learning in each of the three courses. Schools and community agencies support the utilization of service-learning by informing the unit about their needs. Students find their own sites for service or use the campuswide service office to find sites with specific needs. No formal partnerships exist between the unit and community agencies, within the exception of schools and day care centers; however, the community is perceived as welcoming to students. Adjunct faculty from local schools, acting as clinical teachers, provide informal community voice in the department and help with identifying needs and welcoming service sites.

Over the years, the grant-driven initiative has been pushed aside by other, more pressing matters. The faculty member who directed the initial grant moved on to an administrative position with increasing responsibilities. She had been the primary champion of service-learning, but her new duties require that she focus her energies on other, more pressing issues. She notes that "service-learning has stagnated." There is one new faculty member who has since taken the lead, but she is not tenured and needs to work on her scholarship.

Key Points

At Institution D service as part of the mission has not been enough to ensure institutionalization of service-learning because:

- The all-important champion did not seem either to be present or to be able to carry on with the integration effort past the initial stage.

- Schools and local agencies did not form partnerships with the education department;
- Little understanding of service-learning extended beyond its suitability for teaching.
- Administrative changes at both college and department levels created an environment in which service-learning became something that fit a specific niche (assessing admission to the program).
- There were neither incentives nor interest in expanding and exploring service-learning.

Institution E

Service-learning was integrated into the teacher education program at Institution E primarily due to the efforts of the service-learning champion, a tenured, senior faculty member, and the director of the university Office of Service-Learning, who were able to include a specific reference to increasing the use of service-learning across campus in the institutional strategic plan. The president of the university also played an important role in getting service-learning included in the strategic plan and by channeling funds to support the Office of Service-Learning. A common definition of service-learning was developed collaboratively by the seven College of Education (COE) faculty who regularly use it, although other COE faculty are not aware of this definition. Service-learning is not included in the COE mission or strategic plan. The faculty champion and the director of the Office of Service-Learning each have written and received federal grants to enhance service-learning efforts but service-learning is not linked to any other high-profile initiatives.

The faculty champion's direct, personal contact with other faculty members and the former dean of the COE were the primary method used to gain understanding of and acceptance for service-learning. Currently, 5 of the 15 COE faculty members use service-learning, but only one of them (the faculty champion) is an influential, senior faculty member.

Students' main experience with service-learning occurs in the first course they take in the teacher education program. In all sections of this course, 220 students per year are introduced to service-learning, taught how to use it as a pedagogy, and required to design and implement a service-learning project in conjunction with K–12 teachers and students. Students and administrators acknowledge that this placement of service-learning in the first course in the program is problematic. Students feel it is too early in the program for them to know what is happening in schools and, as a result, they rely on their cooperating teachers too heavily to carry out the service-learning requirement. This in turn produces some resentment among the cooperating teachers and principals who then communicate this to the COE dean.

The faculty champion developed strong personal relationships with many K–12 teachers and administrators and with many community-based organizations, enabling him to arrange service-learning placements and projects for students. Many community partners noted that the faculty champion was the key to success. But he could only do so much. There is a need for larger, long-term service-learning projects that are schoolwide and that include a deeper relationship with community partners. The K–12 teachers also need more training in how to use service-learning as a pedagogy.

The Office of the Vice-Provost for Academic Affairs has provided funds to support the use of service-learning in the COE for 6 years, but this funding is competitive and not assured. During the first 5 years that service-learning was included in the curriculum, the COE provided support in the form of limited funds for training and travel to conferences, but the past 3 years this support has been withdrawn by a new dean who does not understand or support service-learning.

Key Points

Although Institution E was able to gradually expand service-learning in the COE, due to the efforts of the faculty champion, the director of the university Office of Service-Learning, and with active support from the department chair, COE dean, and university president, as well as supplemental support from external grants, service-learning institutionalization has stalled because of:

- Too great a reliance on the efforts of a single individual (the faculty champion);
- The loss of the supportive president, dean, and department chair and replacement with people that do not support service-learning use;
- A university financial crisis causing budget cutbacks limiting development or expansion of low-priority programs; and
- Loss of a large federal grant to greatly expand the Office of Service-Learning.

CONCLUSIONS

Conclusions presented below are organized as responses to each of the four primary research questions.

Question One. What policies, practices, and infrastructure are in place at each SCDE that have helped or hindered the institutionalization of service-learning?

The most helpful institutional characteristic in terms of supporting service-learning was having an institutional mission and/or goals in a strategic plan that could be successfully achieved through the use of service-learning. Providing support for a campuswide Service-Learning Center and supporting faculty in obtaining outside grant funds to develop service-learning practice were also key practices. SCDEs with the greatest degree of service-learning institutionalization were quite emphatic in pointing out that policies were not what caused their success with service-learning. Policies were developed last, only after individual faculty's and administrators' hearts and minds were won over to service-learning, and after service-learning practice was at a consistently high level.

The two main hindrances to service-learning institutionalization appear to be interrelated. The first of these is a lack of understanding of what service-learning can accomplish and an attitude that results in blocking, or not actively supporting, service-learning initiatives. The second hindrance was an intense focus on reaching teacher education program accreditation standards that precluded a willingness to explore service-learning and other new projects. The inability to see ways in which service-learning could directly help achieve accreditation standards limited success in both areas.

Question Two. What processes and activities did SCDE faculty, administrators, and others engage in to achieve the current state of service-learning institutionalization?

Processes and activities can be delineated for each of the three stages in the Furco rubric.

Stage One: Critical Mass Building. In the early stages of service-learning institutionalization, it is essential that the SCDE have a service-learning champion: a tenured, well-respected faculty member who is willing to take on the time and work necessary to gain acceptance for service-learning among key faculty and administrators and to develop relationships with community partners. Without such a person service-learning would not have been successful at any of the five SCDEs in this study. Early on, the champion and others must be sure that service-learning is presented in a way that allows key decision-makers to see that it is clearly and directly linked to the institutional mission and strategic plan. The champion then needs to educate SCDE faculty, administrators, and students to understand the benefits of service-learning, as well as how to successfully put service-learning into practice. In many cases, this education was supported by grant funds the champion had obtained for this purpose. The champion also needed to establish successful relationships with K–12 and other community-based organizations in order to have sites for teacher candidates to engage in service-learning. This relationship building could be supported by a campuswide service-learning center, but in the early stages was accomplished primarily by the champion. Although these community partners were essential for success with service-learning, in most cases, they did not have much influence within the SCDE regarding use of service-learning.

Stage Two: Quality Building. In the second stage of institutionalization many of the service-learning champions focused on engaging SCDE faculty and administrators in discussing and developing a definition of service-learning to be used to guide all SCDE service-learning activities. At this point, the campuswide service-learning center often began playing a stronger role in arranging service-learning placements, solidifying partnerships with community-based organizations, and in educating students and faculty regarding service-learning. Also, at this stage SCDE and campuswide administrative support proved helpful, or even necessary, to obtain grant funds, to travel to service-learning conferences, to provide rewards and recognition for faculty and student service-learning success, and to move forward with K–12 partnerships. This administrative advocacy and support for service-learning was not seen as essential in the first stage, and some faculty and administrators saw it as detrimental to service-learning during the early stage of institutionalization.

Stage Three: Sustained Institutionalization. During Stage Three, it was helpful to hire new faculty and administrators that demonstrated not only an interest in service-learning, but expressed a commitment to its use. At this point, it was also productive to establish written policies that placed service-learning in key SCDE documents such as strategic plans and promotion and tenure guidelines. At this stage, some SCDEs were also beginning to link teacher program accreditation standards to specific service-learning practices. Finally, it was helpful for the SCDE or institution to pick up grant-supported service-learning activities and fund them through internal sources.

Question Three. Was there a linear sequence in which these activities were conducted, or did issues re-emerge in a spiral-like process? How long did institutionalization take?

The response to the above question describes three stages of service-learning institutionalization. Although service-learning activities tended to occur in a linear sequence within these stages it was also true that crucial issues kept reemerging throughout the institutionalization process. These issues included the continuing need for a faculty service-learning champion; a positive relationship with K–12 and other community partners, and the necessity of either external or internal funding support for service-learning.

It is also noteworthy that none of the SCDEs in this study reported that student influence, needs, or advocacy played an important role in the development of service-learning courses or its institutionalization.

Although the degree to which service-learning was institutionalized varied by SCDE, in each case it was time-consuming, taking from 5 to 7 years before faculty could claim successful institutionalization. It also appeared that the institutionalization process can occur more rapidly at smaller institutions, perhaps because there are fewer people that need to be convinced of its efficacy.

FINAL THOUGHTS

The institutionalization of service-learning in SCDEs is a highly complex endeavor to both conduct and to study. Many teacher educators are seeking recommendations, or even a cookbook of steps to follow to achieve success with service-learning at their institution. The results of this study support Furco's notion of the existence of stages in the institutionalization process but do not allow us to delineate a linear series of steps to follow to ensure service-learning success. Rather, the authors believe other institutions can learn from the experiences of the five SCDEs in this study and can chart their progress with the help of the three-stage model, but they should be careful not to try to replicate the process followed by any of the SCDEs included here. Instead, they should build on their own history, mission, values, and community needs and assets. They would also do well to be patient with the process. Service-learning institutionalization takes considerable time, even in SCDEs that have near-universal agreement that it is an important goal.

ACKNOWLEDGMENTS

The project described in this chapter was supported in part by grants from the Corporation for National and Community Service and Seattle University.

REFERENCES

Anderson, J. B., & Erickson, J. A. (2003). Service-learning in preservice teacher education. *Academic Exchange Quarterly, 7*(2), 111–115.

Billig, S. H. (2002). Adoption, implementation, and sustainability of K–12 service-learning. In A. Furco & S. H. Billig (Eds.), *Advances in service-learning: Vol. 1. Service-learning: The essence of the pedagogy* (pp. 245–267). Greenwich, CT: Information Age Publishing.

Bringle, R. G., & Hatcher, J. A. (2000). Institutionalization of service-learning in higher education. *Journal of Higher Education, 71*(3), 273–290.

36 J.B. ANDERSON and J. CALLAHAN

Callahan, J., & Root, S. (2003). The diffusion of academic service-learning in teacher education: A case study approach. In J. Eyler & S. H. Billig (Eds.), *Advances in service-learning: Vol. 3. Deconstructing service-learning: Research exploring context, participation, and impacts* (pp. 77–101). Greenwich, CT: Information Age Publishing.

Furco, A. (1999). *Self-assessment rubric for the institutionalization of service-learning in higher education.* Berkeley: University of California, Berkeley.

Furco, A. (2002). Institutionalizing service-learning in higher education. *Journal of Public Affairs, 6*(1), 39–68.

Holland, B. (1997). Analyzing institutional commitment to service: A model of key organizational factors. *Michigan Journal of Community Service Learning, 4*, 30–41.

Holland, B. (2000, Fall). Institutional impacts and organizational issues related to service-learning. *Michigan Journal of Community Service Learning* [Special issue], 52–60.

Keckes, K., & Muyllaert, J. (1997). *Benchmark worksheet for the Western Region Campus Compact Consortium grants program.* Bellingham: Western Washington University.

Miles, M. B., & Huberman, A. M. (1984). *Qualitative data analysis: A sourcebook of new methods.* Beverly Hills, CA: Sage.

CHAPTER 3

DEVELOPING ADVOCATES AND LEADERS THROUGH SERVICE-LEARNING IN PRESERVICE AND INSERVICE SPECIAL EDUCATION PROGRAMS

Jean Gonsier-Gerdin and Joanna Royce-Davis

ABSTRACT

This chapter presents a case study of two collaboratively taught special education courses that incorporated service-learning projects as a pedagogical response to students' self-identified learning needs. The chapter describes and analyzes instructors' and students' post-course learning outcomes related to their participation in service-learning. In particular, this study examines how participation in service-learning contributes to student development of critical competencies, such as advocacy and leadership, associated with the role of special educator. Findings suggest that student participation in service-learning influences: (a) their awareness of social justice issues; (b) their development of and confidence in leadership skills;

Improving Service-Learning Practice: Research on Models to Enhance Impacts, pages 37–57
37

(c) their commitment to advocacy and leadership roles; and (d) their professional role development. Findings also include insights into the process of using service-learning and co-teaching as pedagogical tools in teacher education from the instructor's perspective. Implications, recommendations, and questions for future research into the role of service-learning in special education teacher preparation are provided.

INTRODUCTION

Despite great strides in the provision of services to students with disabilities and their families over the last 25 years, the need for advocacy by special education professionals has no end in sight. Reasons for this need include, but are not limited to, the following:

- Historical discrimination experienced by students with disabilities;
- Frequent denial of the educational rights and needs of students with disabilities;
- Schools as bureaucratic entities;
- The lack of parental advocacy; and
- Findings from research on special education outcomes that indicate students are not successful in post-school community adjustment (Fiedler, 2000).

Furthermore, the successes of current and future school reform efforts are seen as tremendously dependent upon all teachers, including special education professionals, being leaders and change agents (Cobb, 2001; Restine, 1997). Advocacy efforts by special education professionals are necessary to secure new rights, to preserve existing programs, to increase service capacity, to improve program quality, to support change in education systems, and to generate public awareness of key issues faced by individuals with disabilities and their families (Fiedler, 2000).

The dispositions, knowledge, and skills that have been identified necessary for effective special education advocates and leaders include:

- Knowledge of special education practices, laws, and regulations;
- Knowledge of dispute resolution mechanisms;
- Knowledge of systems change;
- Interpersonal communication skills;
- Collaboration skills;
- Conflict resolution skills;
- Ethical analysis skills;
- Willingness to take risks to benefit students;
- Problem-solving skills; and

- Critical thinking skills (Fiedler, 2000; Gartin, Murdick, Thompson, & Dyches, 2002).

If there is the expectation that teachers are to fulfill these roles and responsibilities, teacher education programs cannot assume that all candidates intuitively possess the dispositions and predispositions for these skills essential to advocacy and leadership. Clearly, the dispositions, behaviors, and skills required for teacher leadership need to be part of the preservice and professional development of teachers, as noted by Forster (1997):

> Teacher education institutions must develop an understanding and commitment on the part of preservice teachers that leadership is not a separate role or position to be assumed under specific circumstances. Rather, they must come to believe that leadership is inherent in their role as teachers and professionals, and that they have a responsibility to fulfill that role and develop the capacity to do so. (p. 9)

The challenge then becomes to identify what are the most effective methods available in teacher education coursework that will cultivate these necessary dispositions, knowledge bases, and skills. Service-learning has emerged as one of these methods (Mayhew & Welch, 2001).

SERVICE-LEARNING AND TEACHER EDUCATION

The definition of service-learning remains broad. Currently, over 200 published definitions of service-learning exist in the professional literature (Furco, 2003). Butin (2003) suggested that conceptualizations of service-learning may be placed into four categories:

1. A vehicle for achieving particular student outcomes;
2. As an intentional context for student meaning making, particularly in relation to understanding themselves as community members and in relation to social issues;
3. As a political process used to influence change; and
4. As a means for understanding the consistency and disruption of constructs such as teaching, learning, and self.

The study in this chapter uses the second operational definition of service-learning while also acknowledging the technical parameters of the pedagogy that are emphasized in the first conceptualization. Not only does service-learning provide students and community members with an opportunity to co-construct meaning, service-learning also engages students in a three-part process: (1) classroom preparation through explanation and analysis of theories and ideas; (2) service activity that emerges from and informs classroom context; and (3) structured reflection tying service experience back to specific learning goals (Jeavons, 1995).

Service-learning extends the assumption that direct experience is necessary for learning by adding the criticality of providing learning contexts that are most relevant and meaningful to the learning objectives at hand (Dodd & Lilly, 2000). This form of applied learning is necessary to substantiate student and instructor understandings of locality-based dynamics of advocacy and leadership. Thus, service-learning is a pedagogical tool with the potential to influence social change.

Based on these conceptions, service-learning has a logical place in the teacher education curriculum, particularly in developing skills sets, such as those associated with leadership, that require application in real settings to achieve competency. In fact, service-learning has been described as contributing these types of outcomes to the process of teacher education (Feiman-Nemser, 2001; Sileo, Prater, Luckner, Rhine, & Rude, 1998). Among the learning outcomes reported in the literature as being gained by preservice teachers as a result of their participation in service-learning are:

- Increased critical thinking about teaching practice;
- Accentuation of the multiple roles played by teachers;
- Socialization into the moral and civil obligations of the teaching role, including advocating for social justice within the realm of education; and
- Increased knowledge about diversity (Anderson, 1998; Billig, 2000; Malone, Jones, & Stallings, 2002; Potthoff et al., 2000; Wade, 2003; Wade, Boyle-Baise, & O'Grady, 2001).

Each of these outcomes is also significant for the development of effective special educators, but typically is not intentionally or directly addressed in "traditional" forms of practicum and fieldwork. Service-learning provides a needed forum for preservice special educators to focus specifically on the development of advocacy and leadership skills within meaningful contexts while simultaneously developing their roles as contributing members of the educational community.

There are some isolated examples of preservice special education courses that do include service-learning as a pedagogical tool. One advanced methods course in an undergraduate special education teacher program provided a 25-hour service-learning experience in which students worked collaboratively with their field-based cooperating teachers and university professor to plan, implement, and evaluate instruction to meet the needs of students with disabilities, their families, and the faculty who work with them (Muscott, 2001). In another special education teacher training program, students were matched with a mentor special education teacher in a rural school district and spent time living in homes of community families. Through the development and implementation of a service-learning project, these preservice teachers identified and analyzed the community needs and incorporated these needs as the focus for a meaningful school curriculum for students with special needs (Davis, Emery, & Lane, 1998). While these are helpful examples to guide practice, service-learning methodology continues to be underutilized in the preparation of special education leaders and advocates.

The purpose of this chapter is to present a case study of two collaboratively taught special education courses that incorporated service-learning projects as a pedagogical response to students' self-identified learning needs. This chapter describes and analyzes instructors' and students' post-course learning outcomes related to their participation in service-learning. In particular, this study examines how participation in service-learning contributes to student development of critical competencies, such as advocacy and leadership, associated with the role of special educator.

METHODOLOGY

A case-study design (Taylor & Bogdan, 1998) was selected for this study because the boundaries between course-bound and other influences on "becoming a special educator" are not always easy to separate. Specifically, this case study utilized a phenomenological framework in an attempt to focus on the structure or essence of becoming a special educator, with particular attention to students' development of the inherent roles of advocate and leader, and the potential impact of the service-learning component of courses on these outcomes. Husserl (1931), one of the original phenomenologists, described essence as the condition or quality that makes a phenomenon what it is, as well as the commonalities or universalities between individual experiences and understandings of a phenomenon.

SETTING, CONTEXT, AND PARTICIPANTS

These courses took place at a small private university in northern California—a comprehensive university with an overall enrollment of approximately 6,000 students. The main campus is composed of the core liberal arts college and a variety of professional schools. The students at this campus are an eclectic mix (although approximately 75% of those enrolled are from northern California) with nearly 60% of the undergraduates being women and an ethnic composition that is 49.6% white, 26.5% Asian/Pacific Islander, 10.1% Hispanic, 3.1% African American, and .8% American Indian.

In his critique of the service-learning literature, Furco (2003) proposed that service-learning research focus on the individual as the unit of study, rather than larger units of study, which miss the nuances associated with individual experiences and outcomes of service-learning activity. This focus on individual experiences becomes even more relevant when using a definition of service-learning that requires an examination and understanding of how individuals make meaning of the experience of becoming a special educator. Ultimately, the present study attempts to tease out individual meanings within the context of collective experience. Interestingly, this focus on unique needs of individual learners is consistent with the approach to special education itself.

The participants in the study included 15 students enrolled in undergraduate and graduate special education courses as well as the two instructors who co-taught these courses. This sample was selected because these two classes represented courses typically found in the special education credential requirements, and the students enrolled, based on sample size, provided maximum variation in terms of their diversity based on age, ethnicity, and their years of experience in the field of education. According to Patton (1990), "Findings from even a small sample of great diversity yield important shared patterns that cut across cases and derive their significance from having emerged out of heterogeneity" (p. 172).

The authors of this chapter collaboratively served as instructor for both courses. One instructor was a full-time assistant professor in the School of Education who served as the director of special education programs. The other instructor was a part-time faculty member in the School of Education and a university administrator in the Career Resource Center where she was actively involved coordinating experiential learning programs across the university campus, including service-learning opportunities. The two instructors created this co-teaching arrangement in order to model collaboration and to maximize their varied experiences and expertise in the field of special education and disability studies. Both identify themselves and are considered by others to be advocates for social justice and inclusion issues, particularly those related to the needs of individuals with disabilities.

SPED 166: Building Family–Professional Partnerships. This course provides future educators with the opportunity to:

- Demonstrate understanding and uses of basic concepts and theories in counseling, advocacy, and problem solving that are appropriate for students with disabilities and their families;
- Know and understand techniques, strategies, and resources available to educate parents/family members of students with special needs and strategies to promote family involvement and support;
- Develop an understanding of the implications of ethnic, linguistic, and cultural diversity for family–school relations;
- Acquire a knowledge base about education law and parental/family rights;
- demonstrate familiarity with various family support systems, practices, and strategies;
- Increase awareness of family-centered and family-directed services, practices, and advocacy;
- Become an advocate for students with disabilities and their families; and
- Develop skills that promote professional ethics and self-improvement.

In fall 2002, six undergraduate students and one graduate student were enrolled in Building Family–Professional Partnerships. Students represented a variety of majors, including education, special education, psychology, and speech-language pathology.

Building family–professional partnerships Web advocacy project. During the evolution of this course, one of the chapter authors collaborated with her students to develop a group advocacy project. Since spring 2002, the group advocacy project has been Web-based in nature and therefore serves a larger audience/community, even though these projects initially involved a variety of media in terms of the end product. Moreover, a service-learning orientation has come to frame the assignment.

The Web-based group advocacy projects provide future educators with the opportunity to creatively explore, reflect upon, and synthesize information, concepts, and strategies regarding building meaningful, cooperative, and productive relationships between professionals and families with children who have special needs. These Web sites are intended to be useful for teachers, family members, other professionals, teacher educators, and advocates for individuals who have special needs. In order to develop successful Web sites, students need to not only utilize and integrate concepts and information from the course, but to develop an understanding of the needs of stakeholders (i.e., initially local community members who would access the Web site) and to evaluate and reflect upon their own roles and skills as community members and advocates.

The process of Web site development began early in the semester with brainstorming possible topic areas with facilitation by instructors. Students formed groups by interest area. An initial challenge facing students was that they had to learn the technology and negotiate it as well as develop mastery of the content area. It also was necessary for them to develop skills to communicate with a range of audiences/constituencies. The fact that these Web sites were developed in groups of two to three members made it inevitable that students needed to grapple with collaboration between group members as well as involvement with community stakeholders. Furthermore, students were required to reflect on how well the Web sites served the communities for which they were originally developed and the much larger potential community (i.e., anyone with access to the Internet).

In fall 2002, the students created three Web sites:

1. Advice for Parents and Advocates—The purpose of this Web site is to empower parents, educators, and advocates who work with children with special education needs. This site provides useful information about special education laws through resources and links, as well as advice and information on advocacy skills;

2. Got Support? A Basic Guide to Starting a Support Group—The goal of this Web site is to empower families of children with disabilities to help face the challenges of raising a special needs child; and

3. Family and Educator Resources for Child Abuse—The purpose of this Web site is to provide families and educators the knowledge and power to effectively use local organizations, councils, and agencies to prevent, stop, and report child abuse and maltreatment.

SPED 295a: Crucial Issues in Special Education. This course provides graduate students in education and related fields an opportunity to:

- Increase students' familiarity with current and emerging issues in the field of special education;
- Develop an understanding of the related services provided for children with disabilities;
- Investigate the role of the federal government in the progress of children with disabilities;
- Gain knowledge about regional, state, and national trends in education and their long- and short-term effects;
- Critically analyze research in order to develop positions on issues;
- Explore and respond to issues in special education as they relate to social justice and student outcomes; and
- Understand issues in special education legislation and litigation as they pertain to the learning community: families, teachers, school districts, and students with disabilities.

In the fall of 2002, enrollment for Crucial Issues in Special Education included eight graduate students; seven in a master's degree or credential program and one in a doctoral degree program. The group included one international student who contributed multiple cultural and class perspectives and experiences to course discussions. Students' exposure to the teaching field ranged from 0 to 20 years of direct teaching or education-related experience.

Crucial issues in special education policy analysis project. During the course of analyzing and discussing current issues covered in the course syllabus, students shared feelings of intense frustration regarding how they were directly affected by some of these issues and their related inability to challenge or change current problems connected with the provision of special education services. In particular, students expressed concern about the day-to-day interpretation of various parts of the Individuals with Disabilities Education Act (IDEA) and the implications of the No Child Left Behind Act for students with special needs.

Service-learning was identified as the best pedagogical response to students' current learning, developmental, and emotional needs. Service-learning provided the opportunity for students to enhance their learning about pressing issues in the field of education while empowering them to respond and reinforcing the leadership and advocacy dimensions of their special educator or administrator role. The students and instructors recreated a research assignment included in the original syllabus as a participatory action research project where the findings would directly benefit or serve the participants and members of their extended community. The project was thus reframed in a way that the dissemination and use of the findings was as important as the academic research process.

Students formed groups based on their communities of residence or employment. Topics selected included:

- The current status of teacher and family knowledge about the *No Child Left Behind Act;*
- Administrators' knowledge of and plans for implementation of the *No Child Left Behind Act;*
- The meaning of "natural environment" in early childhood services; and
- The local interpretation of the "Free and Appropriate Public Education" (FAPE) component of IDEA.

The contexts where students completed their service-learning projects were directly meaningful to students as constituents and stakeholders as these were the communities where they lived and continued to provide service. Student findings immediately informed their teaching practice and created opportunities for them to be leaders in the communities of which they continue to be a part.

As advocated in the service-learning literature (Jacoby & Associates, 1996), intentional reflection was an essential part of student learning and for integration of the projects into community outcomes. Intellectual reflections on crucial issues occurred both in class and on a Web-based forum and included insights about the learning process and the course curriculum. Reflections also focused on students' emotional and intellectual relationships to leadership and advocacy issues within their community contexts, including shared frustrations and common experiences at their district and school sites. To facilitate reflection the course instructors continually asked the questions, "As an emerging leader in special education, what can you do to generate or contribute to a solution? How can you make a difference?"

DATA COLLECTION

Data were collected from six different sources for the purpose of triangulation of themes. Data sources included:

- Field notes by the instructors throughout the semester of observations of participants;
- Students' written reflections posted on blackboard.com course sites during and at the end of the experience;
- Artifacts associated with actual service-learning projects;
- Course evaluations containing closed and open-ended questions completed by the students;
- Field notes by instructors of ongoing conversations between instructors and students subsequent to the project; and
- Students' responses to survey and interview questions 3 months after the completion of the two courses.

Additional data came in the form of instructors' field notes and reflections on student learning outcomes and their collaborative teaching efforts in the tradition of heuristic inquiry and in their roles as "participant as observer."

DATA ANALYSIS

According to Moustakas (1994), the goal of phenomenological data analysis is to reduce textural meanings, or the "what" of experience and structural meanings, or the "how" of an experience to a brief description that typifies the experience of a phenomenon for all of the participants in a study. Because all individuals experience the phenomenon in some form, it is a reduction to the "essentials" of the experience. Using the phenomenological approach, data was analyzed to arrive at structural descriptions of service-learning and related course influences on students' development of advocacy and leadership roles within the context of becoming special educators.

The raw data as recorded was transcribed verbatim for each participant. Non-recorded interviews and participant observations were written up as field notes immediately following the data collection. Survey responses were also treated as transcripts and coded as such.

Phenomenological analysis took place using the following five-step process suggested by Moustakas (1994): (1) bracketing, (2) horizontalization, (3) identification of themes, (4) textural description, and (5) structural description. Each investigator completed the five-step process, including writing up categorical descriptions individually. The investigators then met and compared initial findings, paying particular attention to themes that were absent from either of the independent analyses or where the researchers disagreed about interpretation of the data. Independently, they each reviewed the data again to look for negative cases and met a second time to compare findings, omissions, and interpretations. Finally, the investigators shared their findings with the study participants to verify accuracy and identify missed relationships within the data. After this third review of themes, final categories of meaning were determined and descriptive detail expanded.

CREDIBILITY OF FINDINGS

In qualitative research, validity is defined as the confidence placed in study data and data analysis (McLeod, 2003; Neuman, 1997) or recognition that the conclusions and ideas presented after data analysis are well grounded and well supported by the data and are credible (Polkinghorne, 1989). Furthermore, a phenomenological study is considered to be valid when the descriptions and analysis provided in the study make possible an understanding of the meanings and essences of the experience being studied (Boyatzis, 1998; Moustakas, 1994). In this study, the following methods were used to enhance the credibility of the findings (Miles & Huberman, 1994):

- Prolonged engagement with the participants resulting in rich, thick description;
- Triangulation through the use of multiple data sources;

- Confirmation of the data analysis and findings through member checks with the study participants;
- Negative case analysis or examination of events and perceptions that did not fit emerging themes; and
- Continued clarification of the co-investigators' biases.

FINDINGS

Student Outcomes

The findings of this study are congruent with learning outcomes generally discussed in teacher education and service-learning literature, and they add additional insights into the meaning and process of achieving these outcomes for students in undergraduate and graduate special education programs. Findings suggest that student participation in service-learning influences:

- Their awareness of social justice issues;
- Their development of and confidence in leadership skills;
- Their commitment to advocacy and leadership roles; and
- Their professional role development.

From awareness of social justice issues to action. The content of the course provided a purposeful structure for reviewing issues related to social justice. These seemingly remote topics became more relevant as students experienced individual catalysts that personalized their reactions and responses. For example, for one group of students, participation in the former Assistant Secretary for Elementary and Secondary Education's presentation on No Child Left Behind (NCLB) served as a "call to arms" for them, as current special educators, to challenge the impact of the legislation in a state as diverse as California. For another group of students, recognition of social justice issues and related emotion about potential social outcomes emerged from the process of choosing a project topic. Finally, for the majority of students, the process of reviewing professional literature, combined with interviewing stakeholders, created a sense of urgency related to the seriousness of their responsibility as special educators.

Students reported a greater awareness of family challenges, ethical dilemmas for professionals, educational access issues, and limitations on disability rights. According to one team, "[We] have a better sense of the real issues of access and choice that families face when they have a kid with a disability. This project gave us a better picture of what it's really like to not have power to affect your life."

Students also shared that these learning outcomes were enhanced by the interaction between course content and service-learning activities. These outcomes led to a deeper understanding of the reality that, in order to create an environment for necessary changes and increased social justice, advocacy is required. Dana articulated this understanding,

> I realize that there needs to be more lobbying done locally, at the community, district, and at the state level, to help teach the legislators who help make the laws to show them what it's really like in the classroom.

Development of and confidence in leadership skills. Student engagement with social justice issues, in turn, functioned as the context for learning, practicing, and honing competencies associated with leadership and advocacy. Students first became aware of the necessary and available tools for promoting social change and then began to identify the skills needed to utilize those tools. For example, in SPED 166 and the Web-based group advocacy project, the students quickly recognized the use of the Internet and Web sites as far-reaching communication, advocacy, and educational vehicles. Students subsequently were motivated to learn how to use the Internet effectively to reach target audiences and make related social impact. According to Patricia, "It was also very informative to try to make a product for people that informs, teaches, and gives them places to find more information." In a second example, graduate students in SPED 295a recognized the power of raising questions and of serving as a voice for their constituencies. Reba often shared the questions that she posed to the formal leadership, including the representative of the teacher's union, at her district and the related outcome of those individuals pausing to reflect on the status quo.

The service-learning projects also emphasized the criticality of collaboration for effective leadership. Students realized that the practice of collaboration was essential to their ability to move ideas for change and advocacy beyond themselves and their classmates. Indeed, they began to perceive leadership as a shared responsibility. Participation in these activities resulted in a self-evaluation of students' available skill sets, particularly in reference to organizational and systemic change. Students also arrived at an increased understanding of the complexity of collaboration. When one Web site design group was unable to resolve conflict around a number of issues, including the division of labor and consensus building, the group members recognized the importance of and challenges to creating a shared vision and its implications for the productivity and outcomes of their group's work. According to Rachel, one of the group members, collaborators need "to agree on the vision of the page [or other outcome] and not assume that partners share your own [vision]." In other words, students acknowledged that the success and quality of their projects could be attributed to the collaborative efforts of group members and their mutual commitment to the issue being investigated.

In addition, students commented on the power of these service projects for cultivating competence in leadership and advocacy skill sets. When Madison shared, "I also learned how to work with a partner better than I have in the past," she specifically reflected on the impact on her collaborative skills. Students also honed necessary research skills that ranged from the ability to locate and secure credible information to skill in reading documents such as research studies and legislation from an informed, critical perspective. Madison's experience was as follows: "I learned how to perform better research skills. I did not realize it until I completed the project, but I really enjoyed keeping up on such an important issue." Perhaps more importantly, students developed their ability to conduct research about attitudes, awareness, and other variables affecting special education services and individuals with disabilities. As these skills evolved so did the students' sense of the significance, broader meaning, and personal relevance of research activities. Inez eloquently illustrated this point:

> I was afraid of research. I never, how do you say, got that understanding, and creating it was important to my worth when working with people at the university and in the schools. People look at me differently—hear me—hear what the families say. I began to understand this in the Crucial Issues project and it made even more sense in the research class. But, Crucial Issues made the importance of this knowledge and skills clear. I understand now the need to struggle with research for the sake of the struggle that my students and families go through. I am the one who has to take a stand and use this for them.

Commitment to advocacy and leadership roles. The growth in students' advocacy and leadership skills triggered a level of commitment to ongoing involvement in project-related issues. Several months after the courses ended, students shared varying levels of continued engagement with community issues. On one end of the continuum, students expressed increased effort dedicated to maintaining informed awareness of developments related to the social justice issues (e.g., reading professional journals, talking with colleagues). Dana clearly articulated the need to stay involved:

> By doing the policy chapter, I became more aware of how much we are unaware of what happens when we aren't involved or "tuned in"—how much goes on at the federal level that no one has any idea about unless they are "tuned in."

On the other end of the continuum, students were actively involved in educating colleagues in the community and field and planning for future advocacy. Reba described her activism:

> I continually challenge my site staff and leadership about doing what is right. I take the opportunity to share what I have learned through my reading and research and hope that it changes their thinking about what happens to kids with disabilities. I also teach families how to work through a system that does not support them. I ask the questions and encourage them to ask too. I can't sit by knowing what I know.

Professional role development. As the semester progressed, it became evident during discussions inside and outside of the classroom that the above-mentioned commitment to advocacy and leadership helped students shape and even reframe their professional identity as a special educator. For Tanya, this included confirming her career choice:

> This experience made me want to be a special educator—to find the place where I could make change. It also made me realize that I have a lot to learn and that [I] need to make that happen so things can be different for students with disabilities and their families.

Moreover, the students moved from a position of viewing their job as solely to work with students to understanding the ecological nature of their work in special education. That is, the students recognized and acknowledged that to be an effective advocate and leader they would be required to serve as a bridge between multiple interrelated systems (i.e., education, social services, legal, etc.) and individual students with special needs and their families. In this professional role, the students began to see themselves as central to the communication with and between decisionmakers, colleagues, families, and students.

Finally, the service-learning projects even supported students' decisions regarding continued professional development and employment opportunities. For example, two students who had been teaching while completing their credential and master's degree program chose to continue their education in educational administration and leadership. Their goals were to pursue the position of decision-maker as a way of influencing change. For Inez, who was beginning her search for a teaching position, her commitment to advocacy influenced the choices that she made regarding the schools and school districts in which she sought employment.

INSTRUCTOR OUTCOMES

While the initial intent of the study was to explore the student outcomes associated with participation in service-learning, the study findings clearly provide insights into the process of teacher education from the instructor's perspective using service-learning and co-teaching as pedagogical tools. The following themes reflect the essence of the instructors' experiences:

- Service-learning as educational intervention;
- Service-learning projects as process;
- Instructor as learning community member; and
- The need to alter instructor roles and responsibilities.

Service-learning as educational intervention. As a result of facilitating the service-learning projects in both courses, the instructors learned that these projects can be used as vehicles for learning and practicing advocacy and leadership skills in a real applied manner. (See discussion of student outcomes for further details.) They also concluded that service-learning opportunities can emerge from the course learning community in particular types of courses, rather than having to be pre-established by instructors. In fact, the projects for both courses were revisions of already existing assignments to be more responsive to the students' unique learning, emotional, and professional needs.

Service-learning projects as process. In order to effectively support students, the instructors discovered that it was useful to focus on the service-learning projects as a process. For both courses, the process included, but was not limited to, inviting students to become engaged in social change endeavors, brainstorming topics, forming groups, engaging with the community (e.g., interviewing school district personnel, researching on the Internet), teaching and learning technical skills (e.g., Web design, research, interviewing, data analysis), and problem-solving group dynamics. Throughout the various stages of the service-learning process, the instructors spent time together in active reflection and then incorporated their insights into their teaching practice and scaffolding of students' abilities.

A noteworthy part of the process was the timing of community immersion. Prior to students being engaged with the community, the instructors needed to set the stage for students to enter into the experience skilled enough to become involved (e.g., having sufficient content knowledge, able to ask relevant questions), but still in a place where the experience furthered their growth and competency.

Instructor as learning community member. Without a doubt, instructor facilitation and active participation in the learning community was a critical part of the effectiveness of the service-learning process and projects. This membership role went well beyond the expected, limited opportunities for comments on student assignments to ongoing opportunities to brainstorm and to reflect upon the process of the service-learning projects. For the Web-based group advocacy project, both of the instructors spent time outside of class in the computer lab to provide access to computer technology and to assist students to tease out the essentials of educating the general and/or targeted population about their issue as well as to reinforce instructional concepts discussed in earlier classes. For the policy analysis project, the instructors met with teams outside of class in person and via the Internet to support students in defining and addressing the real issues at hand, to review interview questions, to offer feedback on data analysis and conclusions, and to encourage dissemination of findings.

Clearly, it was crucial for the instructors to be responsive to the personality and dynamics of each cohort group. As a result, the instructors really became partners of each team or cohort group. Students valued this partnership with instructors that occurred during the service-learning projects and still frequently seek out the instructors to discuss project-related topics and to problem solve day-to-day evidence of related social issues in their work environments.

Need to alter instructor roles and responsibilities. Not surprisingly, as the instructors became learning community members and partners, the typical instructor roles and responsibilities changed as well. It became expected and essential that instructors be role models for service, community engagement, advocacy, and leadership. The instructors shared with students the ways in which they were involved in social change efforts within their own departments, the university as a whole, and the community at large. They also needed to model the give and take of collaboration and productive dialogue among colleagues and the creative problem solving utilized for conflict management and resolution.

IMPLICATIONS AND RECOMMENDATIONS

With the 21st century and the real changes to federal educational legislation (e.g., NCLB and IDEA), special education preparation programs are challenged more than ever with developing special educators qualified to be leaders, advocates, and agents of change. Consequently, university faculty are exploring instructional strategies and opportunities that build these critical competencies. In the present case study, service-learning projects and processes served as productive vehicles for the teaching and learning of advocacy and leadership dispositions, knowledge, and skills in support of social justice. Indeed, these opportunities to reach the community in less traditionally defined ways resulted in significant student and instructor outcomes as well as reciprocal benefits to a broader community membership.

Before presenting implications for practice, a few limitations must be noted when considering the findings of this study. Due to the small sample size, in terms of the number of courses, instructors, and students involved, caution must be used when generalizing the results to other contexts. While similar outcomes may occur across service-learning experiences, the context and community-bound nature of service-learning activities does uniquely influence how students and instructors may interpret or make meaning of these experiences. The self study nature of the investigation may also imply possible bias in understanding and interpreting the data. Finally, there is the limitation shared by all service-learning research: the lack of a common definition of service-learning. Ultimately, these limitations do not invalidate the purpose of this research, which was to explore and describe the relevance of service-learning for advancing specific learning objectives associated with preparing special educators, rather than to be applicable to every service-learning experience and to all academic disciplines.

Given the purpose of the current study, several noteworthy implications for teacher education practice exist. First, service-learning is a viable method for guiding students through a process of becoming aware of discipline and/or field-based critical issues, identifying and developing skills necessary to contribute to specific practical outcomes in that field, and then generalizing this problem-solving approach to other professional and personal life situations. While in the present case study this process involved the field of special education and the focus was on leadership and advocacy skills, the process described above could be implemented in other disciplines or fields for the purpose of developing other essential skill sets. Furthermore, an implied expectation for instructors involved in this process is that they serve as role models for service and engagement as well as demonstrate associated behaviors.

Another implication is that service-learning activities can serve simultaneously as a social change endeavor and a pedagogical tool. Beyond the acquisition of academic knowledge and skills and the growth of community awareness and involvement, students engaged in service-learning come to recognize and assume their roles as active community citizens. This feature is consistent with Battistoni's suggestion (1997) that a civic approach to service-learning promotes recognition and participation in individually defined, yet interdependent communities. Students become more confident and competent in their ability to influence change because their definitions of community are derived from and through their personal and/or professional relationships and the reciprocity inherent in these relationships. Moreover, students' community activism is powered by a sense of obligation and responsibility to the relationships found within each defined community of which a student is a part. As Pompa (2002) noted, "Service-learning provides both an incubator for and impetus for change. It is transformative education at its best" (p. 75).

As social change efforts, service-learning activities require and involve risk, disrupting the status quo, and potential professional and personal consequences for both the students and instructors. For example, when early career teachers or faculty members raise questions and concerns about current practices as part of the service-learning process within their respective organizations and communities, their job security may be threatened. In this quest for social justice, the nature of the instructor–student relationship changes. The instructor(s) becomes a team member(s)/partner(s) in the students' endeavors and, in turn, the instructor(s) and students become connected long term by the common experience and the implications of responsibility to the community and the field. In short, the necessity for collaborative partnerships and the reciprocity created through collaboration as colleagues alter the traditional teacher–student relationship.

We encourage other university instructors to consider the implementation of service-learning projects in their special education teacher preparation programs and offer the following recommendations. Instructors should be willing to allow the service-learning projects to emerge as a pedagogical response to students' self-identified educational and professional needs. To that end, instructors will want to consider broad definitions of what constitutes service-learning. Instructors will also want to be prepared to facilitate the resolution of challenges faced by students, such as those involved with group dynamics, the realities of time constraints, and students' conflicting interpretations of issues and roles.

As with any exploratory study, a number of questions emerged for further research, including the following:

- Does service-learning influence how early career special educators continue to approach their advocacy and leadership roles?
- Do these service-learning efforts support or contribute to community partner efforts toward social justice outcomes?
- Does modeling of service-learning use in teacher preparation lead to those teachers' use of service-learning in their K–12 school settings?

With these and other questions in mind, the decisive demonstration of service-learning's value in preparing future special educators will be documented through the repeated assessment of its effects on social justice outcomes for students with special needs and their families.

REFERENCES

Anderson, J. B. (1998). *Service-learning and teacher-education.* Washington, DC: ERIC Clearinghouse on Teacher and Teacher Education. (ERIC Document Reproduction Service No. ED421481)

Battistoni, R. M. (1997). Service-learning and democratic citizenship. *Theory into Practice, 36,* 150–156.

Billig, S. H. (2000). The effect of service-learning. *School Administrator, 57*(7), 14–18.

Boyatzis, R. (1998). *Transforming qualitative information.* Thousand Oaks, CA: Sage.

Butin, D. W. (2003). Of what use is it? Multiple conceptualizations of service-learning within education. *Teacher Education, 105,* 1674–1692.

Cobb, J. B. (2001). Graduates of professional development school programs: Perceptions of teacher as change agent. *Teacher Education Quarterly, 28*(4), 89–107.

Davis, M. T., Emery, M. J., & Lane, C. (1998). *Serve to learn: Making connections in rural communities.* Charleston, SC: Conference Proceedings of the American Council on Rural Special Education. (ERIC Document Reproduction Service No. ED417890)

Dodd, E. L., & Lilly, D. H. (2000). Learning within communities: An investigation of community service-learning in teacher education. *Action in Teacher Education, 22*(3), 77–85.

Feiman-Nemser, S. (2001). From preparation to practice: Designing a continuum to strengthen and sustain teaching. *Teachers College Record, 103,* 1013–1055.

Fiedler, C. R. (2000). *Making a difference: Advocacy competencies for special education professionals.* Boston: Allyn & Bacon.

Forster, E. M. (1997). Teacher leadership: Professional right and responsibility. *Action in Teacher Education, 19,* 82–94.

Furco, A. (2003). Issues of definition and program diversity in the study of service-learning. In S. H. Billig & A. S. Waterman (Eds.), *Studying service-learning: Innovations in education research methodology* (pp. 13–33). Mahwah, NJ: Lawrence Erlbaum Associates.

Gartin, B. C., Murdick, N. L., Thompson, J. R., & Dyches, T. T. (2002). Issues and challenges facing educators who advocate for students with disabilities. *Education and Training in Mental Retardation and Developmental Disabilities, 37,* 3–13.

Husserl, E. (1931). *Ideas: General introduction to pure phenomenology.* New York: Macmillan.

Jacoby, B., & Associates. (1996). *Service-learning in higher education: Concepts and practices.* San Francisco: Jossey-Bass.

Jeavons, T. H. (1995). Service-learning and liberal learning: A marriage of convenience. *Michigan Journal of Community Service Learning, 2,* 134–140.

Malone, D., Jones, B. D., & Stallings, D. T. (2002). Perspective transformation: Effects of a service-learning tutoring experience on prospective teachers. *Teacher Education Quarterly, 29*(1), 61–81.

Mayhew, J., & Welch, M. (2001). A call to service: Service-learning as a pedagogy in special education programs. *Teacher Education and Special Education, 24*(3), 208–219.

McLeod, J. (2003). *Doing counseling research.* Thousand Oaks, CA: Sage.

Miles, M., & Huberman, A. (1994). *Qualitative data analysis.* Thousand Oaks, CA: Sage.

Moustakas, C. (1994). *Phenomenological research methods.* Thousand Oaks, CA: Sage.

Muscott, H. S. (2001). Using service-learning to enhance the preparation of preservice special education teachers at Rivier College. In J. B. Anderson, K. J. Swick, & J. Yff (Eds.), *Service-learning in teacher education: Enhancing the growth of new teachers, their students, and communities* (pp. 188–192). Washington, DC: American Association of Colleges for Teacher Education Publications.

Neuman, W. (1997). *Social research methods.* Needham Heights, MA: Allyn & Bacon.

Patton, M. Q. (1990). *Qualitative evaluation methods* (2nd ed.). Thousand Oaks, CA: Sage.

Polkinghorne, D. E. (1989). Phenomenological research methods. In R. Valle & S. Halling (Eds.), *Existentialism and phenomenological perspectives in psychology* (pp. 41–60). New York: Plenum Press.

Pompa, L. (2002, Fall). Service-learning as crucible: Reflections on immersion, context, power, and transformation. *Michigan Journal of Community Service Learning, 9,* 67–76.

Potthoff, D. E., Dinsmore, J., Eifler, K., Stirtz, G., Walsh, T., & Ziebarth, J. (2000). Preparing for democracy and diversity: The impact of a community-based field experience on preservice teachers' knowledge, skills, and attitudes. *Action in Research, 22*(1), 79–92.

Restine, N. (1997). Learning and development in the context(s) of leadership preparation. *Peabody Journal of Education, 72,* 117–130.

Sileo, T. W., Prater, M. A., Luckner, J. L., Rhine, B., & Rude, H. A. (1998). Strategies to facilitate preservice teachers' active involvement in learning. *Teacher Education and Special Education, 21*(3), 187–204.

Taylor, S., & Bogdan, R. (1998). *Introduction to qualitative research methods* (3rd ed.). New York: Wiley.

Wade, R. C. (2003). Teaching pre-service social studies teachers to be advocates for social change. *Social Studies. 94*(3), 129–133.

Wade, R. C., Boyle-Baise, M., & O'Grady, C. (2001). Multicultural service-learning in teacher education. In J. B. Anderson, K. J. Swick, & J. Yff (Eds.), *Service-learning in teacher education: Enhancing the growth of new teachers, their students, and communities* (pp. 248–259). Washington, DC: American Association of Colleges for Teacher Education Publications.

Section II

IMPLEMENTATION MODELS, IMPACTS, AND ISSUES

CHAPTER 4

COLLEGE STUDENTS' PREFERRED APPROACHES TO COMMUNITY SERVICE

Charity and Social Change Paradigms

Barbara E. Moely and Devi Miron

ABSTRACT

Morton's (1995) model of paradigms of service was used to assess student preferences for community service activities. Reliable assessment of student preferences for the Charity and Social Change paradigms was shown. College students, especially women and younger students, showed strong preferences for service activities typical of the Charity orientation. Students with service experience during high school were more likely to endorse Social Change. Both orientations predicted plans for future community involvement. Implications for the structuring of service activities in service-learning and for future research are discussed.

Improving Service-Learning Practice: Research on Models to Enhance Impacts, pages 61–78
Copyright © 2005 by Information Age Publishing
All rights of reproduction in any form reserved.

INTRODUCTION

In recent years, researchers have amassed considerable evidence of the benefits college students gain through participation in service-learning. Among the benefits are increasingly positive self-evaluations for interpersonal and leadership skills, increased awareness of social issues, greater concern for social issues and social justice, and plans for future involvement in community service (Astin & Sax, 1998; Eyler & Giles, 1999; Moely, McFarland, Miron, Mercer, & Ilustre, 2002). As we look more closely at the impact of service-learning, however, questions arise concerning the ways in which characteristics of participating students and the nature of their service-learning experiences may moderate the impact of participation. Several efforts have been made to characterize the attitudes and beliefs that the individual brings to the service experience. Clary and his colleagues (1998), for example, delineated six different motivational beliefs that individuals may hold regarding community service involvement. These functions of service include motives focused on:

- Personal well-being (Protective, Enhancement, Career);
- Interpersonal connections (Social); and
- Self-actualization (Values, Understanding) (pp. 1517–1518).

Clary's work and that of others (e.g., Hynes & Nykiel, 2005) has shown that the individual's evaluation of a particular service experience is affected by the extent to which the experience involves opportunities that correspond with his or her preferred motives.

In 1995, Morton published a groundbreaking paper concerning our assumptions about the nature of community-based activities in service-learning. He proposed that these assumptions underlie our goals for students and affect the ways in which we design courses, service experiences, and service-learning programs. Specifically, Morton was addressing the assumption that there is a continuum of service in which students begin community involvement with rather basic, simple "helping" behaviors, such as tutoring a child, delivering newsletters for an organization, planning a day's recreation for a senior center, and so forth, and continue through to a concern about social justice and social change. Through initial helping activities, it is assumed students come to see the larger social-political issues surrounding the social structures within which they serve. This energizes them to become active in working for social change, where they will assume advocacy functions and contribute to significant changes in the way social groups and governments function.

Through his discussions with students, faculty, administrators, and community representatives, Morton rejected the continuum model. Rather than assuming a single path of development, he proposed several different orientations or "paradigms of service" that students may conceptualize and adopt as their own, leading them to seek out certain kinds of experiences, to value certain aspects of their community contacts, and to evaluate their successes or failures in community service in a particular way. Morton (1995) proposed three such orientations.

1. The *Charity* paradigm involves "giving of the self, expecting nothing in return, and with no expectation that any lasting impact will be made" (1995, p. 20). Charity is characterized by direct service to one or a few individuals, for a limited period of time. The service provider retains power to plan activities and make decisions about the nature and extent of service. The potential gain through such service is learning about the individual served. Two possible negative outcomes of service organized around this paradigm are that the service creates a long-term dependency of those served and that the server's stereotypes or preconceptions about the individual and the source of his or her problems are maintained or strengthened, since there is no emphasis on the structural causes of problems.

2. The *Project Development* paradigm includes service models that

   > focus on defining problems and their solutions and implementing well-conceived plans for achieving those solutions.... The organizing principle...lies in the development of partnerships of organizations that collectively have access to the resources necessary to "make something happen." (p. 22)

   The server carries out a well-articulated plan that was created by an organization or "expert" to produce a useful product for a particular social group. The service activity ideally lasts until the product is completed and is based on some consideration of the structural causes of the social problem addressed. As with Charity, power resides with the service provider and decisions are made without the input of those served. Service from this paradigm is somewhat rigid, based on preconceived notions about the nature of problems and their solutions, so that rather than producing ameliorative effects, Project Development may have no impact or even produce negative outcomes.

3. The *Social Change* paradigm "is change oriented, and implies an agenda—speaking to others with a powerful voice. Acts of service are steps in a larger strategy to bring about change, quite often assessed as the redistribution of resources or social capital" (p. 20). In contrast to the two other models, Social Change involves participation by both server and served in a planning and decision-making process through which major, long-term change in a social system is sought. Relationships are built, creating a learning environment that enables

the server to reconceptualize societal problems in terms of structural factors that can be addressed through collaborative action.

According to Morton, a person working from the Social Change perspective

> sees the problems of the poor and oppressed, not as basically functional, but as rooted in and perpetuated by the structural organization of society—as a process whereby they are excluded from economic gain and political power by strategies which preserve the concentration of privilege in society. (p. 23, quoting the *Guidelines for Development* of the Christian Conference of Asia, 1980)

The aim of the service is to empower the disenfranchised, "helping people to do for themselves, in the world as it is, not as we wish it to be" (p. 23).

Morton's model has been elaborated by other authors. Kahne and Westheimer (1996), for example, described differing moral, political, and intellectual goals that may be held by those who support and promote "Charity" and "Change" models in service-learning. They encourage a politically aware and socially active approach to service-learning, one that focuses students' thinking on structural changes to create a more just society. In more recent work, Kahne, Westheimer, and Rogers (2000) and Westheimer and Kahne (2004) elaborated their model into three views of citizenship that they observed in high school service-learning classes:

1. The *Responsible Citizen* is described as "... someone with a job, who votes, pays taxes, gives blood, and obeys the law."

2. The *Participatory Citizen* is "... someone who is active in community affairs, planning community events and participating on local boards, for example."

3. The *Social Reformer* is "... someone who seeks to understand the causes of societal problems and address them at the root" (quotes from Kahne et al., 2000, p. 44).

The authors argued that service-learning programs reflect one or another of these perspectives in choices of activities, topics of reflection, and interpretations of the service experience, thereby affecting the orientations toward community and civic engagement that students adopt. Along the same lines, Perreault (1997) urged an examination of the assumptions that guide the structuring of volunteer programs for college students. Perreault described the *charity* orientation and contrasted it with preferred approaches that are more concerned with societal structures (*service-learning*) and sociopolitical action (*citizen leader*).

Although these models have been articulated in several conceptual papers, analysis of how students view their roles with regard to community service has received limited research attention to date. The present study relies on Morton's conceptualization to explore students' views. The first aim of the study was to attempt to validate Morton's model as a way of describing students' preferences for different kinds of community service. A second question concerned personal characteristics that may be related to paradigm preferences. Such information gives hints about factors in the individual and his or her experiences that may affect preferences. Finally, the authors wanted to address the implications of the paradigm model for service-learning course and program design. Since the study is exploratory in nature, several questions, rather than formal hypotheses, guided data collection and analysis. These research questions were as follows:

1. Can the three paradigms described by Morton be assessed reliably in a sample of college student service participants?
2. To what extent do students show preferences for each paradigm of service?
3. What factors in the individual or in his or her past experience might bring about development of a particular paradigm preference?
4. Do paradigm preferences predict students' plans for future engagement in community service?

METHOD

Research Participants

A group of 183 students (Sample 1) from a private, southern, research university completed a questionnaire in the spring of 2003. Some additions to the questionnaire were made on the basis of information obtained, and a new group of 285 students (Sample 2) completed the revised form in the fall of 2003. Students were recruited from service-learning courses representing a range of academic disciplines (8 courses in spring 2003 and 14 courses in fall 2003). During the fall semester, students were also recruited from the student volunteer organization on campus (approximately 10% of that sample).

The samples were predominantly white (85%), reflecting the student body of the university. More women (73%) than men (27%) took part in the research. Students from the second through fourth years of undergraduate study were about equally represented (24% to 30% of all participants), with a smaller number of first-year college students (19% of all participants). The mean age was just over 20 years for each sample.

Students were quite strong academically, reporting an average college GPA of B+ (3.2 on a 4-point scale, for each sample). They held high expectations for their own academic attainment: Only 16% to 17% expected the bachelor's to be their terminal degree, with the remainder about equally divided between terminal master's (37% to 40%) and doctoral or professional program completion (41% to 44%). Because of the ways in which research participants were recruited, the two samples varied in students' major interest areas. In the first sample, psychology was the most popular major, while majors in the arts and humanities and in business fields were predominant in the second.

Measuring Paradigm Preferences

Starting with Morton's (1995) research and his descriptions of the paradigms, two scales were created, varying in the nature of item descriptions and in the kinds of responses requested. Through this multimethod approach, the authors hoped to obtain a picture of student preferences that was relatively independent of item characteristics. Instructions for each scale and sample items are shown in Figures 4.1 and 4.2.

The *Approaches Scale* consisted of brief statement descriptions of the kinds of service. Students read triads of items, one representing each paradigm, and indicated their first, second, and third choice within each triad. The four sets of items are shown in Figure 4.1. Responses were reverse coded, so that a larger score indicates a stronger preference; these scores were averaged to obtain a total score for each paradigm preference.

Internal consistencies of the measures derived from the Approaches Scale were just adequate for the Charity scale ($\alpha = .69$ [$N = 183$] and .63 [$N = 268$]) for Samples 1 and 2, respectively. Internal consistency was satisfactory for the Social Change scale (α coefficients were .74 for Sample 1 and .72 for Sample 2). The Project Development scale had low internal consistencies in each sample (α less than .50).

The *Activities Scale* contained short paragraph descriptions of service activities, with four items designed to represent each of the three paradigms of service (12 items total). Items were created by considering different kinds of service described in publications and Web sites on service-learning as well as activities carried out by students in the university's service-learning program. Students used a 5-point scale to rate the extent to which they would like to engage in each activity. Sample items, all focused on the field of education, are shown in Figure 4.2. Other items on the Activities Scale were concerned with service in health agencies, nonprofit organizations, and government offices. Items were coded so that a high score indicated a strong preference for the activity described. Scores for each paradigm were obtained by averaging scores for each item in that category.

Instructions: *Please rank the following sets of items from most to least important, where 1 = Most Important to You, 2 = Somewhat Important, and 3 = Least Important.*

Set One: Rank the following 1–3 in order of importance to you
___ Helping those in need. C
___ Designing Project Developments that will benefit the whole community. PD
___ Working to reshape the world we live in. SC

Set Two: Rank 1–3
___ Working to address a major social ill confronting our society. SC
___ Working to give others the necessities that they lack. C
___ Working with a group of people to solve a community problem. PD

Set Three: Rank 1–3
___ Contributing to a group or Project Development that benefits the community. PD
___ Changing public policy for the benefit of people. SC
___ Making a major difference in a person's life. C

Set Four: Rank 1–4
___ A service placement where you can really become involved in helping individuals. C
___ A service placement where you can contribute to social change that affects us all. SC
___ A service placement where you can help a group of people improve their situation. PD

Note: C, Charity; PD, Project Development; SC, Social Change.

Figure 4.1.   The Approaches Scale for Assessing Service Paradigm Preferences.

Instructions: *The following scenarios describe different kinds of community service activities. Please rate each scenario as to how much you would like to engage in this kind of community service. 1 = Would very much like to do this kind of service; 2 = Would somewhat like this; 3 = Not sure; 4 = Would not like this very much; 5 = Would very much dislike this kind of service.*

___ Sarah goes to a local middle school twice a week to tutor a seventh grader. She reads to the student and helps the student understand new vocabulary words. C

___ Matt works at a school specifically geared toward children who have special needs. Matt has developed a diagram game to help the kids deal with spatial and memory issues. The diagram will be distributed to all the classrooms so that teachers can utilize it in helping the children. PD

___ Jane attends the local school board meetings. She is a very vocal participant in the discussions about administrative and financial practices especially affecting the public schools. She is organizing a group of college students to influence the school board members. SC

Note: C, Charity; PD, Project Development; SC, Social Change.

Figure 4.2.   Instructions and sample items from the Activities Scale for Assessing Service Paradigm Preferences.

For each sample, Activities Scale items were subjected to a principal components analysis with Varimax rotation. Three factors accounted for 52% of the variance in Sample 1 and 47% in Sample 2. The three factors that emerged from this analysis reflected the three approaches to service. In the analysis of Sample 1, items designed to assess Social Change loaded on the first factor, and items designed to assess the Charity approach loaded on the second factor. Three of the four items designed to assess the Project Development approach loaded on the third factor, while the fourth item loaded on Social Change. In the second sample, the factor analysis largely grouped items by paradigm but with some slippage: One Social Change item loaded on the Project Development factor and one Charity item loaded both with the Charity and Social Change groups. Internal consistencies of the measures derived from the Activities Scale were assessed. For the Charity Scale, α = .67 for Sample 1 (N = 183) and .65 for Sample 2 (N = 268). For the Social Change Scale, α = .63 for Sample 1 but only .49 for Sample 2. For the Project Development Scale, *alphas* were .59 and .55, for Samples 1 and 2, respectively.

Thus, considering both the Approaches and Activities Scales, it was possible to achieve reasonably good measurement of the Charity and Social Change orientations. The low internal consistencies for the Project Development items may occur because an individual's endorsement of this approach is dependent on very specific characteristics of the Project Development activity rather than on a more general and stable perspective, or because the limited number of items made it difficult to appropriately represent the Project Development approach. In any case, further work is needed to develop an adequate assessment of preferences for that paradigm.

RESULTS

In addressing the research questions posed above, the authors looked for findings that would hold over both the Approaches and Activities Scales and that would be consistent for the two samples.

Research Question 1. Can the three paradigms or orientations described by Morton (1995) be assessed reliably?

The measurement characteristics described through factor analyses and internal consistency assessments (above) indicate that the Charity and Social Change paradigms were assessed with some consistency by means of our scales. The next question concerned the extent to which students showed consistent preferences across the Approaches and Activities Scales. Correlations of scores obtained on these two measures were statistically significant at $p < .001$ for both Charity and Social Change. For the Charity orientation, the Approaches and Activities measures correlated .38 and .35 for Samples 1 and 2, respectively. For Social Change, correlation coefficients were .34 and .28. The scores obtained for Project Development orientation did not show significant correlations. As with the reliability assessments, then, the authors did not find evidence for a consistent evaluation of the Project Development paradigm.

Research Question 2. Do students show preferences for any one of the paradigms?

An overall preference for the Charity orientation was shown by students in each sample, on both the Approaches and Activities Scales. Analyses summarized in Exhibit 4.1 showed significant mean differences favoring the Charity approach over the others on both scales and in both samples.

Individual respondents' scores were examined for each scale separately and the paradigm receiving the highest mean score was taken as that person's preference. As indicated in Exhibit 4.2, approximately 75% of the students expressed a preference for the Charity orientation on each scale. Consistency across the Approaches and Activities Scales is seen, with approximately 70% of the students who expressed a preference showing the same preference on each measure. More than 60% of the sample expressed a preference for the Charity orientation on both the Approaches and Activities Scales.

Exhibit 4.1.   Means and Standard Deviations for Students' Preferences for Each Paradigm of Service

	Sample One*				Sample Two**			
	Approaches Scale (N = 183)		Activities Scale (N = 183)		Approaches Scale (N = 264)		Activities Scale (N = 267)	
	M	SD	M	SD	M	SD	M	SD
Charity	2.49	.53	4.02	.77	2.50	.49	3.95	.79
Project Development	1.85	.42	2.59	.82	1.94	.41	2.66	.81
Social Change	1.66	.58	3.11	.84	1.55	.55	3.20	.74

* Sample 1, Approaches Scale: Mean differences between paradigms significant, $F(2, 180) = 42.49$, $p < .001$
  Sample 1, Activities Scale: Mean differences significant, $F(2, 180) = 61.57$, $p < .001$
** Sample 2, Approaches Scale: Mean differences significant, $F(2, 261) = 96.45$, $p < .001$
  Sample 2, Activities Scale: Mean differences significant, $F(2, 264) = 92.72$, $p < .001$

Exhibit 4.2.   Percentages of Students Who Selected Each Paradigm as Their Preferred Service Option

	Sample One			Sample Two		
	Approaches Scale (N = 172)	Activities Scale (N = 169)	Both Scales (N = 169)	Approaches Scale (N = 232)	Activities Scale (N = 242)	Both Scales (N = 202)
Charity	71	75	62	75	74	63
Project Development	12	10	2	12	11	2
Social Change	17	15	7	13	15	5

Research Question 3. Do factors in the individual or in his or her past experiences relate to development of a particular paradigm preference?

The next research question concerned personal characteristics that might predict preferences. The characteristics considered were gender, age, year in college, and area of academic study. Students' past experiences with service activities were also considered.

Gender. As indicated in Exhibit 4.3, women were stronger than men in their preference for the Charity paradigm, while men rated the Social Change activities higher. The gender difference in evaluations of the Charity orientation held for both samples on both the Approaches and Activities Scales, while men's preference for Social Change was seen in three of the four comparisons shown in Exhibit 4.3. Gender by paradigm interactions were significant on each measure, for each sample.

Exhibit 4.3.   Mean Scores (and Standard Deviations) for Men and Women on Approaches and Activities Scales: Gender Differences in Student Preferences

	Sample One[*]				Sample Two[**]			
	Men (N = 44)		Women (N = 139)		Men (N = 72)		Women (N = 192)	
	M	SD	M	SD	M	SD	M	SD
	Approaches Scale							
Charity	2.23	.57	2.57	.49	2.38	.53	2.55	.46
Social Change	1.90	.61	1.58	.55	1.73	.61	1.49	.52
	Activities Scale							
Charity	3.68	.83	4.13	.72	3.49	.81	4.13	.70
Social Change	3.35	.88	3.04	.82	3.12	.84	3.23	.69

[*] Sample 1, Approaches Scale: Gender × Paradigm interaction significant, $F(1, 181) = 14.96$ $p < .001$
Sample 1, Activities Scale: Gender × Paradigm interaction significant, $F(1, 181) = 18.16$, $p < .001$
[**] Sample 2, Approaches Scale: Gender × Paradigm interaction significant, $F(1, 262) = 9.68$, $p < .01$
Sample 2, Activities Scale: Gender × Paradigm interaction significant, $F(1, 265) = 14.85$, $p = .001$

Age and Year in College. Chronological age and year in college were taken as rough indices of student maturity and their relation to paradigm preferences was examined. A consistent finding across samples was that more mature individuals were less likely to endorse the Charity paradigm on the Activities Scale than were younger individuals. Correlations with the Charity scale for Sample 1 were $r = -.24$ for age and $-.18$ for year, both $p < .01$ for $N = 183$. For Sample 2, both age and year negatively predicted Charity preferences on the Activities Scale, $r = -.12$ with $N = 268$, $p < .05$. No such pattern was shown for the Approaches measure.

Area of Academic Study. Undergraduate students reported a wide range of majors, which were classified for analysis into academic areas that included the sciences, social sciences, humanities and fine arts, psychology, and (in Sample 2 only) business. Comparisons of individuals in these four groups showed consistency across samples and measures in evaluations of the Charity orientations, as indicated in Exhibit 4.4. Psychology majors strongly endorsed the Charity paradigm, while social science majors (sociology, economics) were the least favorable of all groups toward the Charity paradigm, in three out of four comparisons.

Exhibit 4.4. Preferences for the Charity Orientation (Mean Scores) Expressed by Students Electing Different Major Areas of Study

	N	*Approaches Scale: Charity*	*Activities Scale: Charity*
Sample One[*]			
Humanities/Arts	34	2.49	3.92
Psychology	80	2.66	4.21
Sciences	18	2.33	4.08
Social Sciences	31	2.19	3.67
Sample Two[**]	N		
Humanities/Arts	78	2.49	4.00
Psychology	51	2.60	4.19
Sciences	24	2.51	3.95
Social Sciences	25	2.26	4.01
Business	57	2.58	3.73

[*] Sample 1, Approaches Scale: Mean differences significant, $F(3, 159) = 7.57$, $p < .001$
Sample 1, Activities Scale: Mean differences significant, $F(3, 159) = 4.58$, $p < .01$
[**] Sample 2, Approaches Scale: Mean differences significant, $F(4, 218) = 2.69$, $p < .05$
Sample 2, Activities Scale: Mean differences significant, $F(4, 220) = 2.41$, $p = .05$

Previous Community Service. Information on previous service activities was obtained only for Sample 2. In this group, 90% of students reported community service experience during high school. During college, nearly half (48%) had served through a religious organization, 35% had previously taken part in the university's volunteer program, 19% had previously engaged in service-learning, and 11% had done federal work study in the community.

Regression analyses were run to determine whether prior experience with these five different service experiences would predict current paradigm preferences. Some consistent patterns emerged: Most dramatically, on both the Approaches and Activities Scales, endorsement of Social Change was related to having performed community service during high school (Exhibit 4.5).

Exhibit 4.5. Predicting Preference for the Social Change Paradigm from Prior Community Experiences: Regression Analyses for Sample Two

Dependent Variable	*Approaches Scale: Social Change (N = 261)*			*Activities Scale: Social Change (N = 266)*		
Predictor	*B*	*SE B*	*β*	*B*	*SE B*	*β*
Gender	−.233	.078	−.188**	.129	.104	.078
Year in College	.057	.030	.121	.018	.041	.028
High School Service	.252	.128	.121*	.460	.173	.164**
College Service-Learning	.053	.088	.039	−.126	.115	−.069
Federal Work Study Service	.106	.109	.061	.294	.141	.130*
Volunteer Service	−.069	.077	−.060	−.107	.103	−.070
Religious-Based Service	−.127	.069	−.115	−.073	.092	−.049

Note. * $p < .05$, ** $p < .01$
Overall prediction for Approaches scale significant at $p < .01$, $F(7,253) = 2.926$.
Adjusted $R^2 = .049$
Overall prediction for Activities scale significant at $p < .05$, $F(7, 258) = 2.147$.
Adjusted $R^2 = .029$

The Charity orientation, as measured by the Activities Scale (Exhibit 4.6) was related to various kinds of college service (service-learning, volunteer service, and service through a religious organization). On the Approaches Scale, however, the Charity orientation was not significantly predicted from prior service.

Exhibit 4.6. Predicting Preference for the Charity Paradigm from Prior Community Experiences: Regression Analyses for Sample Two

Dependent Variable	Approaches Scale: Charity (N = 261)			Activities Scale: Charity (N = 266)		
Predictor	B	SE B	β	B	SE B	β
Gender	.135	.070	.124	.515	.099	.294[**]
Year in College	−.049	.027	−.118	−.123	.039	−.183[**]
High School Service	−.083	.114	−.046	.311	.165	.104
College Service-Learning	.040	.078	.033	.221	.110	.114[*]
Federal Work Study Service	.061	.097	.040	.071	.134	.030
Volunteer Service	.058	.069	.058	.322	.099	.198[**]
Religious-Based Service	.114	.061	.118	.202	.088	.129[*]

Note. $* p < .05, ** p < .01$
Overall prediction for Approaches scale not significant at $F(7,253) = 1.97, p = .06$.
Adjusted $R^2 = .025$
Overall prediction for Activities scale significant at $p < .001, F(7, 258) = 11.69$.
Adjusted $R^2 = .220$

Research Question 4. Do paradigm preferences predict students' plans for future engagement in community service?

In addressing the importance of preferences in determining students' plans for engagement in community service, the authors looked at Sample 2, where two indices reflected students' plans for community service in the future:

1. A question asked specifically whether or not students planned to participate in community service activities during the upcoming semester.

2. The Civic Action Scale of the CASQ (Moely, Mercer, Ilustre, Miron, & McFarland, 2002) was administered to students to assess their plans for future engagement in the community.

Students who indicated on these two measures high likelihood of future community service indicated endorsement of both Charity and Social Change paradigms on the Activities Scale. Correlations were $r = .23$ and $.42$ for Charity with the first and second index, respectively, and $.17$ and $.21$ for Social Change with each index ($p < .01$, for each correlation). It appears that both Charity and Social Change perspectives can serve as the impetus to involvement in the community.

DISCUSSION

The study addressed several questions concerning student preferences for different kinds of community service. With regard to the first research question, the validity of Morton's (1995) characterization of service through the Charity and Social Change paradigms was supported. These orientations are expressed in a reliable and consistent fashion by students and their responses are related both to prior service experiences and plans for future engagement in their communities. The authors were not successful in creating a reliable measure of the Project Development orientation, for which preferences may depend more on specific aspects of the experience than on an overriding preference for this as a "type" of service. Future efforts to assess this orientation will need to include a larger number and wider variety of items, so as to tap the range of experiences that are included in Morton's description.

Investigation of the second research question yielded a dramatic finding: Students showed a strong and consistent preference for the Charity orientation. Students appear to be more comfortable with the activities involved in "helping" than with activities that attempt societal change. Upon reflection, this is not as surprising as it first seems—when students think about community service, it is likely that an activity typical of the Charity orientation will be imagined. Public service announcements stress helping activities rather than activities focused toward societal change, and encouragement of community service through agencies like the Points of Light Foundation also characterize service in the Charity paradigm. For example, the Points of Light Web site (www.pointsoflight .org/programs) emphasizes the importance of "promoting compassion" and describes sample activities that include {indent this as block quote}"holding food drives for the needy, participating in crafts and games with nursing home residents, organizing parties and art project developments for underprivileged children, assisting with major community events, and having numerous fundraisers to buy holiday presents for the needy in the community." Typical descriptions of community service less often include activities that will change a social system or government policy, activities that very likely will require time, commitment, and expertise beyond that expected of the typical citizen volunteer.

Consideration of the third research question yielded several findings suggesting the importance of experience on student perspectives. First, there were differences between students enrolled in different major areas of study. Psychology as a discipline emphasizes the individual, in contrast to the focus on societal structures seen in sociology. Student majors showed differences in their evaluations of the Charity approach that reflected the principles of their major areas of study. A second finding of interest concerned the importance of previous community service: Students with service experiences during high school showed increased endorsement of the Social Change perspective, suggesting the importance of community experience in shaping views. Finally, the finding of less enthusiasm for the Charity orientation among more mature students may support the "continuum of service" that Morton (1995) argued against. However, this effect was not strong and no corresponding change with age was shown for the Social Change measures, so the finding remains open to other interpretations.

A feature of Morton's approach that is particularly interesting is the notion of change within paradigms. A student beginning community service with a Charity orientation might develop in a positive way by deepening and elaborating this perspective on service, rather than by shifting to another paradigm. Development with age in the quality of the Charity orientation was beyond the scope of this study, but future research based on feminist theory is encouraged. Feminist theorists have suggested development within the "ethic of care" that Foos (1998) associated with the Charity approach. Keller, Nelson, and Wick (2003) used Tronto's (1993) explication of stages of development in the ethic of care to describe changes in the nature of helping or care activities:

> While doing service, students come face to face with how economic injustice, racism, sexism, violence, and poverty affect real people—but in addition, they see hope and encounter people actively engaged in working for justice and equality....As they explore differences and similarities between themselves and the people with whom they are working, the systemic nature of oppression becomes more obvious. (p. 43)

Within an ethic of care, development involves a broadening perspective on sociopolitical factors that affect both the individuals served and those performing the service. Future research may benefit by a consideration of Tronto's (1993) model in attempting to assess change within the Charity paradigm.

What are the implications of these findings for the structuring of service-learning programs? Plans for future community involvement were predicted by endorsement of both the Charity and Social Change paradigms. Both of these orientations can be the impetus to service, though the nature of the service to be sought and activities performed will likely vary considerably. Clary and colleagues (1998) showed that individuals value service experiences most positively when there is a correspondence between their functional motives and the opportunities provided by the service experience. Similarly, Hynes and Nykiel (2005) show that such correspondence results in more enthusiastic plans for future civic engagement as well as greater satisfaction with the service experience. At the same time, many have urged that service-learning programs provide students with experiences that focus on social justice and social change (Mendel-Reyes, 1998; Perreault, 1997; Vogelgesang & Rhoads, 2005; Westheimer & Kahne, 2004). The question for practitioners, then, is: Given the strong endorsement of the Charity orientation, how do service-learning practitioners ensure positive student outcomes while encouraging concerns for social justice and work toward structural changes in society? Kahne and Westheimer (1996) viewed the moral goal of the change orientation as involving care for another, thus suggesting a way in which the individual could elaborate and deepen a Charity orientation, by maintaining an emphasis on care but adding a concern for action with regard to those societal structures affecting the well-being of the cared-for individual. Through meaningful connection with the individuals served, the server is motivated to move into more active roles. An effective service-learning course, then, might involve charity-type work combined with instruction in and activity toward social action. For example, students might form relationships with elementary school students they are tutoring while they learn about school board policies and procedures and attend board meetings to support initiatives that will benefit the children. Or, similarly, students who help families file applications for the Earned Income Tax Credit study government policies affecting poor families and communicate with their elected representatives about pending legislation. Such experiences can provide the basis for students to benefit from opportunities to develop as citizen leaders (Perreault, 1997), with the one-on-one relationships established through service motivating action. Internships, capstone experiences, and leadership opportunities for students can encourage them to go deeper into the Charity orientation to more intensive and effective community engagement. Future research should focus on the ways in which different kinds of service activities are received by and affect the views of individuals who come to service-learning with varied preferences, beliefs, and developmental levels.

ACKNOWLEDGMENTS

We would like to thank the Tulane students, faculty members, and representatives of CACTUS (student volunteer organization) whose cooperation made this research possible. We also thank research colleagues Megan McFarland, Marilyn Fragioudakis, Amanda Pierce, Vincent Ilustre, and Jenna Kellam for their contributions to the development of the research design and methodology. Finally, we are grateful to all of our colleagues at the Office of Service-Learning for their continued support and assistance. For more information about measures used or the findings of this research, contact Barbara Moely at moely@tulane.edu or Devi Miron at dmiron@tulane.edu.

REFERENCES

Astin, A. W., & Sax, L. (1998). How undergraduates are affected by service participation. *Journal of College Student Development, 39,* 251–263.

Clary, E. G., Copeland, J., Haugen, J., Miene, P., Ridge, R. D., Snyder, M., & Stukas, A. A. (1998). Understanding and assessing the motivations of volunteers: A functional approach. *Journal of Personality and Social Psychology, 74,* 1516–1530.

Eyler, J., & Giles, D. E., Jr. (1999). *Where's the learning in service-learning?* San Francisco: Jossey-Bass.

Foos, C. L. (1998). The "different voice" of service. *Michigan Journal of Community Service Learning, 5,* 14–21.

Hynes, R. A., & Nykiel, A. I. (2005). Maximizing outcomes of volunteer programs through a functional approach to motivation. *Journal of College and Character, 2.* Retrieved March 1, 2005, from http://www.collegevalues.org/pdfs/Hynes.pdf

Kahne, J., & Westheimer, J. (1996). In the service of what? The politics of service learning. *Phi Delta Kappan, 77,* 592–599.

Kahne, J., Westheimer, J., & Rogers, B. (2000). Service-learning and citizenship: Directions for research. *Michigan Journal of Community Service Learning, 7,* 42–51.

Keller, J., Nelson, S., & Wick, R. (2003). Care ethics, service-learning, and social change. *Michigan Journal of Community Service Learning, 10,* 39–50.

Mendel-Reyes, M. (1998). A pedagogy for citizenship: Service learning and democratic education. In R. A. Rhoads & J. P. F. Howard (Eds.), *Academic service learning: A pedagogy of action and reflection* (pp. 31–38). *New Directions for Teaching and Learning, 73.* San Francisco: Jossey-Bass.

Moely, B. E., McFarland, M., Miron, D., Mercer, S., & Ilustre, V. (2002). Changes in college students' attitudes and intentions for civic involvement as a function of service-learning experiences. *Michigan Journal of Community Service Learning, 9,* 18–26.

Moely, B. E., Mercer, S. H., Ilustre, V., Miron, D., & McFarland, M. (2002). Psychometric properties and correlates of the Civic Attitudes and Skills Questionnaire (CASQ): A measure of students' attitudes related to service learning. *Michigan Journal of Community Service Learning, 8,* 15–26.

Morton, K. (1995). The irony of service: Charity, Project Development, and social change in service learning. *Michigan Journal of Community Service Learning, 2,* 19–32.

Perreault, G. (1997). Citizen leader: A community service option for college students. *NASPA Journal, 34,* 147–156.

Tronto, J. C. (1993). *Moral boundaries: A political argument for an ethic of care.* New York: Routledge.

Vogelgesang, L. J., & Rhoads, R. A. (2005). Advancing a broad notion of public engagement: The limitations of contemporary service learning. *Journal of College and Character, 2.* Retrieved March 2, 2005, from http://www.collegevalues.org/articles.cfm?a=1&id=1017

Westheimer, J., & Kahne, J. (2004). What kind of citizen? The politics of educating for democracy. *American Educational Research Journal, 41,* 237–269.

CHAPTER 5

THE JOB CHARACTERISTICS MODEL AND PLACEMENT QUALITY

Marcy H. Schnitzer

ABSTRACT

Key themes in service-learning research include the impacts of placement quality on attitudinal change, as well as the impact of service-learning on commitment and citizenship. This chapter applies a motivational theory of work, the Job Characteristics Model, as a basis for linking placement quality to commitment. The definition of placement quality and methodology utilized by Eyler and Giles (1999) in *Where's the Learning in Service-Learning* serves as a comparison point. Implications for this model in terms of pedagogy, service design, and role-based learning are discussed.

INTRODUCTION

Implicit outcomes of service-learning programs include fostering a service ethic and continued service. To achieve this, a positive service-learning experience is essential. Eyler and Giles (1999) identified placement quality, among other findings, as a key contributor to positive service-learning

Improving Service-Learning Practice: Research on Models to Enhance Impacts, pages 79–96
Copyright © 2005 by Information Age Publishing

outcomes. While their book focuses principally on student outcomes, the issue of placement quality suggests a more holistic approach. What do we know about the task environment of community placements? How does placement influence long-range commitment? And finally, what theories can help us understand the relationship between placement and outcomes?

To date, the field of service-learning has focused a great deal of attention on student attitudinal outcomes from participation in a service-learning course (Eyler, Giles, Stenson, & Gray, 2001). At the same time, the field has been challenged to broaden student outcomes to include a more long-range perspective (Eyler, 2000). Additionally, the need for greater focus on community outcomes has been noted (Cruz & Giles, 2000; Eyler, 2000; Sigmon, 1998). Lastly, the need for a more theoretical base has also been advanced (Bringle, 2003; Furco & Billig, 2002). This chapter focuses on a theoretical model for understanding the placement context of service-learning and its potential for motivating students and encouraging continued commitment to community organizations. The Job Characteristics Model (Hackman & Oldham, 1980; Hackman, Oldham, Janson, & Purdy, 1975), a motivational theory of work, serves as a foundation for this study.

This chapter begins by examining what we know about placement quality. It then examines the literature on service and motivation, particularly as it pertains to continuing service. The Job Characteristics Model (JCM) and its associated constructs are explored, with connections drawn between the measures presented in this model, and those used by Eyler and Giles (1999) in their extensive research. The survey methodology associated with this model is reviewed with attention to how it could be used in a service-learning setting. Finally, research considerations for studying continued service among participants in a higher education service-learning program are explored.

PLACEMENT AND MOTIVATION

Eyler and Giles (1999) discussed the critical role of placement quality in the service-learning experience: "Placement quality provides a context in which students can exercise initiative, take responsibility, and work as peers with practitioners and community members" (p. 169). Placement quality was determined to be a significant predictor of stereotyping, personal development, interpersonal development, citizenship, learning and application, problem solving/critical thinking, and perspective transformation. The authors listed the following characteristics of high-quality placements:

- Students do meaningful work;
- Students have important responsibilities;
- Students have varied or challenging tasks;
- Students work directly with community partners;
- Students receive support and feedback from agency staff; and
- The service continues over a sustained period (pp. 190–191).

While the authors were interested in how student attitudes toward service change over the course of one semester, others have looked at whether students believe they will continue to serve (Payne & Bennett, 1999; Stukas, Snyder, & Clary, 1999; Tartter, 1996; Vogelgesang & Astin, 2000). Still others (Astin, Sax, & Avalos, 1999; Schnitzer & Parker-Gwin, 2003; Warchal & Ruiz, 2004) conducted long-range studies to look at actual commitments to service after college. Can aspects of placement quality contribute not only to positive outcomes immediately following service, but also to continued commitment to service?

Here, we enter the realm of "volunteerism"; and while this concept is distinct from service-learning, there is an implicit, largely unexamined assumption that service-learning should lead to continued *voluntary* community involvement. Long-range analysis of student participation takes place *after* the student's initial semester of involvement, at which point the student has the *choice* of continuing service. In this case, service-learning can be regarded as a threshold experience, and motivation to continue will occur solely in a voluntary context.

In considering motivation to serve, it is important to distinguish between "recruitment, performance, and retention motivations" (Clary & Snyder, 1999; Gluck, 1975; Smith, 1981). The factors that may motivate a service participant to get involved with a particular organization (recruitment motivations) are viewed here as distinct from the factors that influence performance and promote *continued* involvement (performance and retention motivations). The emphasis on continued service is significant, as turnover is a persistent problem for service organizations, necessitating ongoing costs in recruitment and training. Retaining service-learning students would therefore be perceived as beneficial to these organizations. In addition, continuity of service would also provide a bridge to understanding post-college attitudes toward community and civic participation.

REVIEW OF THE LITERATURE

Measures of Motivation and Continued Service

Research into the theoretical basis for service motivations has focused on a variety of factors. These include altruistic motives, instrumental motives, integrative motives, and ideological motives (Sherer, 2004). Altruistic motives (Phillips, 1982; Sherer, 2004) are a frequent focus in the literature. However, Smith (1981) and others have taken issue with altruism as a motivational construct, citing in particular that altruism is a socially desirable response on self-report surveys. Furthermore, it is problematic to disentangle "altruistic" motives from other aspects of intrinsic motivation, or the desire to be approved of as an altruistic person. For this reason, others have incorporated the measure of altruism into a broader concept of "values." Altruism may work better in explaining recruitment motivations than persistence motivations.

Several studies have attempted to apply motivational theories to voluntary service. Clary, Snyder, and Stukas (1996) developed an approach based on "functional theories of beliefs and behaviors." Six motivational dimensions are proposed:

1. Values (inclusive of altruism);
2. Career (professional development);
3. Understanding (increased knowledge);
4. Social (involvement with a particular social group);
5. Enhancement (esteem building); and
6. Protective (reducing guilt and inferiority) (p. 487).

Career and understanding motives were found to be more important for new volunteers than for continuing volunteers. Tschirhart, Mesch, Perry, Miller, and Lee (2001) utilized goal-setting theory to advance a similar set of motivations: instrumental (career), avoidance (escape from alienation, boredom, and other problems), self-esteem, social, and altruistic. Both of these theories are dependent upon motivational factors specific to volunteers (i.e., volunteers vary on the motivational dimensions discussed above and will be more likely to stay with a position that matches their interests).

Schnitzer and Parker-Gwin (2003), in their long-range study of service-learning alumni, cast doubt on significant preservice value differences between service-learning and non-service-learning students. In their study of 873 students entering college over a 5-year period, they found that the future service-learning students did not express significant value differences from the rest of their freshman cohort. Differences emerged post-college with service-learning alumni expressing more interest in continuing with community service than their counterparts. This indicates that aspects of the service experience may motivate continued service.

Stenson, Eyler, and Giles (2003) reviewed the work of Clary and others in exploring student intrinsic motivation to serve. They utilized cognitive evaluation theory (CET), in which intrinsic motivation is "the process of doing an activity for its own sake...for the sake of the feelings of excitement, accomplishment, and personal satisfaction" (Deci, 1995, p. 21). Stenson and colleagues (2003) cited items they would include in a survey of intrinsic motivation in service-learning. These items included:

- "It is important that I see the results of my work";
- "It is important that I do interesting tasks at work";
- "It is important that I have a chance to do the things I do best at work" (p. 208)

While feelings and values about service are outside of our control in motivating continued service, other intrinsic factors, such as the characteristics of the service itself, can be negotiated. Utilizing factors identified by Andrews (1995), a theory based on characteristics of service, could be advanced (Stenson et al., 2003).

Fortunately, a serviceable theory already exists. The JCM is a motivational theory that focuses on factors specific to a job that lead to commitment and satisfaction. Dailey (1986) specifically applied the JCM to the study of organizational commitment for volunteers. Dailey's study is instructive, in that it extends the outcomes of the JCM to the overall outcome of *organizational commitment.* Drawing on the research of Porter, Steers, Mowday, and Boulian (1974), organizational commitment is a direct result of job satisfaction, a predicted outcome of the JCM. Using multiple regression analysis, Dailey found strong positive correlations between all of the job characteristics, job satisfaction, and commitment.

Dailey (1986) also incorporated a variable called *job involvement* to account for the apparent exclusion of the social environment of work from the JCM, and investigated aspects of McClelland's (1978) manifest needs theory by including measures of the *need for achievement* and *need for affiliation.* The *job involvement* variable is problematic for the following reasons: several of the elements of job involvement, as defined by Rabinowitz and Hall (1977), are confounding of the existing variables of the JCM (identification with the job, active participation in the job). In addition, this variable was found to be negatively related to organizational commitment. Need for achievement was found to be significantly related to satisfaction and commitment, but need for affiliation was not.

Dailey's (1986) mixed findings on social motives may have more to do with his operationalization than in the construct itself. Harrison (1995) noted the importance of social motives in episodic volunteerism. Verba, Schlozman, and Brady (1995) noted the importance of *being asked* as a motivator of volunteer participation. Smith, in his 1994 literature review on voluntary association participation, echoed this finding, as well as *having friends in the organization.* Self's (1991) study of a developmental approach to organizational commitment also identified socialization as influential in developing identification with an organization. Socialization motives are partially accounted for in the JCM, as discussed below.

Finally, consideration is given to demographic factors associated with volunteering. Gender, age, and education, as well as prior service participation, have all been reported to play a role in service (Wilson, 2000). However, given the focus on service-learning, particularly in higher education, the unit of analysis is skewed toward traditionally aged college students. Therefore, the influence of age and education has limited applicability in *this particular population of study*; however, gender, race, and prior participation can be assessed as demographic variables.

THEORETICAL FRAMEWORK

In the Job Characteristics Model, Hackman and colleagues (1975), and later Hackman and Oldham (1980), highlighted aspects of the task environment of service itself, which can lead to continued commitment. For this reason, it can be particularly helpful in connecting *placement quality* to *continued* service with an organization beyond the initial semester of involvement. The JCM posits a relationship between five specific characteristics of work (skill variety, task identity, task significance, autonomy, and feedback), which influence "critical psychological states" (experienced meaningfulness of the work, experienced responsibility for outcomes of the work, and knowledge of the actual results of the work), which then lead to high intrinsic work motivation (including increased job performance, job satisfaction, and low absenteeism and turnover). The variable *growth needs strength* is thought to moderate the relationship between characteristics and outcomes (Hackman & Oldham, 1980). The proposed relationship is depicted in Figure 5.1. Key variables are described below.

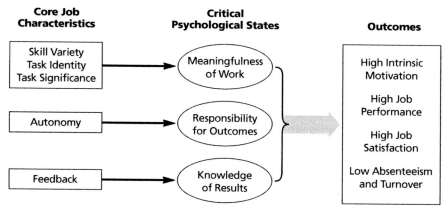

Figure 5.1.   The Job Characteristics Model (Hackman & Oldham, 1980).

Hackman and Oldham (1980) listed the following independent variables:

- *Skill variety.* The degree to which a job requires a variety of different activities in carrying out the work, involving the use of a number of different skills and talents of the person.
- *Task identity.* The degree to which a job requires completion of a "whole" and identifiable piece of work; that is, doing a job from beginning to end with a visible outcome.
- *Task significance.* The degree to which the job has a substantial impact on the lives of other people, whether those people are in the immediate organization or in the world at large.
- *Autonomy.* The degree to which the job provides substantial freedom, independence, and discretion to the individual in scheduling the work and in determining the procedures to be used in carrying it out.
- *Feedback.* The degree to which carrying out the work activities required by the job provides the individual with direct and clear information about the effectiveness of his or her performance. This definition of feedback is distinct in that it focuses on feedback from the *job itself* (as opposed to a supervisor), and the individual realizing the fruits of his or her labor (pp. 78–80).

Dependent variables include intrinsic *motivation, performance, satisfaction,* and *absenteeism/turnover* (p. 90). These outcomes are said to result from an "enriched" work environment created by the maximization of the five job characteristics variables (Hackman & Oldham, 1980).

The five independent variables are combined in the following equation to yield a *motivating potential score* (MPS):

$$(MPS) = \frac{(\text{Skill Variety} + \text{Task Identity} + \text{Task Significance})}{3} + \text{Autonomy} + \text{Feedback}$$

Fried and Ferris (1987) noted that a revision of the equation may be equally, if not more predictive.

$$MPS = \text{Skill variety} + \text{Task identity} + \text{Task significance} + \text{Autonomy} + \text{Feedback}$$

The motivating potential scores have been calculated for various types of paid jobs in the public and for-profit sectors, indicating the extent to which the characteristics of these jobs lead to satisfaction and performance. The further relationship between satisfaction and organizational commitment has been explicated by Mowday, Porter, and Steers (1982).

There has been some critique of the JCM, to the effect that it insufficiently accounts for the social environment of work. However, it is noted that socialization with service recipients is partially accounted for in the JCM, in terms of *task significance* (the degree to which the job has a substantial impact on the lives of other people, whether those people are in the immediate organization or in the world at large), *autonomy*, and *feedback* (for further discussion, see Hackman et al., 1975). Furthermore, Hackman and Oldham (1980) have included an additional variable, *dealing with others*, in their questionnaire, but not in the model itself. This relational aspect is not considered a stable characteristic of a job; however, because its impact on continued commitment can be analyzed, this factor effectively constitutes a sixth job characteristic.

The Relationship between Job Characteristics and "Placement Quality"

There is evidence that the JCM has applicability in service-learning research. Eyler and Giles (1999) identified *placement quality* as a key variable found to correlate significantly with variables such as tolerance, personal efficacy, leadership skills, communications skills, career skills, community efficacy, value of service, and future intent to serve (see Exhibit 5.1). In their research, *placement quality* was operationalized to include the following items that relate to the five job characteristics variables—"During my community service: *[sic]*"

- Had important responsibilities (task significance);
- Had challenging tasks (skill variety);
- Made important decisions (autonomy);
- Did things myself instead of observing (autonomy);
- Talked with people receiving service (task significance, feedback);

- Had a variety of tasks to do (task variety);
- Felt I made a contribution (feedback); and
- Free *[sic]* to develop and use my ideas (autonomy) (pp. 240–241).

Exhibit 5.1.   Correlation of Placement Quality With Service-Learning Outcomes

	b	$\alpha<$
High-Quality Service-Learning	0.47	.001
Learned More in Service-Learning	0.21	.001
Intellectually Challenged in Service-Learning	0.15	.001
Motivated to Work Harder[†]	0.32	.001
Needy Are Like Me	0.11	.01
Know Self Better	0.15	.001
Spiritual Growth	0.11	.01
Rewarding to Help[†]	0.19	.001
Learn to Work With Others[†]	0.22	.001
Specific Skills	0.15	.001
See Issues in New Way	0.08	.05
Close to Faculty During Service-Learning	0.18	.001
Close to Other Students During Service-Learning	0.09	.05
Tolerance	0.12	.001
Personal Efficacy	0.15	.001
Leadership Skills	0.14	.001
Communication Skills	0.14	.001
Career Skills	0.07	.05
Community Efficacy	0.10	.01
Future Volunteer Time Commitment[†]	0.09	.05

Adapted from Eyler & Giles (1999), Tables E.1–E.5.
[†] Indicates variable in the Job Characteristics Model

Exhibit 5.2 presents items from the JCM scale alongside items from the Fund for the Improvement of Postsecondary Education (FIPSE) scale used by Eyler and Giles (1999). (It is noted that Eyler and Giles derived their scale from the prior work of Owens and Owen [1979] and Moore [1981], who found task-related reasons to be most highly rated over social reasons in reporting a community experience as an excellent learning opportunity. This is among the reasons task-related measures are included in the survey

Exhibit 5.2.   Survey Questions by Variable for the Job Characteristics Model as Compared with the FIPSE Survey Employed in *Where's the Learning in Service-Learning?*

Job Diagnostic Survey	*FIPSE Survey (Eyler & Giles)*
Skill variety	
How much variety is there in your job? That is, to what extent does the job require you to do many different things at work, using a variety of your skills and talents? (Section 1, item 4)	Had challenging tasks (item 11)
The job requires me to use a number of complex or high-level skills (Section 2, item 1)	Had a variety of tasks to do onsite* (item 18)
The job is quite simple and repetitive (reverse scored) (Section 2, item 5)	
Task identity	
To what extent does your job involve doing a *"whole" and identifiable piece of work?* That is, is the job a complete piece of work that has an obvious beginning and end? Or is it only a small part of the overall piece of work, which is finished by other people ? (Section 1, item 3)	(none)
The job allows me the chance to completely finish the pieces of work I begin (Section 2, item 11)	
The job is arranged so that I do *not* have the chance to do an entire piece of work from beginning to end. (reverse scored) (Section 2, item 3)	
Task significance	
In general, how significant or important is your job? That is, are the results of your work likely to affect the lives or well-being of other people? (Section 1, item 5)	Had important responsibilities (item 10)
This job is one where a lot of other people can be affected by how well the work gets done. (Section 2, item 8)	Talked with people receiving service (item 15)
The job itself is *not* very significant or important in the broader scheme of things. (reverse scored) (Section 2, item 14)	Felt I made a real contribution (item 20)
Autonomy	
How much *autonomy* is there in your job? That is, to what extent does the (your) job permit you to decide *on your own* how to go about doing the work? (Section 1, item 2)	Made important decisions (item 12)
The job gives me considerable opportunity for independence and freedom in how I do the work (Section 2, item 13)	Did things myself instead of observing (item 14)
The job denies me any chance to use my personal initiative or judgment in carrying out the work (reverse scored) (Section 2, item 9)	Free to develop and use my ideas (item 21)

Exhibit 5.2.   Survey Questions by Variable for the Job Characteristics Model as Compared with the FIPSE Survey Employed in *Where's the Learning in Service-Learning?* (Cont.)

Job Diagnostic Survey	*FIPSE Survey (Eyler & Giles)*
Feedback	
To what extent does *doing the job itself* provide you with information about your work performance? That is, does the actual *work itself* provide clues about how well you are doing—aside from any "feedback" co-workers or supervisors may provide? (Section 1, item 7)	Was appreciated when I did a good job (item 19) *(Note: This notion of feedback differs from that expounded in the JCM.)*
Just doing the work required by the job provides many chances for me to figure out how well I am doing. (Section 2, item 4)	
The job itself provides very few clues about whether or not I am performing well. (reverse scored) (Section 2, item 12)	
Dealing with others[*]	
To what extent does your job require you to *work closely with other people* (either "clients," or people in related jobs in the your own organization)? (Section 1, item 1)	(Several items that do not closely parallel this construct)
The job requires a lot of cooperative work with other people (Section 2, item 2)	
The job can be done adequately by a person working alone—without talking or checking with other people (reverse scored) (Section 2, item 6)	

Eyler & Giles (1999, pp. 240–241); Hackman & Oldham (1980, pp. 275–302)
[*] Not accounted for in the original model

methodology to begin with.) Eyler and Giles's research focused on the task environment in enhancing student *learning* and *civic development*; however, long-range studies have not studied the impact of the task environment in determining whether or not students actually continue to serve with a particular organization. This relationship could be important in understanding future commitment to serve, and certainly could provide us with information of importance to community organizations as a long-range benefit of their partnership with campus service-learning programs.

Figure 5.2 relates the list of characteristics of high-quality placements articulated by Eyler and Giles (1999) in terms of four of the five JCM variables. If these relationships hold, then continued, sustained service could be predicted, based on the model.

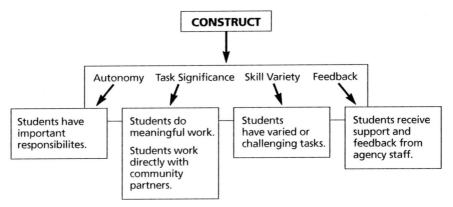

Figure 5.2.   Relationship between job characteristics and student outcomes.

SURVEY METHODOLOGY

This section discusses the survey methodology associated with the JCM. Exhibit 5.2 shows most of the items can be directly compared with items on the FIPSE survey used by Eyler and Giles (1999). This indicates that we have already been measuring job characteristics, and, by extension, could expand our methodology to utilize JCM to study continued service.

The JCM survey methodology comprises two separate but parallel survey instruments. The first, administered to work participants, is the Job Diagnostic Survey (JDS). The second, administered to managers or supervisors, is the Job Rating Form (JRF). These instruments, discussed below, allow for comparison between job holders and supervisors. The JDS, short form (Hackman & Oldham, 1980) consists of 39 closed-ended survey items in four sections. The original survey incorporates items relating to compensation, which would not be applicable. Survey respondents are asked to rate their satisfaction with aspects of the job on a 7-point Likert scale ranging from extremely dissatisfied to extremely satisfied. This survey would be administered to students, as "job holders" at the end of the semester of service, or even as a long-range indicator beyond the semester. The survey could then be used to compare between students who remain with their service placements versus students who do not. It would be important, however, to determine further whether the students' service was ended because the project itself was finite, or whether it was due to constraints on the student's availability, graduation, or other reasons.

Likewise, the JRF, which reports the extent to which job characteristics correspond to the independent variables in the JCM, can be used to determine how community service supervisors perceive their service projects. The JRF consists of 25 items in three sections, and closely parallels the JDS. The JRF would be administered to community-based organizations concurrent with the initial semester of service-learning in which the student survey respondents participate. In this manner, it can be ensured that organizations are responding regarding positions occupied by this particular group of students. Organizations can later confirm whether the student has continued with service, and if so, whether the position was time-delimited, seasonal, or no longer needed. Scoring of the JRF and the JDS will utilize the scoring key accompanying both instruments.

Psychometric Properties

Both the JRF and JDS (short form) use three sets of questions to operationalize each variable. As described by Taber and Taylor (1990),

> One item...uses a seven-step rating format with short descriptive phrases anchoring its middle and end points. The other items are in a Likert format. One Likert item is positively worded and one is negatively worded. Using a seven-step scale, respondents rate how "accurately" each statement describes their jobs. (p. 468)

This repetition and reverse coding helps improve internal consistency. In their 1990 review of the psychometric properties of the JDS, Taber and Taylor noted that the instrument has psychometric limitations, "but is able to provide useful information about perceived job properties." They noted that the internal consistency of the scales could be improved by *increasing* the number of parallel questions for each variable. Aldag, Barr, and Brief (1981) found the internal consistency of the instrument to be acceptable. Fried and Ferris (1987), in their review of some 200 studies utilizing the model, found that "the available correlational results are reasonably valid in light of the issues examined." All of the above sources noted, however, that not all of the five factors have emerged across all studies; indeed, the model itself predicts varying degrees of each variable, depending on the job examined.

DISCUSSION

This review of the JCM and prior research into service-learning and service motivations indicates that the JCM can be of use in elucidating the issue of placement quality, and that placement quality has been demonstrated to be significantly related to certain student service outcomes. The model takes into account aspects of the service environment, as well as social relationships of work, and is descriptive of elements of placement quality as articulated by Eyler and Giles (1999). However, in "unpacking" their findings on placement quality in Exhibit 5.1, it is important to address what the model *does* predict, what it *does not* predict, and what it may (or could) predict upon further consideration.

First, the JCM would indeed predict the impact of placement quality on increased motivation to work harder in service-learning ($b = .32$, $p < .001$), as well as the predicted future volunteer time commitment ($b = .09$, $p < .05$). These findings are directly related to the outcomes of high intrinsic motivation, high job performance, and commitment. Furthermore, the perception that it is *rewarding to help* ($b = .19$, $p < .001$) would be an element of the independent variable *feedback,* indicating that the service performed was effective, and that it was significant in impacting the lives of others. *Learning to work with others* ($b = .22$, $p < .001$) would also be predicted to the extent that the service involved *dealing with others*: as discussed above, this variable is measured for in the questionnaire, but not represented in the model itself.

It is noted here that the variables *task identity* and *feedback* are not accounted for in the survey methodology utilized by Eyler and Giles (1999) (see Exhibit 5.2). However, both of these variables may offer explanatory value in determining placement quality. First, *task identity,* the idea that a student would complete a whole, identifiable piece of work, has appeal as a variable of interest. Many service-learning courses are designed with the idea of students producing a whole "product" for an organization (a grant proposal, a newsletter). The model would provide a basis for determining whether such a focus yielded greater satisfaction for the students. *Feedback* is often discussed as an important element of service-learning and service in general. However, the focus of the JCM is to assess how feedback is obtained from the job itself. It is intriguing to consider how this might differ from feedback given by others, which is subject to the amount of contact and the relationship a student has with a supervisor.

In developing or identifying a theoretical base for the field, it is also important to note that no theory can account for all perceived variation in a system, and that exclusionary principles are also necessary. For this reason, while it is intriguing to speculate on the possible relationships with other outcomes, it is not likely that the JCM will be of much predictive value in explaining the relationships not emphasized in Exhibit 5.1. What is certainly worth examining are the reported learning outcomes (learned more, was intellectually challenged, needy are like me, know self better). Is it possible that an enriched job (service) environment entails opportunities for reflection? The distinction drawn on *feedback* by Hackman and Oldham (1980) points us in this direction—that it is not merely a function of someone telling us how we are doing on a job, but on how *we perceive* our effectiveness on the job. This relates to role-based learning, which is (arguably) implicitly at the center of service-learning as a pedagogy. And here, the JCM has the potential to measure aspects not just of the service itself, but of the service as integrated into a larger classroom experience.

While considering this idea, it is well to note and echo the caution of Eyler and Giles (1999) regarding how researchers and practitioners perceive the role of placement quality. It is not simply the case that one can go out and find the highest quality service-learning placement, and thereby predict the most pronounced positive outcomes for our students. A fully integrated service-learning experience would entail dialogues between the faculty and community organizer, such that working together in an enriched service experience can be designed with the five job characteristics in mind. In this manner, one could envision that perceptions of task significance, as well as job feedback, would be enhanced through reflection and full integration into the classroom experience. As well, the variable *task identity* could be further examined to determine whether performing a whole and identifiable service project, as opposed to a piecemeal project, increased students' commitment to their project, their perceived learning, and their motivation to continue to serve.

Future studies could merge items from the JDS into current survey methodology to test for continued service. This would necessitate instigating some "mid-range" studies to determine whether students persist in service beyond the initial semester. The JRF enables a parallel measure that can be used to match the responses of community partners with those of students. Such studies could then be linked with long-range research findings about the relationship between service-learning and commitment to serve broadly. As indicated, the variables *task identity* and *feedback*, as defined by the JCM, could be the subject of expanded research. Finally, the theory could be extended to examine the relationship of job characteristics (as a measure of placement quality) on learning outcomes.

CONCLUSION

This chapter is intended to assess the appropriateness of the JCM in explaining job turnover and satisfaction for service-learning students. The five independent variables of the model—Skill Variety, Task Identity, Task Significance, Autonomy, and Feedback—relate to similar measures used by Eyler and Giles (1999) to indicate *placement quality*. Furthermore, the model is predictive of some of their findings, that *placement quality* is related to greater work motivation and intent to serve. While few studies have focused on continuity of service beyond one semester, the model can be of great use here. It can further elucidate the findings of long-range studies that indicate greater interest on the part of service-learning alumni in serving their communities. But perhaps its most significant contribution could be in suggesting ways to "enrich" the service-learning experience such that placement quality was meaningfully determined as a product of *both* the community organization and the classroom. So considered, service-learning project design, with an eye to skill variety, task identity, task significance, autonomy, and feedback, could lead to greater learning for students. The model and its associated surveys provide a basis for further study.

REFERENCES

Aldag, R., Barr, S., & Brief, A. (1981). Measurement of perceived task characteristics. *Psychological Bulletin, 90,* 425–431.

Andrews, G. (1995) *Factors affecting volunteer motivation: The importance of intrinsic motivations, extrinsic motivations, and situational facilities on volunteer work.* Unpublished dissertation, Kent State University, Kent, OH.

Astin, A., Sax, L., & Avalos, J. (1999). Long-term effects of volunteerism during the undergraduate years. *Review of Higher Education, 22*(2), 187–202.

Bringle, R. (2003). Enhancing theory-based research on service-learning. In S. H. Billig & J. Eyler (Eds.), *Advances in service-learning: Vol. 3. Deconstructing service-learning: Research exploring context, participation, and impacts* (pp. 3–24). Greenwich, CT: Information Age Publishing.

Clary, E., & Snyder, M. (1999). The motivations to volunteer: Theoretical and practical considerations. *Current Directions in Psychological Science, 8*(5), 156–159.

Clary, E., Snyder, M., & Stukas, A. (1996). Volunteers' motivations: Findings from a national survey. *Nonprofit and Voluntary Sector Quarterly, 25*(4), 485–505.

Cruz, N., & Giles, D. (2000, Fall). Where's the community in service-learning research? *Michigan Journal of Community Service Learning* [Special issue], 28–34.

Dailey, R. (1986). Understanding organizational commitment for volunteers: Empirical and managerial implications. *Journal of Voluntary Action Research, 15*(1), 19–31.

Deci, E. (1995). *Why do we do what we do: The dynamics of personal autonomy.* New York: G.P. Putnam's Sons.

Eyler, J. (2000, Fall). What do we most need to know about the impact of service-learning on student learning? *Michigan Journal of Community Service Learning* [Special issue], 11–17.

Eyler, J., & Giles, D. (1999). *Where's the learning in service-learning,* San Francisco: Jossey-Bass.

Eyler, J., Giles, D., Stenson, C., & Gray, C. (2001). *At a glance: What we know about the effects of service-learning on college students, faculty, institutions and communities,*

1993–2000 (3rd ed.). Washington, DC: Corporation for National Service, Learn and Serve America, National Service Learning Clearinghouse.

Fried, Y., & Ferris, G. (1987). The validity of the job characteristics model: A review and meta-analysis. *Personnel Psychology, 40,* 287–322.

Furco, A., & Billig, S. H. (2002). Establishing norms for scientific inquiry in service-learning. In S. H. Billig & A. Furco (Eds.), *Advances in service-learning: Vol. 2. Service-learning: through a multidisciplinary lens* (pp. 15–32). Greenwich, CT: Information Age Publishing.

Gluck, P. (1975). An exchange theory of incentives of urban political party organization. *Journal of Voluntary Action Research, 12*(1), 20–35.

Hackman, J., & Oldham, G. (1980). *Work redesign.* Reading, MA: Addison-Wesley.

Hackman, J., Oldham, G., Janson, R., & Purdy, K. (1975). A new strategy for job enrichment. *California Management Review, 17*(4), 57–71.

Harrison, D. (1995). Volunteer motivation and attendance decisions: Competitive theory testing in multiple samples from a homeless shelter. *Journal of Applied Psychology, 80*(3), 371–385.

McClelland, D. (1978). Managing motivation to expand human freedom. *American Psychologist, 33,* 201–210.

Moore, D. (1981). Discovering the pedagogy of experience. *Harvard Educational Review, 51*(2), 286–300.

Mowday, R., Porter, L., & Steers, R. (1982). *Employee-organizational linkage.* New York: Academic Press.

Owens, T., & Owen, S. (1979). Enhancing the quality of community learning experiences. *Alternative Higher Education, 4*(2), 103–112.

Payne, C., & Bennett, E. (1999). Service-learning and changes in community involvement preferences among undergraduates. *NASPA Journal, 37*(1), 337–348.

Phillips, M. (1982). Motivation and expectation in successful volunteerism. *Journal of Voluntary Action Research, 11*(2), 118–125.

Porter, L., Steers, R., Mowday, R., & Boulian, P. (1974). Organizational commitment, job satisfaction and turnover among psychiatric technicians. *Journal of Applied Psychology, 59,* 603–609.

Rabinowitz, S., & Hall, D. (1977). Job scope and individual differences as predictors of job involvement. *Academy of Management Journal, 20,* 273–281.

Schnitzer, M., & Parker-Gwin, R. (2003, November). *Service-learning outcomes: Perspectives from alumni.* Presentation at the 3rd Annual International Conference on Service-Learning Research, Salt Lake City, UT.

Self, R. (1991). The development of organizational commitment: A conceptual approach, *Proceedings from the Southern Management Association Conference,* pp. 232–236.

Sherer, M. (2004). National service in Israel: Motivations, volunteer characteristics, and levels of content. *Nonprofit and Voluntary Sector Quarterly, 33*(1), 94–108.

Sigmon, R. (1998). *Building sustainable partnerships: linking communities and educational institutions* [Monograph]. Washington, DC: Corporation for National Service.

Smith, D. (1981). Altruism, volunteers and volunteerism. *Journal of Voluntary Action Research, 10*(1), 21–36.

Smith, D. (1994). Determinants of voluntary association participation and volunteering: A literature review. *Nonprofit and Voluntary Sector Quarterly, 23*(3), 243–263.

Stenson, C., Eyler, J., & Giles, D. (2003). Service and motivation to serve: An exploration and model. In S. H. Billig & J. Eyler (Eds.), *Advances in service-learning: Vol. 3. Deconstructing service-learning: Research exploring context, participation, and impacts* (pp. 195–212). Greenwich, CT: Information Age Publishing.

Stukas, A., Snyder, M., & Clary, E. (1999). The effects of "mandatory volunteerism" on intentions to volunteer. *Psychological Science, 10*(1), 59–64.

Taber, T., & Taylor, E. (1990). A review and evaluation of the psychometric properties of the job diagnostic survey. *Personnel Psychology, 43,* 467–500.

Tartter, V. (1996). *City College report to FIPSE.* New York: City College Research Foundation.

Tschirhart, M., Mesch, D., Perry, J. L., Miller, T. K., & Lee, G. (2001). Stipended volunteers: Their goals, experiences, satisfaction, and likelihood of future service. *Nonprofit and Voluntary Sector Quarterly, 30*(3), 422–443.

Verba, S., Schlozman, K., & Brady, H. (1995). *Voice and equality: Civic voluntarism in American politics.* Cambridge, MA: Harvard University Press.

Vogelgesang, L., & Astin, A. (2000). Comparing the effects of service-learning and community service. *Michigan Journal of Community Service Learning, 7,* 25–34.

Warchal, J., & Ruiz, A. (2004). The long-term effects of undergraduate service-learning programs on postgraduate employment choices, community engagement, and civic leadership. In M. Welch & S. H. Billig (Eds.), *Advances in service-learning research: Vol. 4. New perspectives in service-learning: Research to advance the field* (pp. 87–106). Greenwich, CT: Information Age Publishing.

Wilson, J. (2000). Volunteering. *Annual Review of Sociology, 26,* 215–240.

CHAPTER 6

THE RELATIONSHIP BETWEEN THE QUALITY INDICATORS OF SERVICE-LEARNING AND STUDENT OUTCOMES

Testing Professional Wisdom

Shelley H. Billig, Susan Root, and Dan Jesse

ABSTRACT

This study examined the effects of service-learning on high school students' civic engagement and the elements of quality that were associated with the strongest outcomes. The sample included over 1,000 students who were in service-learning and non service-learning classrooms matched for grade level, subject matter, demographics, and achievement profiles. Results showed that service-learning was associated with enjoyment of school and intention to vote, with few other differences apparent between the students in the service-learning and non service-learning groups. Particular characteristics of the service-learning experience, such as cognitive challenge, meeting genuine needs, valuing diversity, and student preparation, were associated with specific increases in academic and civic outcomes.

Improving Service-Learning Practice: Research on Models to Enhance Impacts, pages 97–115

INTRODUCTION

Service-learning intentionally ties the provision of community service to academic learning. According to Skinner and Chapman (1999), service-learning is practiced in half of all public high schools. Private school participation is estimated to be even stronger, with nearly 80% implementing service-learning (Pritchard, 2002).

A gradually accumulating body of evidence suggests that service-learning can help students develop knowledge of community needs, commit to an ethic of service, develop more sophisticated understandings of politics and morality, gain a greater sense of civic responsibility and feelings of efficacy, and increase their desire to become active contributors to society (Billig, 2000; Westheimer & Kahne, 2000a, 2000b; Youniss, McLellan, & Yates, 1997; Youniss & Yates, 1997). Service-learning can also positively influence students' academic achievement, attitudes toward school, and engagement in school learning (Ammon, Furco, Chi, & Middaugh., 2001; Billig & Klute, 2003; Melchior, 1999; Meyer, Billig, & Hofschire, 2004).

Given the wide range of types of service-learning programs and the range of quality within each type of program, programs can be expected to vary substantially in the extent to which they are successful in promoting civic development and academic attainment. While the potential for service-learning is considerable, the research shows that unless certain practices within service-learning are in place, its impacts may not be maximized. In the mid 1990s, practitioners and researchers convened to identify those elements that they believed represented best practice. The group identified 11 Essential Elements (National Service-Learning Cooperative, 1998), shown in Figure 6.1. These Elements were widely disseminated and used as the basis for professional development to help teachers implement high-quality programs.

The purpose of this study was to advance the knowledge about moderators of service-learning impacts by investigating the contribution of the Essential Elements and other perceived quality indicators to high school participants' civic and academic development through service-learning.

Service-Learning Element

1. Clear educational goals.
2. Involve students in cognitively challenging tasks.
3. Assessment used to enhance student learning and evaluate how well students have met content and skill standards.
4. Students are engaged in service tasks with clear goals that meet genuine community needs and have significant consequences.
5. Use of evaluation.
6. Youth voice in selecting, designing, implementing, and evaluating service-learning projects.
7. Valuing diversity.
8. Communication, interaction, partnerships, and collaboration with the community.
9. Students are prepared for all aspects of their service work.
10. Use of reflection.
11. Celebration and acknowledgment of service work.

Figure 6.1.   Essential Elements of Service-Learning.
Source: National Service Learning Cooperative, 1998

METHODOLOGY

This study addressed the following research questions:

1. To what extent do students who participate in service-learning show increases over time on measures of a variety of aspects of civic engagement and academic and civic knowledge and skill acquisition as compared with students in the same or matched schools who participate in classes on the same subject matter and do not participate in service-learning?

2. To what extent do aspects of program quality including the Essential Elements and other features of the service-learning experience moderate the association between participation in service-learning and civic outcomes? What teacher characteristics and practices serve to moderate outcomes?

Five sites were selected for participation in the study based on the reported quality of the site, the availability of a comparison group, and the approval of the school and district. An effort to gain a broadly representative sample from different regions of the country, locales, and socioeconomic and ethnic backgrounds was an additional selection criterion. A total of 1,052 students comprised the sample, 645 of whom were service-learning participants and 407 of whom were comparison group students. Nearly 60% of the sample was comprised of seniors and nearly 60% was female. Hispanics were the largest ethnic group represented. Just over 60% of the sample spoke English at home. Most of the remainder spoke Spanish. Exhibit 6.1 shows the final study sites.

Student surveys were administered in the fall and spring of the 2003–2004 school year. In addition to questions about student characteristics, student surveys included measures of civic outcomes and attitudes toward school. Civic outcomes addressed by the surveys comprised civic knowledge, skills, dispositions, civic engagement, and efficacy.

Civic knowledge was measured through items from the National Assessment of Academic Progress (NAEP), about government institutions, leaders, and the like, as well as a single question about local community service organizations. A second knowledge measure ("self-reported civic knowledge") asked students to rate how well informed they were about various aspects of politics (e.g., registering to vote, the difference between democracy and socialism, etc.). *Civic skills* were assessed by asking students to rate their ability to perform particular activities required for effective civic participation such as their ability to lead others, conduct a campaign to get someone elected, or work to solve a community problem.

The measure of *community attachment* tapped indicators of positive student community feeling such as contributing to, taking pride in, or being viewed as a valued part of the neighborhood or local community. The *civic dispositions* measure assessed civic responsibility (e.g., through questions about the degree to which students acted to help the needy). Student *efficacy* was measured by two items that addressed feelings of making a difference and having adult responsibilities. Finally, the measure of *civic engagement* measured political and civic participation such as how often students discussed politics, attended rallies, raised funds for a cause, or wrote letters to public officials.

Academic outcomes addressed in the study included academic engagement, valuing school; school attachment, enjoyment of math and science, and enjoyment of reading, language arts, and social studies. The measure of *academic engagement* asked students about the degree to which they were cognitively, affectively, and behaviorally engaged in school. The *valuing school* items were designed to capture the extent to which students felt that schoolwork was meaningful and important. The *school attachment* measure assessed students' sense of connection to school (e.g., belonging, making a contribution, doing things to make the school a better place). Several items asked students about the extent to which they *enjoyed specific school subjects*.

Exhibit 6.1. Sample Site Characteristics

Site	Service-Learning High School	Comparison School	Subject Matter	Grade Levels	Number of Service-Learning Classes	Number of Comparison Classes
A	1	Similar	• TV production • Environmental science • Art	9–12	4	3
B	2	Similar	• Government and economics • World history	11–12	2	2
C	3	Same	• American government	11–12	1	1
	4	Same	• Government and economics	12	6	6
	5	Same	• World history and government	11–12	4	4
	6	Same	• American government	11–12	4	2
	7	Same	• English	11–12	3	3
D	8	Similar	• Senior project matched with government and economics	12	1	2
E	9	Similar	• Senior class	12	1	1

This study also investigated the moderating influence of several categories of indicators that the literature in service-learning suggests may enhance or diminish the outcomes of service-learning, including student perceptions of characteristics of the service-learning experience, teacher attributes, and teacher practices, one component of which was service-learning practice. Specifically, student surveys included measures asking students to rate:

- The *quality* of their service-learning experience, including the degree to which they had had opportunities to reflect, make important decisions, develop and use their own ideas, feel that they had made a contribution, experience challenge, or experience adult criticism (reverse scored).
- The *extent to which they believed that they had acquired academic and work-related skills* as a result of their service-learning experience.
- A *measure of engagement in service-learning*, that is, the degree to which students worked hard on the service-learning project, enjoyed school more when working on service-learning, and/or whether they just acted as if they were working on service-learning (reverse scored).

Exhibit 6.2 displays characteristics of these moderators.

Exhibit 6.2.   Characteristics of Student Service-Learning Subscales

Subscale	Mean or Average	Number of Items	Range	Internal Reliability
Service-learning quality	3.74	8	1–5	.844
Perceived gains in reading, writing, and computer	1.13	3	0–3	.758
Perceived gains in math/science skills	0.45	2	0–2	.689
Perceived gains in work-related skills	1.81	3	0–3	.674
Overall service-learning engagement	3.35	11	1–5	.829

Teacher surveys were administered to both service-learning and comparison teachers. All teachers were asked about their field of certification, teaching experience, frequency of use of various instructional methods (e.g., lecture, debate, mock trials, cooperative learning, community service, etc.), coverage of civics topics, and perceived student growth in civic knowledge and skills. The service-learning teacher survey incorporated questions about the respondent's experience in implementing service-learning and about aspects of his or her service-learning practice, including duration, focus, type, and quality of current project(s).

To examine the quality of service-learning, subscales were created by combining items on the teacher survey intended to measure the degree to which service-learning reflected the 11 Essential Elements of Service-Learning (National Service-Learning Cooperative, 1998).

A two (pre-test vs. post-test) by two (service-learning vs. comparison) mixed multivariate analysis of variance (MANOVA) model, with pre-test and post-test as repeated measures, was initially used to analyze the effects of service-learning on subscale scores and on individual survey items. In order to control for context, student grade level, and subject area, hierarchical MANOVAS with repeated measures using nested pairs (service-learning vs. comparison groups at each study site) were subsequently used to analyze student outcomes, and ANOVAs were used to explore results of statistically significant MANOVAs. Multivariate t tests were also used to compare student groups when appropriate.

In order to determine the contribution of particular moderating variables (e.g., engagement in service-learning) to the outcomes, two approaches were used. Multivariate regression analyses were conducted to determine relationships between more than one continuous predictor variable and a dependent variable. When multiple dependent measures and independent measures were involved, a canonical correlation approach was used. Results of statistically significant canonical correlational analyses were followed by additional analyses to further explore the results.

AGGREGATED RESULTS

Civic Development

Civic Knowledge. On the measure of factual knowledge, both the service-learning and comparison groups scored higher on the post-survey. Differences were not significant. On the self-reported measure, civic knowledge, the comparison group described themselves as being better informed than the service-learning group, while the service-learning group demonstrated greater gains over time. However, these differences were not statistically significant.

Civic Disposition. Results for the civic dispositions measure showed that students generally tended to be favorably disposed to being civically engaged. Service-learning students had slightly higher scores on this measure than comparison students at both points in time; however, these differences were not significant.

Civic Skills. Differences between the service-learning students and comparison students on the civic skills measure slightly favored the service-learning students. In the analysis of specific skills items, group differences were found for those that pertained most directly to service-learning. Over time, the service-learning participants were more likely to report that they knew how to work with others to solve a community problem and that they knew how to identify community needs. However, these differences were not statistically significant.

Civic Participation.   When asked about the frequency with which they engaged in a variety of activities related to civic life, students' responses averaged between "seldom" and "sometimes" on most activities. Differences between groups were not statistically significant. Results also showed no differences between the service-learning and comparison groups on the efficacy subscale. Both groups felt that they sometimes made a lot of difference in people's lives, and both groups reported increases in having adult responsibilities.

In summary, although service-learning students scored higher than comparison students on several civic outcomes, most of these differences were not statistically significant.

Attitudes Toward School

It was hypothesized that students who were engaged in service-learning would outscore others on measures of attitudes toward school, such as valuing school, enjoyment of school subjects, engagement in learning, and school attachment. Results showed that both service-learning and comparison students sometimes or often found school to be meaningful and important for later life, but that their ratings of the value of school declined over time. A repeated measures ANOVA revealed only slight, nonsignificant differences between the service-learning and comparison groups on this measure.

School Enjoyment.   Mean scores on the measure of enjoyment in school are displayed in Figure 6.2. The results showed a difference approaching statistical significance in school enjoyment favoring both pre-test and post-test responses for the service-learning group. There were no significant differences in ratings of enjoyment of specific subject matters.

Academic Engagement.   Analyses of the academic engagement measure showed that all participants rated their engagement higher at the pre-test than the post-test. Differences between service-learning and comparison students were not statistically significant.

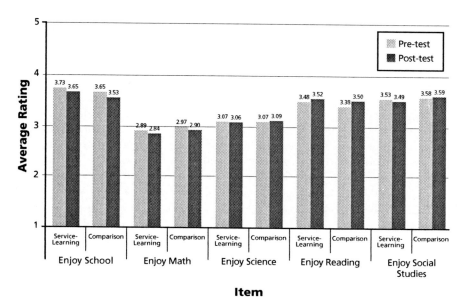

Figure 6.2.   Service-learning and comparison student ratings of enjoyment of school and specific content areas.
Note. Items range from 1 to 5 with 1 = Never/Almost Never, 5 = Always/Almost Always.

School Attachment.   On a final measure of school-related attitudes, school attachment, service-learning students scored slightly higher than the comparison group in both fall and spring. However, the differences were not statistically significant.

Subsequent to the analyses of overall differences, a second set of analyses was conducted to determine pre/post differences between service-learning and matched comparison students at each study site. *Aggregated results of these comparisons revealed statistically significant differences in the pre/post change scores for service-learning and comparison students on two subscales: Civic Knowledge, $\underline{F}(9, 1,033) = 6.535$, $\underline{p} = < .001$, and Civic Dispositions, $\underline{F}(9, 1,025) = 3.045$, $\underline{p} = .001$. Results approached statistical significance for Valuing School, $\underline{F}(9, 1,028) = 1.869$, $\underline{p} = .053$.*

MODERATORS OF IMPACT

Results showed large disparities between sites. The finding of differential outcomes for service-learning students may be attributable to variations in aspects of the service-learning experience. Informal observations conducted by study staff revealed broad variations in the ways in which service-learning was being practiced within different programs. For example, at three schools, all students completed year-long projects that were closely linked to class goals and explicitly focused on skills needed for effective democratic engagement such as problem analysis, collaborative problem solving, civic dialogue, and the ability to work within the political system to improve society. Other projects observed in the study were similarly extensive, but not directly linked to civic skills. In some programs, service-learning involved very limited time and/or student participation. These variations suggested the need to test for differences in moderating variables across programs and for relationships between moderators and student outcomes. Measures of quality included the Essential Elements, so these elements were tested as potential moderators, along with other purported elements of quality.

Multivariate analyses of variance showed a statistically significant overall difference across programs in students' ratings of the quality of their service-learning experiences, $F(64, 4{,}912) = 2.219$, $p < .001$, Eta squared = .028. Univariate tests revealed statistically significant differences between programs in several specific elements of quality including exposure to challenging tasks, making important decisions, discussing experiences with teachers, feeling criticized by adults, and feeling efficacious. Exhibit 6.3 displays the results of univariate tests for the Quality of the Service-Learning Experience scale, showing the areas of quality that had the greatest variation among schools.

Exhibit 6.3.   School Differences in Student Ratings of Quality of the Service-Learning Experience

	df	F	p	Partial Eta squared
Had real responsibilities	8	1.120	.348	.014
Had challenging tasks	8	2.271	.021	.029[*]
Made important decisions	8	2.366	.016	.030[*]
Discussed my experience(s) with my teacher(s)	8	3.264	.001	.041[**]
Did things myself instead of observing	8	1.611	.118	.021
Had freedom to develop and use my own ideas	8	1.695	.096	.022
Adults criticized me or my work	8	2.930	.003	.037[**]
Felt I made a contribution	8	3.195	.001	.040[**]

[*] $p < .05$, two-tailed test; [**] $p < .01$, two-tailed test

A multiple regression analysis was conducted to determine whether there was a relationship between students' overall scores on the measure of quality and their post-test scores. Results of this analysis were highly significant, $F(12, 600) = 28.041$, $p < .001$, $R^2 = .359$. Students' perception of the quality of their service-learning experience was a strong, positive predictor of their post-test scores on school attachment and civic knowledge, in particular.

A multivariate regression analysis was conducted to test for a relationship between student engagement in service-learning and the outcome measures. Results of this analysis were highly significant as well, $F(12, 593) = 37.598$, $p < .001$, Eta squared = .432. Follow-up analyses revealed that student engagement was significantly positively associated with every outcome measure except one (civic knowledge). Exhibit 6.4 displays the results for the overall service-learning engagement score and its relationships to each of the student outcome measures.

Exhibit 6.4. Service-Learning Engagement as a Moderator of Student Outcomes

Dependent Variable	F	p	Partial Eta squared
Academic Engagement	200.901	.000	.250***
Valuing School	175.162	.000	.225***
School Attachment	130.944	.000	.178***
Enjoyment of Math and Science	25.391	.000	.040***
Enjoyment of Reading/Language Arts and Social Studies	59.232	.000	.089***
Civic Knowledge	.070	.792	.000
Self-Reported Civic Knowledge	23.592	.000	.038***
Civic Skills	109.269	.000	.153***
Community Attachment	108.774	.000	.153***
Civic Dispositions	80.811	.000	.118***
Efficacy	175.764	.000	.225***
Civic Engagement	103.500	.000	.146***

*** $p < .001$, two-tailed test

Data analyses were also conducted on the relationship between moderating variables assessed on the teacher survey and student outcomes.

Duration. To investigate the degree to which service-learning duration was associated with student outcomes, teachers were asked to estimate the length of time their classes spent on all activities associated with the service-learning project, including the service activity itself and the steps of preparation, reflection, and celebration/demonstration. Four categories of duration were identified: (1) less than 1 month, (2) one to two months, (3) one semester, and (4) one year.

A one-way MANOVA revealed statistically significant effects for the duration of the service-learning experience on students' overall post-test scores, $F(36, 1,866) = 6.326$, $p < .001$, Eta squared = .109. Univariate tests showed that duration significantly influenced post-test scores on academic engagement, valuing school, school attachment, enjoyment of math and science, enjoyment of reading/language arts and social studies, civic knowledge, self-reported civic knowledge, and community attachment, shown in Exhibit 6.5. Subsequent analyses showed that academic engagement, valuing school, and enjoyment of subject matter scores were highest when projects were of one or two months' duration. School attachment, civic skills, and community attachment were rated highest by students in programs of one semester. Civic knowledge was highest when projects were a year in length.

Exhibit 6.5.   Effect Sizes for Service-Learning Duration and Student Outcomes

Post-Test Student Outcomes	df	F	p	Partial Eta squared
Academic Engagement	3	4.283	.005	.020**
Valuing School	3	5.058	.002	.023**
School Attachment	3	15.041	.000	.067***
Enjoying Math and Science	3	6.511	.000	.030***
Enjoying Reading/Language Arts and Social Studies	3	15.018	.000	.067***
Civic Knowledge	3	13.062	.000	.058***
Civic Knowledge Self-Ratings	3	6.379	.000	.029***
Civic Skills	3	2.666	.047	.013*
Civic Dispositions	3	1.027	.380	.005
Community Attachment	3	9.620	.000	.044***
Efficacy	3	0.800	.494	.004
Civic Engagement	3	2.193	.088	.010

* $p < .05$, two-tailed test; ** $p < .01$, two-tailed test; *** $p < .001$, two-tailed test

Service Issue.   This study also explored the question of whether the service issue targeted by students and their teachers was associated with the outcomes. Based on teachers' descriptions, issues for service were categorized as varied (student selected), civic, or environmental. A one-way MANOVA to determine the effects of the service issue on participants' overall post-test scores was statistically significant, $F(24, 1,244) = 5.593$, $p < .001$, Eta squared = .097. Post hoc tests revealed differences in three outcomes due to the service issue: civic knowledge, self-reported civic knowledge, and community attachment.

Student Choice.   Students who chose their service activity made significantly greater gains in civic knowledge than those that focused on a teacher-selected civic problem or an environmental issue. Students who addressed a teacher-selected civic issue made greater gains than those whose projects focused on an environmental problem. For self-reported civic knowledge, students whose teachers selected civic issues performed better than students who selected topics themselves. Both of these groups exceeded those students who worked on the environment. Finally, students who chose their service projects rated themselves as more attached to the community than students who worked on the environment. Both of these groups had higher community attachment scores than those that worked on civic issues.

Type of Service Activity.   The study also investigated the hypothesis that the type of service activity performed by students would serve as a moderating variable. To test this hypothesis, student service activities were categorized as direct (involving contact with the intended beneficiaries or target of the project), indirect (involving efforts to benefit recipients or the target without direct contact), or political and civic action (involving efforts to influence political institutions or processes). The MANOVA analysis of the effects of the service activity on the post-test scores was significant, $F(24, 1{,}028) = 5.326$, $p < .001$, Eta squared = .111. In follow-up univariate tests, service type was significantly related to scores on two-thirds of the subscales, as shown in Exhibit 6.6.

Exhibit 6.6.   Relationship Between Types of Service Activity and Student Outcomes

Post-Test Student Outcomes	df	F	p	Partial Eta squared
Academic Engagement	2	4.761	.009	.018**
Valuing School	2	4.082	.017	.015*
School Attachment	2	1.825	.162	.007
Enjoying Math and Science	2	5.810	.003	.022**
Enjoying Reading/Language Arts and Social Studies	2	13.000	.000	.048***
Civic Knowledge	2	13.612	.000	.049***
Self-Reported Civic Knowledge	2	9.577	.000	.035***
Civic Skills	2	0.549	.578	.002
Civic Dispositions	2	5.921	.003	.022**
Community Attachment	2	3.705	.025	.014*
Efficacy	2	1.994	.137	.008
Civic Engagement	2	0.310	.734	.001

* $p < .05$, two-tailed test; ** $p < .01$, two-tailed test; *** $p < .001$, two-tailed test

Specifically:

- Students who participated in civic or political action had higher post-test civic knowledge and self-reported civic knowledge scores than those involved in indirect or direct service.
- Students who engaged in civic or political action scored higher than others on civic dispositions.
- Students who performed direct service had higher scores on community attachment.
- Indirect service was associated with higher levels of academic engagement, valuing school, and enjoyment of specific subject matters than direct service or civic or political action.

Finally, a composite score of service-learning quality was created by averaging responses to the 38 items on the teacher survey derived from the Essential Elements of Service-Learning. Results of an analysis using a canonical correlation approach showed that this composite score was significantly correlated with student outcomes, $F(12, 622) = 5.045$, $p < .001$, $R^2 = .089$. As displayed in Exhibit 6.7, follow-up analyses indicated that total teacher-reported quality was positively correlated with multiple measures of student civic and academic attainment, including school attachment, civic knowledge, self-reported civic knowledge, civic skills, civic dispositions, and civic engagement.

Exhibit 6.7. Correlations Between Total Teacher Ratings of Service-Learning Quality and Student Post-Test Outcomes

Student Outcome	N	r	p
Academic Engagement	667	−.020	.612
Valuing School	666	−.077[*]	.046
School Attachment	666	.153[***]	.000
Enjoyment of Math and Science	646	−.042	.287
Enjoyment of Reading/Language Arts and Social Studies	659	−.007	.848
Civic Knowledge	667	.155[***]	.000
Self-Reported Civic Knowledge	666	.130[**]	.001
Civic Skills	665	.119[**]	.002
Community Attachment	666	.053	.169
Civic Dispositions	665	.101[**]	.009
Efficacy	662	.064	.099
Civic Engagement	664	.122[**]	.002

[*] $p < .05$, two-tailed test; [**] $p < .01$, two-tailed test; [***] $p < .001$, two-tailed test

To determine the relationships between specific Essential Elements and the dependent variables, a correlation analysis was performed. Results, displayed in Exhibit 6.8, revealed important differences between individual elements and the outcome measures. The Essential Elements with the greatest positive correlations with outcomes were student engagement in challenging tasks (Element 2), activities that meet the genuine needs of the community (Element 4), valuing diversity (Element 7), and student preparation (Element 9). Elements 5 (use of evaluation) and 11 (celebration) were not positively related to any of the outcomes measured in this study, and several elements had negative relationships to outcomes.

These findings suggest the need to reconsider recommendations regarding the inclusion of all the Essential Elements in service-learning practice and the importance of additional study to determine the elements that are most strongly associated with the desired results of a particular program.

CONCLUSIONS

This study examined the impact of participation in service-learning on high school students' attitudes toward school and civic development. Using a national sample of classrooms of students that participated in service-learning matched with classrooms of students of similar demographic and achievement background that did not participate in service-learning, the study investigated the effect of service-learning participation on students' academic engagement; valuing school; attachment to school; and civic knowledge, skills, dispositions, and activities. Additionally, the study examined the degree to which many of the variables related to the service-learning experience served as moderators of outcomes.

A variety of methodologies was used to collect data. Students in service-learning classes and students at the same school or a demographically matched school at the same grade level taking classes in the same content area responded to surveys in the fall and spring. Teachers completed surveys in the spring. Subscales were created from survey items, and differences between students who participated in service-learning relative to those that did not participate were analyzed, both in terms of the overall sample and using the matched classroom design.

Results showed that, although service-learning students scored higher than comparison students on several outcomes, most differences were not statistically significant. Service-learning students had slightly higher scores on enjoyment of school overall than comparison group peers. No differences were found in enjoyment of specific content areas. Service-learning students were significantly more likely than comparison group members to report that they intended to vote.

Exhibit 6.8. Correlations Between the Essential Elements and Student Outcome Measures (*N* = 635)

Student Outcome	Service-Learning Element										
	1	*2*	*3*	*4*	*5*	*6*	*7*	*8*	*9*	*10*	*11*
Academic Engagement	-.020	.009	.053	.029	-.034	-.109*	.125**	-.054	.142**	-.069	-.041
Valuing School	.057	.050	-.051	-.008	-.157**	-.188**	.176**	-.109**	.106**	-.136**	-.020
School Attachment	-.041	.175**	.130**	.163**	-.012	.032	-.026	.167**	-.011	.142**	-.040
Enjoy Math/Science	-.032	.001	.043	.017	-.042	-.130**	.146**	-.084*	.153**	-.103**	-.021
Enjoy Reading/Language/Social Studies	-.007	.016	.114**	-.003	-.033	-.168**	.111**	.057	.150**	-.045	-.200**
Civic Knowledge	.107**	.202**	-.033	.125**	-.037	.124**	-.067	.193**	-.112**	.171**	-.011
Self Reported Civic Knowledge	.089*	.066	-.009	.058	.047	.145**	-.088*	.153**	-.038	.162**	-.047
Civic Skills	.074	.162**	.015	.139**	-.044	.021	.065	.073	.063	.086*	.005
Community Attachment	-.176**	.005	.175**	.038	.057	.007	-.118**	.121**	-.077	.073	-.049
Civic Dispositions	.179**	.181**	-.078*	.134**	-.111**	.023	.103**	.062	.081*	.067	-.006
Efficacy	.107**	.123**	-.070	.090*	-.089*	.019	.068	-.013	.026	.039	.064
Civic Engagement	.108**	.154**	.015	.123**	-.035	.033	.078*	.098*	.084*	.089*	-.027

* $p < .05$; ** $p < .01$, two-tailed test

The students in this study who participated in service-learning had very different experiences, which led to wide variations in student perceptions of service-learning and the impact that it had. Analysis of matched pairs of students showed that just a few of the classrooms in the sample accounted for many of the differences.

A variety of hypotheses related to the service-learning experiences and outcomes were tested.

The hypothesis that service-learning was inherently engaging was supported in some schools and in some ways.

Over half of the participants in service-learning said that they often worked hard on their service-learning projects, tried to learn from them, and paid attention.

Engagement in service-learning was a strong predictor of all student outcomes, except for the civic knowledge measure.

Students who reported stronger engagement in service-learning were statistically significantly more likely to be academically engaged; to value schooling; to become attached to school and community; to enjoy content courses; to perceive a gain in civic knowledge, skills, and dispositions; to become more civically engaged; and to feel greater efficacy.

Students who chose the issue for their service-learning project made greater gains on the objective questions of civic knowledge than others, while those who worked on a teacher-selected civic issue made greater gains than those who worked on an environmental service project.

Students who worked on the teacher-selected civic activities perceived that they made greater gains in civic knowledge than others.

The type of service activity performed (direct, indirect, or civic or political action) was related to nearly all outcome measures.

Participating in civic or political action was positively related to civic knowledge and civic dispositions. Direct service activities were associated with community attachment, while indirect activities were associated with higher post-test scores on academic engagement, valuing school, and enjoyment of subject matters.

Duration of the service-learning experience was also significantly related to most of the outcome areas.

Generally, those service-learning activities that were one to two months in duration had the highest academic impacts while those that were a semester long had the greatest civic impacts.

All of the civic outcome areas, except community attachment, were strongly related to teacher-reported service-learning program quality.

School attachment was also strongly related to program quality. However, the most commonly used indicators of quality—the Essential Elements of Service-Learning—did not predict outcomes evenly. Rather, specific elements were much more highly related to outcomes, and some elements were not positively related to outcomes at all. These data show that students had vastly different experiences with service-learning during the year, and these differences illuminate potential reasons for the results. As repeatedly shown in service-learning research, there is a strong need for high-quality service-learning practice, whether quality is measured directly through quality indicators, or less directly through assessments of student engagement in service-learning.

LIMITATIONS OF THE STUDY

As is often the case, the results of this study call for more investigation in order to yield greater understanding. This study has multiple limitations. First, it relies heavily on self-report. While it has a strong matched comparison group design, the design was undermined by the fact that there was very uneven quality within the sites so that the main hypotheses could not be tested well. There were too few controls on the parameters and content of service-learning to provide definitive conclusions, though the data were suggestive of many of the variables that served as moderators of outcomes.

The results of this study can best be described as suggestive and worthy of consideration by service-learning practitioners in the field. When service-learning is of high quality, at best it appears to be as good as other instructional strategies in producing civic engagement outcomes. However, more data are needed to understand how impact can be maximized.

REFERENCES

Ammon, M. S., Furco, A., Chi, B., & Middaugh, E. (2001). *Service-learning in California: A profile of the CalServe service-learning partnerships, 1997–2000.* Sacramento: California Department of Education.

Billig, S. H. (2000, May). Research on K–12 school based service-learning: The evidence builds. *Phi Delta Kappan, 81*(9), 658–664.

Billig, S. H., & Klute, M. M. (2003, April). *The impact of service-learning on MEAP: A large-scale study of Michigan Learn and Serve grantees.* Presentation at the National Service-Learning Conference, Minneapolis, MN.

Melchior, A., (1999). *Summary report: National evaluation of Learn and Serve America.* Waltham, MA: Brandeis University, Center for Human Resources.

Meyer, S. J., Billig, S. H., & Hofschire, L. (2004). The impact of K–12 school-based service-learning on academic achievement and student engagement in Michigan. In S. H. Billig & M. Welch (Eds.), *Advances in service-learning research: Vol. 4. New perspectives in service-learning: Research to advance the field* (pp. 61–85). Greenwich, CT: Information Age Publishing.

National Service-Learning Cooperative. (1998, April). *Essential elements of service-learning.* St. Paul, MN: National Youth Leadership Council. Retrieved from http://www.nylc.org/publications.cfm

Pritchard, I. (2002). *Community service and service-learning in America.* In A. Furco & S. H. Billig (Eds.), *Advances in service-learning research: Vol. 1. Service-learning: The essence of the pedagogy* (pp. 3–21). Greenwich, CT: Information Age Publishing.

Skinner, R., & Chapman, C. (1999). *Service-learning and community service in K–12 public schools* (NCES Statistical Brief 1999–043). Washington, DC: U.S. Department of Education, Office of Educational Research and Improvement.

Westheimer, J., & Kahne, J. (2000a, April). *Assessment and the democratic purposes of schooling.* Paper presented at the American Educational Research Association, New Orleans, LA.

Westheimer, J., & Kahne, J. (2000b). *Report to the Surdna Board–D.V.I.* New York: Surdna Foundation.

Youniss, J., McLellan, I. A., & Yates, M. (1997). What we know about engendering civic identity. *American Behavioral Scientist, 40*(5), 620–631.

Youniss, J., & Yates, M. (1997). *Community service and social responsibility in youth.* Chicago: University of Chicago Press.

Section III

METHODOLOGICAL MODELS AND ISSUES

CHAPTER 7

RECIPROCAL VALIDITY

Description and Outcomes
of a Hybrid Approach of Triangulated
Qualitative Analysis in the Research
of Civic Engagement

Marshall Welch, Peter Miller, and Kirsten Davies

ABSTRACT

Providing opportunities for students to assimilate skills of civic engagement has generated a new and provocative dialogue of higher education's role in this process. However, constructs of civic education skills have generally been conceptualized and proposed by scholars or by policymakers in public or higher education. It is equally important to validate these components, especially within authentic settings and from practitioners' perspectives. Likewise, it is necessary to consider the ramifications of discrepancies that might emerge from multiple perspectives. This can be accomplished by incorporating a new methodology referred to as reciprocal validity that is described in this chapter. Reciprocal validity is a hybrid approach of triangulation that combines salient features of theoretical models with other types of validity using Delphi technique to form a new qualitative

Improving Service-Learning Practice: Research on Models to Enhance Impacts, pages 119–139
Copyright © 2005 by Information Age Publishing
All rights of reproduction in any form reserved.   119

methodology in social and behavioral science to study civic engagement and service-learning. The chapter begins by reviewing and describing civic engagement skills that have been presented in the professional literature and continues with an illustration of how reciprocal validity was employed in the analysis of those skills.

The current professional literature reflects a growing interest on the topic of civic engagement that emerged in 1985 from a report by the Carnegie Foundation for the Advancement of Teaching (Newman, 1985). Since then, a number of research and other reports continue to document the need for promoting civic education and civic engagement. For example, a report from the National Assessment of Education Progress (Lutkus, Weiss, Campbell, Mazzeo, & Lazer, 1999) revealed students do not know or understand American social and political institutions. The Carnegie Corporation and the Center for Information and Research on Civic Learning and Engagement (2003) reported on the decrease of civic education in K–12 settings. Within higher education, The Kettering Foundation (London, 2001) conducted a series of discussions with university administrators, faculty, students, and community partners. Participants of that study argued for a new way of thinking about and teaching civic engagement. In partnership with Campus Compact, college and university presidents recommitted their institutions to promote civic engagement in the *Presidents' Declaration on the Civic Responsibility of Higher Education* (Ehrlich & Hollander, 1999).

As a result, a new discussion has emerged as to what constitutes or characterizes civic engagement skills as well as the role of higher education to provide the necessary skills to students to empower them to be good citizens. Providing opportunities for students to assimilate these skills of civic engagement has generated a new and provocative dialogue of higher education's role in this process. The American Association of Higher Education has focused on civic education in its publications, *Change* and *AAHE Bulletin*. Likewise, the American Association of University Professors devoted the entire issue of the summer 2000 publication of *Academe* to the topic, as did special issues of the *Journal of Public Affairs*.

It is important to note, however, that the constructs of civic education skills have generally been conceptualized and proposed by scholars or by policymakers in public or higher education. It is equally important and necessary to validate these components, especially within authentic settings and from practitioners' perspectives. Likewise, it is necessary to consider the ramifications of discrepancies that might emerge from multiple perspectives. This can be accomplished by incorporating a new methodology referred to as reciprocal validity, which is described in this chapter. We begin by reviewing and describing civic engagement skills that have been presented in the professional literature and continue with an illustration of how reciprocal validity was employed in the analysis of those skills.

CIVIC ENGAGEMENT SKILLS

In terms of skills, Saltmarsh (2002) argued the need to teach students how to problem solve and think critically to initiate social action in community settings. Battistoni (2002) noted that to be engaged citizens, students need specific skills such as political knowledge and critical thinking, communication, public problem solving, civic judgment, civic imagination and creativity, collective action, community/coalition building, and organizational analysis.

1. Political knowledge and critical thinking skills;
2. Communication skills;
3. Public problem solving;
4. Civic judgment;
5. Civic imagination and creativity;
6. Collective action;
7. Community/coalition building; and
8. Organizational analysis.

Similarly, Colby, Ehrlich, Beaumont, and Stephens (2003) identified and described principles of best practice that constitute a pedagogy of engagement. These include active learning, learning as a social process, knowledge shaped by contexts, reflective practice, and capacity to represent an idea in more than one modality.

For the purpose of this investigation, a review of the literature was conducted by using the key words "civic engagement" or "civic engagement skills" with an electronic search engine. A total of 26 references were identified and only 21 were available and obtained for review. Many of these references were characterized as essays or reports articulating the importance and value of civic engagement and the need for teaching civic engagement skills in K–12 and higher education settings. Consequently, only 12 sources included an explicit description or list of skills that were used for this reciprocal validity study. Of these, one was a conference presentation already obtained by one of the authors, three were books, four were reports, and six were chapters from edited books. The sources compiling the literature review are listed in Exhibit 7.1 and the references of this chapter. In general, this list includes skills such as communication,

Exhibit 7.1. Skills of Civic Engagement Focus Group and Literature Comparison

Skills in Current Literature	Source	Students	Faculty/ Staff	Business/ Political	Nonprofit/ Religious
1. Communication	Battistoni, 2002; Colby et al., 2003; Morse, 1992; Ramaley, 2000	X	X	X	X
2. Political knowledge	Battistoni, 2002	X	X	X	X
3. Collaboration	Carnegie Corporation and CIRCLE, 2003; Colby et al., 2003;	X		X	X
4. Wholeness and inclusiveness	Peng, 2000; Ramaley, 2000	X		X	X
5. Listening	Peng, 2000	X	X		X
6. Public discussion of problems	Peng, 2000; Rimmerman, 2001	X	X		X
7. Self-understanding	Colby et al., 2003	X	X		X
8. Community/coalition building	Battistoni, 2002			X	X
9. Understanding of relationship between self and community	Colby et al., 2003; Ramaley, 2000			X	X
10. Collective action	Battistoni, 2002	X			X
11. Compromise	Colby et al., 2003	X			X
12. Cultural awareness		X			X
13. Problem solving	Battistoni, 2002; Carnegie Corporation and CIRCLE, 2003; Colby et al., 2003; Coplin, 1997; Peng, 2000	X			X

Exhibit 7.1. Skills of Civic Engagement Focus Group and Literature Comparison (Cont.)

Skills in Current Literature	Source	Students	Faculty/ Staff	Business/ Political	Nonprofit/ Religious
14. Organizing	Ehrlich, 2000	X			
15. Public speaking	Carnegie Corporation and CIRCLE, 2003	X			
16. Civic judgment	Battistoni, 2002; Carnegie Corporation and CIRCLE, 2003; Peng, 2000; Torney-Purta & Vermeer, 2003		X		
17. Critical thinking	Battistoni, 2002; Colby et al., 2003; Rimmerman, 2001		X		
18. Gathering information	Coplin, 1997		X		
19. Willingness to experiment	Ramaley, 2000			X	
20. Caring, trust, teamwork					X
21. Appreciation of global dimensions of issues	Colby et al., 2003				
22. Assessment					
23. Base of shared values	Ramaley, 2000				
24. Civic imagination and creativity	Battistoni, 2002; Ramaley, 2000				
25. Confidence in importance of community	Ramaley, 2000				
26. Organizational analysis	Battistoni, 2002				
27. Self-responsibility	Ehrlich, 2000				

collaboration, community/coalition building, critical thinking, problem solving, and public speaking, as well as understanding affective and interpersonal dynamics associated with community partnerships. Space does not permit a detailed description of each skill. Of importance here is not so much a description of the skills, but rather consensus or disagreement of those skills across groups. A total of 27 discrete skills for civic engagement were identified from these sources and are listed as referenced by focus groups in Exhibit 7.1.

RECIPROCAL VALIDITY

Reciprocal validity is a hybrid approach of triangulation that combines salient features of theoretical models with types of validity using an Adelphi technique to form a new qualitative methodology in social and behavioral science to study civic engagement and service-learning. Value for the presence of authentic voices of research participants in the reality construction process is a hallmark of constructivist and critical research paradigms. From these perspectives, validity is dependent upon the presence of participant voices. Rather than viewing research as a quest to discover the *one* reality of a given situation, constructivist/critical approaches seek understanding of *multiple* realities that are experienced from diverse perspectives. Constructivist paradigms call for researchers to expand their traditional roles to become describers, consultants, negotiators, and/or catalysts for change (Greene, 1998). To gain broader perspective, we briefly address three paradigms and approaches that, like reciprocal validity, fall under this broad constructivist/critical umbrella and rely upon multiple voices.

THEORETICAL FOUNDATIONS OF RECIPROCAL VALIDITY

The method of reciprocal validity is based on principles from four theoretical models:

1. Constructivism (Freire, 1998; Lincoln & Guba, 2000);
2. Critical race theory (Tate, 1996);
3. Critical pedagogy (Freire, 1982, 1998); and
4. Democratization of knowledge (Benson & Harkavy, 2000; Harkavy, 2004; Harkavy & Benson, 1998).

Constructivism

A constructivist paradigm seeks to understand *some* characteristics of a particular issue or phenomenon, not *the* characteristics of the issue or phenomenon. Central to a constructivist "way of knowing" is the interaction between human actions and perceptions and the surrounding environment. The ontological perspective of this approach is expressed by Freire (1982):

> The concrete reality for many social scientists is a list of particular facts that they would like to capture; for example, the presence or absence of water, problems concerning erosion in the area. For me, the reality is something more than isolated facts. In my view, thinking dialectically, the concrete reality consists not only of concrete facts and (physical) things, but also includes the ways in which the people involved with these facts perceive them. Thus, in the last analysis, for me, the concrete reality is the connection between subjectivity and objectivity, never objectivity isolated from subjectivity. (p. 30)

Thus, from a constructivist perspective, reality is neither static nor immutable; it is dynamic and constantly under construction. Expressed in relation to a qualitative research study, the "reality" of this participant is constantly being built and it varies greatly depending on whose perspective is being described (Schwandt, 2000). Axiologically, a constructivist approach acknowledges that the values and perspectives of both the researcher and the research participants influence the research process (Lincoln & Guba, 2000). Indeed, contrary to positivistic notions that research can (and should) be neutral and objective, constructivist researchers embrace its subjectivity and hold no aspirations for neutrality or objectivity. Freire (1998) further described his thoughts regarding impartiality/objectivity:

> I am not impartial nor objective; not a fixed observer of facts and happenings. I was never able to be an adherent of the traits that falsely claim impartiality or objectivity. That did not prevent me, however, from holding always a rigorously ethical position. Whoever really observes does so from a given point of view. And this does not necessarily mean that the observer's position is erroneous. It is an error when one becomes dogmatic about one's point of view and ignores the fact that, even if one is certain about his or her point of view, it does not mean that one's position is always ethically grounded. (p. 22)

Critical Race Theory

Describing the central dimensions of critical race theory (CRT), Tate (1996) suggested that scholars in education who are interested in equity research must begin to question the appropriateness and potential of their theoretical and conceptual frameworks. Citing the limited effectiveness of traditional methods, CRT emphasizes the validity—even necessity—of incorporating the voices and stories of research participants as central components of emancipatory research (Delgado & Stefancic, 2000). CRT asserts that this perspective lends insight into various social constructions that cannot be gained from research that is conducted in isolation from participants. In this way, CRT has similar foundations as feminist paradigms that work toward social change from an insider's perspective.

Critical Pedagogy

Another critical framework that stresses the incorporation of participants' voices is that of Freire (1982) who contended that every person, no matter how uneducated or ignorant by common societal measures, is capable of looking critically at the world in a dialogical encounter with others. Not only does Freire espouse the power of the people's voices, he claims that *only* common people (the oppressed) can lend authentic insight and perspective to issues of liberation from inequitable societal structures. From a Freirian theorist's viewpoint, those educators who do not engage the oppressed in dialogue only serve to perpetuate existing structures of dominance.

Democratization of Knowledge

A final example, and one that is specifically immersed in the field of civic engagement, is Harkavy's (2004) perspective on the democratization of knowledge. Influenced by historical heavyweights such as Francis Bacon, Benjamin Franklin, and John Dewey, Harkavy criticized Platonic views of the academe as a place for the few privileged elite—a place that is separate from and not responsible for societal ills. Rather, Harkavy described universities as being uniquely obliged to address and capable of addressing complex societal problems. From this perspective, the multiple realities that exist within communities must have great implications for the workings of institutions of higher education. Indeed, educational organizations should serve as a practical vehicle for societal improvement.

The common thread taken from each of these theoretical perspectives is the notion of voice.

PRINCIPLES OF VALIDITY

Additionally, principles of three types of validity have been borrowed to characterize and operationalize reciprocal validity. The first is construct validity, characterized by Kerlinger (1979) as an attempt to understand abstract properties of a concept, process, or phenomenon. A second type is content validity, which is an effort to determine what is actually being discussed, addressed, or measured (Kerlinger, 1979). Social validity is the third type of validity and the most germane to the development of reciprocal validity. Social validity is commonly used in the fields of educational psychology and special education whereby practitioners in school settings assess the practical application of theoretically based interventions. In essence, classroom teachers and service providers determine the degree to which an educational or behavioral intervention program is user-friendly as well as effective in authentic settings. In this way, theoretical constructs are validated by "real people" in "real settings" as an important extension of initial experimental trials in carefully controlled conditions.

Schwartz and Baer (1991) suggested social validity is a two-part process to (1) collect an accurate and representative sample of opinions and, (2) use the information to sustain or change a program to support its feasibility. Finney (1991), referring to clients of psychological consultation and consumers of behavioral intervention programs, succinctly summarized the purpose and concept of social validity with, "Why don't you ask them?" (p. 245). This concept is simple yet profound as it differentiates "we" as scholars from "them" as practitioners or clients and it reflects the philosophical tenets of some of the theoretical constructs such as the democratization of knowledge presented above. This, in turn, raises questions regarding the source of expertise. Baer and Schwartz (1991) did not fail to notice this schism and asked the provocative question if "we [scholars] are presumed more rational than 'they' [practitioners]" (p. 232). In this sense, reciprocal validity means researchers are seeking the expertise and viewpoint of practitioners and/or clients to validate their theoretical work. This information allows researchers to surmise if the theoretical foundations espoused in the literature and taught in college courses are accurate or applicable. This approach lends itself nicely to validating which, if any, skills for civic engagement are applicable in authentic situations.

Triangulation Process

Triangulation, the use of multiple methods of data collection, adds to the credibility and trustworthiness of a research study. According to Denzin and Lincoln (1994), "the combination of multiple methods, empirical materials, perspectives and observers in a single study is best understood, then, as a strategy that adds rigor, breadth, and depth to any investigation" (p. 4). Triangulation is typically employed in qualitative research by comparing the results of data obtained from three distinct procedures. For example, notes from observations are compared with interview transcripts and quantitative survey scores to determine consistent patterns of phenomena. In this way, personal bias of the investigator is minimized as well as maximizing credible and reliable data (Budd, Thorpe, & Donohew, 1967).

The three components of the triangulation process in reciprocal validation include:

1. Enumeration of theoretical constructs;
2. A validation response team (authentic audience); and
3. An interpretation team.

It is important to note that the first two components can be interchanged. The reciprocal process can either begin by identifying and listing constructs from the literature and then validating them with responses from practitioners or vice versa. Either way, triangulation occurs when researchers propose salient features or enumerate theoretical constructs that are then validated by practitioners or consumers in the field followed by objective interpretation of the validation responses by an unbiased or neutral team of reviewers. Hence, the validation process is reciprocal in nature as it is a two-way process to discern if practitioners or a specific group such as students, clients, or consumers are aware of, understand, and implement what scholars theorize. Concomitantly, the process allows scholars an opportunity to become cognizant of perspectives and factors from authentic situations or settings. As such, reciprocal validity reflects the literal definition of "re-search" by "looking again" at knowledge and theoretical constructs from multiple perspectives, including the views from authentic contexts.

There are three possible outcomes from reciprocal validation. First, the process may validate the theoretical constructs, which would suggest they could be taught and ultimately applied. If, however, the results do not validate constructs found in the literature, scholars then must make one of two decisions and choices. First, it may be determined that the theoretical concepts from the literature have limited application in authentic settings.

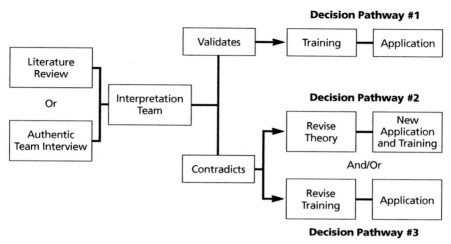

Figure 7.1.   Steps of reciprocal validity.

If this is the case, the theoretical constructs must be revised and then articulated in the literature and profession preparation that enables practitioners (e.g., students) to apply them. Second, scholars may conclude the theoretical constructs are, in fact, valid but have not been articulated or understood in a manner that promotes application. This leads scholars to rethink how they present and teach those constructs. See Figure 7.1.

RECIPROCAL VALIDITY IN ACTION

An innovative, student-driven initiative known as the *Dialogue for Democracy* project (see Brough, Carter-Bake, Davies, Elggren, & Ethington, 2004) is used to illustrate reciprocal validity in action. The primary objective of the project was a Delphi study to identify salient features of civic engagement that could be used to influence policy and practice at the University of Utah. A secondary objective was to employ reciprocal validity to confirm civic engagement skills from multiple perspectives. In this context a cadre of five research student fellows conceptualized and implemented a series of four focus group dialogues with four distinct constituencies using reciprocal validity. The investigation was designed to identify critical components of civic engagement, necessary skills for students to become civically engaged citizens, and the role of an urban research institution to promote civic engagement. For the purposes of this chapter, only the skills of civic engagement will be applied to the reciprocal validation process and be described here. Using the principles and procedures of reciprocal validity, the results from the four focus groups were compared to the extant literature.

Background and Purpose

Harkavy (2004) noted that the historical mission of higher education has been to prepare young men and women to be good citizens in a just and democratic society and pointed out that most institutional mission statements reflect that role. Therefore, it stands to reason that part of the educational experience will and does include teaching civic engagement skills. At the same time, Harkavy continued by arguing that many colleges and universities have lost sight of that mission. In evaluating the mission of the university as a public good, he found, central to this dialogue, the role of higher education in teaching civic engagement and the relationship these institutions have with their surrounding communities. The *Dialogue for Democracy* research project utilized reciprocal validity to explore the degree to which the University of Utah promotes developing civic engagement skills in light of the charge of the university's mission statement to "foster social responsibility."

In seeking to understand the University of Utah's interactions with the larger community, and particularly the ways in which it encourages civic engagement among faculty, staff, and students, the *Dialogue for Democracy* project involved a series of focus groups to define civic engagement and discover the university's role in promoting social responsibility. The student research fellows spoke with university and community stakeholders from student, staff, and faculty communities on campus, and with government, nonprofit, business, and religious leaders from the greater community.

Focus Group Methodology

In November 2003, five undergraduate students were recruited to serve as Civic Engagement Fellows for the Bennion Center and to conduct the *Dialogue for Democracy* research project.

Focus group participants. The collected data consisted of nonexperimental qualitative information collected from four different focus groups: students, faculty/staff, nonprofit/religious, and business/political. These groups took the role of the validation response team as described above. Research fellows identified a number of potential participants through personal networks while others were selected due to their prominence in the community. Due regard was given to invite participants that would contribute a diverse and balanced range of perspectives by identifying and including individuals or representatives from organizations with conservative and liberal viewpoints or political party affiliations, as well as an array of religious perspectives. Attempts were made to have 4–10 persons per group. Approximately 100 potential participants were sent written invitations. Ultimately, 6 students, 10 faculty and staff, 6 nonprofit and religious leaders, and 3 political and business leaders participated in the focus groups.

Focus group procedures. Each focus group discussion was led by an independent facilitator who was a graduate student in the Department of Communications. The facilitator responded to a posted job announcement and was then interviewed, selected, and trained by the student research fellows. A "mock" focus group was conducted with volunteer students to rehearse the process and identify unanticipated procedural problems. Each focus group was led by the facilitator and co-chaired by two fellows. Each discussion lasted approximately one hour and refreshments were provided to the participants. The focus groups asked five primary questions:

1. What does civic engagement mean to you?
2. What are the skills of civic engagement?
3. The university's mission statement says "social responsibility is fostered." Is this a good goal for the university?
4. How does the university do this currently?
5. How can this role be improved?

Responses to the questions of the four sessions were recorded on audiotapes and later transcribed by an outside service.

Analysis. Each transcript was read independently by three of the Civic Engagement Fellows to identify common and notable themes in the responses. This constituted the interpretation team component of reciprocal validity as described previously. When all reviewers met to determine a consensus from their interpretations, triangulation procedures were incorporated. The transcripts were then coded into agreed-upon thematic categories and compared for similarity and disparity in the themes by population. The results were compiled into a formal written and oral report. The oral report was made during a public meeting held in the library auditorium. The audience of approximately 50 attendees included university administration, faculty, students, and representatives from community agencies. In addition to reporting the findings from each of the focus group questions, the fellows made several recommendations for integrating civic engagement into the academic experience. Only the results regarding identified skills of civic engagement are reported and compared to the literature in this chapter.

The analysis in the reciprocal validation process continued by comparing and contrasting the results of the focus groups with skills identified from the literature review described above. This comparison is presented in Exhibit 7.1.

RESULTS

The purpose of reporting the results in this chapter is to compare responses of focus group participants to the extant literature and to compare responses among the four groups to illustrate the utility of reciprocal validity. Since these comparisons are presented in Exhibit 7.1, a detailed description of the identified skills is not provided here. Instead, the objective of the reciprocal validity study conducted was to determine to what extent perceptions of skills identified by representatives of four constituencies are congruent with perceptions of researchers' enumeration of skills in the literature; however, salient themes, consensus, and disagreement are reported and later discussed.

Comparison of Focus Group Responses to the Literature

As shown in Exhibit 7.1, of the 27 skills identified in the review of the literature, only two sets of skills emerged from all four focus groups: communication skills and political knowledge. As displayed in Exhibit 7.2,

- Five skills were articulated by at least three of the four groups;
- Six additional skills were identified in the literature cited by at least two of the four groups;
- Another seven skills were articulated by at least one of the four groups; and
- A total of seven skills from the list of 27 identified skills derived from the literature were never mentioned by any of the four groups.

It is interesting to note that both the student group and nonprofit/religious leaders group articulated 13 skills that had the highest level of agreement with the literature. Conversely, faculty articulated only eight skills and the business/political group only six skills.

Exhibit 7.2. Skills Cited by Groups

Five skills articulated by at least 3 of the 4	*Six additional skills cited by at least 2 of the 4*	*Seven skills articulated by at least 1 of the 4*
1. Collaboration	1. Community building	1. Organizing
2. Inclusiveness	2. Understanding of relationships between self and community	2. Public speaking
3. Listing	3. Collective action	3. Civic judgment
4. Public discussion of problems	4. Compromise	4. Critical thinking
5. Self-understanding	5. Cultural awareness	5. Gathering information
	6. Problem solving	6. Willingness to experiment
		7. Caring/trust/teamwork

Consensus Among Groups

Communication skills emerged as a skill articulated by all four groups. The ability to express oneself through effective communication was mentioned as an important skill of engagement in each group. Though each group described different skills of communication, all regarded this aspect as valuable. Each of the following skills was mentioned in this context: explaining well one's beliefs and objectives to others, articulating reasoning for a position on an issue, and discussing topics in a clear and understandable way. The student group described this as an important way to garner support for one's cause. Public speaking was also mentioned in the student group as a skill of communication and was categorized separately in the literature comparison analysis.

Political knowledge was the second skill that all four groups discussed. "Knowledge of the process" emerged as a central theme from the focus groups. The "process" primarily referred to political systems at the local and state levels, although participants implied other social structures in some instances. One nonprofit/religious group participant described his experience.

> I think we've all had something we really wanted to move forward, we wanted to push forward, and we went forth with vigor and we said, "I'm going to go out and do this," and just became frustrated because the legislature works in a weird way.... I'd work so hard and became so frustrated because I did not understand the system as well as I needed to.

The faculty/staff group described knowledge of the system as "the first step in problem solving," and the lack thereof as a "huge barrier" to achieving social justice. Business/political group participants noted that knowing the system is an "essential" part of effecting change once a person has discovered an exigency in society. The student group also seemed very aware of the need to understand the political and social structures to become civically engaged.

Knowledge of the process is essential to correctly assessing the appropriate political action for a person's cause. Participants suggested knowledge is essential for political action, whether it be organizing protests, contacting representatives at the local and state level, or recruiting people with a vested interest in the cause to attend hearings. Members of the business/political group gave an example of an individual who knows the process and effectively advocates for the homeless.

> She could be down near the viaduct 24 hours a day, seven days a week, and she would be for eons of years...unless we can affect some kind of policy change. And because she is aware of the process and knows how the process works, she takes that experience, and gets under the viaduct and she brings it up to the halls of the legislature and she says, "Okay, here's what is happening. What can we do to stop this from happening?"

Participants identified the role of course curriculum (particularly in government classes), political internships, and volunteer experiences in helping people gain knowledge of the process. They also noted the limited number of internship opportunities available, as well as the lack of publicity for volunteer programs at the University of Utah.

Here the theme of dialogue resurfaces as an important aspect of being politically engaged. The faculty/staff group advocated listening to both sides of the issue, reflecting on what you heard, and expressing your opinion articulately as a skill for civic engagement. Many groups agreed that such communication skills are necessary to build common ground and relationships in the community. Several groups felt that the university is an essential forum for public dialogue. Participants also identified leadership and organizational skills as a part of the knowledge of civic engagement.

Disagreement between Groups

The results presented in Exhibit 7.1 reveal some very interesting patterns of disagreement. It should not be surprising that faculty viewed the skills of civic judgment, critical thinking, and gathering information as important skills as they reflect the nature of academic and empirical work.

As such, it should be noted that none of the other three groups named these skills, suggesting that constituencies outside of academia do not generally consider such "academic" skills. Conversely, collaboration was identified by these three groups and not by faculty. Again, this may reflect the autonomous nature of work in the academic setting and not the reality of skills in authentic settings. This disparity represents one of the important findings that reciprocal validity can facilitate.

Another noticeable pattern of disagreement emerged on the part of business and political leaders. As clearly evidenced in Exhibit 7.1, participants from the business and political leaders group did not identify many of the skills described by other groups, especially the nonprofit/religious groups.

DISCUSSION

The initial results indicate a general consensus of skills identified by focus group participants and those listed in the literature. More importantly, an authentic audience of religious leaders and directors from nonprofit agencies that would be expected to value and practice civic engagement validated 13 (48%) of the skills enumerated in the professional literature. Somewhat surprising is that students also reported 13 skills (48%) found in the literature, although there was some difference from those identified by the nonprofit directors and religious leaders.

We were surprised that faculty only identified eight skills (29%) found in the literature. These findings might be explained by the fact that faculty generally view their responsibilities as teaching and research within their discipline. As such, they are less likely to promote civic engagement in their teaching, let alone practice it if it does not correlate with their research agenda. However, an important side note emerged from the focus group transcripts that was not directly related to the objective of identifying and validating civic engagement skills. Faculty consistently voiced their concern and frustration regarding the reward structure within higher education. They indicated while they may recognize and value preparing college students to be civically engaged citizens, the criteria within the retention, promotion, and tenure review process does not promote nor reward such work.

It is also somewhat ironic that it was the group of political and business leaders who articulated the fewest number of skills. Given that politicians' vocation is that of being civically engaged, it is interesting to note they had the least contributions to the discussion. The one skill that was only identified by this group was that of a willingness to experiment. Curiously, only the nonprofit directors and religious leaders identified caring/trust/ teamwork as an important skill for civic engagement.

These results raise some important questions. First, what frame of reference is more "rational" or "correct"—the skills enumerated in the professional literature or the constituencies interviewed? Are the theoretical constructs of the skill sets found in the literature and listed above truly valid and applicable? Or, are the perspectives of those interviewed merely "out of touch" with empirically validated knowledge? Additionally, the discrepancies between groups present some interesting questions. For example, is the constituency of nonprofit and religious leaders the only group that recognizes and values affective dimensions such as trust and caring? Or, does the context of their civic work accentuate the importance of those affective dimensions that are less applicable in other contexts? If so, how are these types of affective components taught, let alone evaluated or assessed in higher education experiences?

IMPLICATIONS AND FUTURE DIRECTIONS

The implications of results from reciprocal validity are rather striking in two ways. First, it calls into question what might traditionally be viewed as rational. Second, it requires scholars and an instructor to not only carefully consider what is taught in terms of civic engagement, but how it is taught. It is one thing to use a didactic approach to teach discrete skills and terminology on civic engagement and quite another thing to teach complex and abstract concepts that are more affective and social in nature. Similarly, the pragmatic demands facing students and community partners must be taken into consideration. While it is important to give authentic experiences, educators must be mindful of students' balancing act of juggling school, work, and families coupled with the survival mode many community partners face every day. These perspectives are as valid as scholars' theoretical constructs. These implications can be carried over into a variety of fields, including service-learning and cultural education.

Finally, despite the general consensus of these results, the reciprocal validation process described here demonstrates some clear discrepancies in terms of how specific groups view skills for civic education or engagement. This, however, is not problematic in this context. It really should not be surprising that various constituencies identified similar and dissimilar skills. The value of these results is not to reject one set of responses and perspectives, but to be more inclusive as the outcomes of the reciprocal validity present a more complete and comprehensive set of skills than any one constituency alone could articulate. The views of practitioners "out in the trenches" lend authenticity to the skills for civic engagement that are taught to students in higher education. We believe this reflects the theoretical tenets we have used as the foundation for reciprocal validity, especially the notion of the democratization of knowledge. Therefore, in the context of this investigation, it would be prudent to take Decision Pathway #2 as depicted in Figure 7.1 and revise our theoretical constructs from a scholarly perspective of what constitutes civic engagement skills and then teach them. This, in turn, will enable students to be better equipped to be civically engaged citizens than they would be if we relied exclusively on the notions of scholars as to what constitutes skills for civic education and engagement. As such, civic education within higher education becomes more integral and holistic with the beneficiaries being both the students and society at large.

REFERENCES

Baer, D. M., & Schwartz, I. S. (1991). If reliance on epidemiology were to become epidemic, we would need to assess its social validity. *Journal of Applied Behavioral Analysis, 24*, 231–234.

Battistoni, R. M. (2002). *Civic engagement across the curriculum*. Providence, RI: Campus Compact.

Benson, L., & Harkavy, I. (2000). Integrating the American systems of higher, secondary, and primary education to develop civic responsibility. In T. Ehrlich (Ed.), *Civic responsibility and higher education* (pp. 174–196). Phoenix, AZ: Oryx Press.

Brough, T., Carter-Bake, C., Davies, K., Elggren, M., & Ethington, T. (2004). *Dialogue for Democracy: An investigation of civic engagement at the University of Utah*. Salt Lake City: University of Utah, Lowell Bennion Community Service Center.

Budd, R. W., Thorp, R. K., & Donohew, L. (1967). *Content analysis of communications*. New York: Macmillan.

Colby, A., Ehrlich, T., Beaumont, E., & Stephens, J. (2003). *Educating citizens: Preparing America's undergraduates for lives of moral and civic responsibility*. San Francisco: Jossey-Bass.

Coplin, W. D. (1997). Citizenship courses as life-changing experiences. In G. Reeher & J. Cammarano (Eds.), *Education for citizenship: Ideas and innovations in political learning* (pp. 63–80). Lanham, MD: Rowman & Littlefield.

Delgado, R. & Stefancic, J. (2000). *Critical race theory: The cutting edge*. Philadelphia: Temple University Press.

Denzin, N. K., & Lincoln, Y. S. (1994). Introduction: Entering the field of qualitative research. In N. K. Denzin & Y. S. Lincoln (Eds.), *Handbook of qualitative research* (pp. 1–17). Thousand Oaks, CA: Sage.

Ehrlich, T. (2000). *Civic responsibility in higher education*. Phoenix, AZ: Oryx Press.

Ehrlich, T., & Hollander, E. (1999). *Presidents' declaration on the civic responsibility of higher education*. Providence, RI: Campus Compact.

Finney, J. W. (1991). On further development of the concept of social validity. *Journal of Applied Behavior Analysis, 24,* 245–249.

Freire, P. (1982). Creating alternative research methods: Learning to do it by doing it. In B. Hall, A. Gillette, & R. Tandon (Eds.), *Creating knowledge: A monopoly? Participatory research in development.* New Delhi, IN: Society for Participatory Research in Asia.

Freire, P. (1998). *Pedagogy of freedom: Ethics, democracy, and civic courage.* Lanham, MD: Rowman & Littlefield.

Greene, J. C. (1998). Qualitative program evaluation: Practice and promise. In N. K. Denzin & Y. S. Lincoln (Eds.), *Collecting and interpreting qualitative materials* (pp. 372–399). Thousand Oaks, CA: Sage.

Harkavy, I. (2004). Service-learning and the development of democratic universities, democratic schools, and democratic good societies. In M. Welch & S. H. Billig (Eds.), *Advances in service-learning research: Vol.4. New perspectives in service-learning: Research to advance the field* (pp. 3–22). Greenwich, CT: Information Age Publishing.

Harkavy, I., & Benson, L (1998). De-Platonizing and democratizing education as the bases of service-learning. In R. A. Rhoads & J. P. F. Howard (Eds.), *Academic service-learning: A pedagogy of action and reflection* (pp. 11–19). San Francisco: Jossey-Bass.

Kerlinger, F. N. (1979). *Behavioral research: A conceptual approach.* New York: Holt, Rinehart and Winston.

Lincoln, Y. S., & Guba, E. G. (2000). Paradigmatic controversies, contradictions, and emerging confluences. In N. K. Denzin & Y. S. Lincoln (Eds.), *Handbook of qualitative research,* (pp. 163–188). Thousand Oaks, CA: Sage.

London, S. (2001). Higher education and public life: Restoring the bond. *Connections, 11*(2), 15–17.

Lutkus, A. D., Weiss, A. R., Campbell, J. R., Mazzeo, J., & Lazer, S. (1999). *NAEP 1998 Civics report card for the nation* (NCES 2000–457). Washington, DC: U.S. Department of Education, Office of Educational Research and Improvement.

Morse, S. W. (1992). *Politics for the 21st century: What should be done on campus?* Dubuque, IA: Kettering Foundation.

Newman, F. (1985). *Higher education and the American resurgence.* Princeton, NJ: Carnegie Foundation for the Advancement of Teaching.

Peng, L. (2000). Effects of public deliberation on high school students: Bridging the disconnection between young people and public life. In S. Mann & J. J. Patrick (Eds.), *Education for civic engagement in democracy: Service-learning and other promising practices* (pp. 73–86). Bloomington, IN: Educational Resources Information Center.

Ramaley, J. A. (2000). The perspective of a comprehensive university. In T. Ehrlich (Ed.), *Civic responsibility and higher education* (pp. 227–248). Phoenix, AZ: Oryx Press.

Rimmerman, C. A. (2001). *The new citizenship: Unconventional politics, activism, and service.* Boulder, CO: Westview Press.

Saltmarsh, J. (2002). Introduction from the guest editor. *Journal of Public Affairs, 6,* iv–ix.

Schwandt, T. A. (2000). Three epistemological stances for qualitative inquiry: Interpretivism, hermeneutics, and social constructionism. In N. K. Denzin & Y. S. Lincoln (Eds.), *Handbook of qualitative research* (pp. 189–213). Thousand Oaks, CA: Sage.

Schwartz, I. S., & Baer, D. M. (1991). Social validity assessments: Is current practice state of the art? *Journal of Applied Behavior Analysis, 24,* 189-204.

Tate, W. F. (1996). Critical race theory and education: History, theory, and implications. *Review of Research in Education,* 22, 77–82.

The Center for Information and Research on Civic Learning and Engagement and Carnegie Corporation of New York. (2003). *The civic mission of schools.* New York: Authors.

Torney-Purta, J., & Vermeer, S. (2003). *Young people's citizenship competency in nation, community, and school: Background paper for the ECS/NCLC Initiative in Education for Citizenship: Kindergarten to grade 12.* Denver, CO: Education Commission of the States.

CHAPTER 8

USING RANDOMIZED CONTROL FIELD TRIALS IN SERVICE-LEARNING RESEARCH

Keith R. Aronson, Nicole S. Webster, Robert Reason, Patreese Ingram, James Nolan, Kimber Mitchell, and Diane Reed

ABSTRACT

The use of randomized control field trials (RCFTs) in service-learning research would provide the kind of strong-inference research that is needed in the field of service-learning. RCFTs are experiments conducted in the field and thus provide a good measure of internal and external validity. Despite their inherent strengths, RCFTs are rarely used in service-learning research. We describe the challenges associated with conducting RCFTs, as well as strategies that can be used to overcome those challenges. A moderation–mediation conceptual model of service-learning is presented, as well as the design of a RCFT planned to evaluate the model. The authors suggest that service-learning research can be appreciably enhanced by creating theoretical models of service-learning and evaluating them using rigorous methods.

Improving Service-Learning Practice: Research on Models to Enhance Impacts, pages 141–165
Copyright © 2005 by Information Age Publishing

INTRODUCTION

Service-learning is a pedagogical approach that strategically combines academic curriculum with real-world community service to enhance student learning and development. Proponents of service-learning argue that classroom curriculum is brought to life and learning is deepened when students participate in community service that is connected to coursework in ways that make students think, reflect, and feel more deeply about what it is they are learning (Eyler & Giles, 1999; Eyler, Giles, & Schmiede, 1996; Jacoby, 1996). Indeed, a growing body of research has found that service-learning has a positive impact on:

- Academic and cognitive outcomes (Eyler & Giles,1999; Fredericksen, 2001; Giles & Eyler, 1998; Jones & Abes, 2004; Markus, Howard, & King, 1993; Melchior, 1998; O'Bannon, 1999; Shaffer, 1993; Strage, 2000, 2004);
- Cultural sensitivity and awareness (Eyler & Giles, 1999; Melchior, 1998; Shaffer, 1993; Stephens, 1995);
- Character development (Astin & Sax, 1998; Follman & Muldoon, 1998; Jones & Abes, 2004);
- Social and emotional competence (O'Bannon, 1999; Scales & Blyth, 1997);
- Self-esteem and self-efficacy (Shaffer, 1993);
- Social and civic responsibility (Astin & Sax, 1998; Berkas, 1997; Melchior, 1998); and
- Long-term commitment to service (Melchior, 1998; Stephens, 1995).

The benefits of service-learning have been demonstrated in a number of diverse settings, across various ages, using differing methodological approaches. It is important to note, however, that the quality of service-learning research has been criticized on a number of grounds (Billig, 2000a, 2000b, 2003b; Bringle & Hatcher, 2000; Eyler, 2000, 2002; Furco & Billig, 2002). A brief review of those criticisms is presented below.

Criticisms of Service-Learning Research

Perhaps the most significant overarching problem in the field is the lack of theoretical and conceptual models (Bringle, 2003). In 2004, Ziegert and McGoldrick posited that without theory, "any empirical work is by its nature ad hoc and incoherent" (p. 32.), making it more difficult to detect positive effects when they exist, meaningfully interpret research findings, and move an area of inquiry forward (Bordens & Abbott, 1991; Kazdin, 1992; Kerlinger, 1986; Pedhazur & Schmelkin, 1991). Indeed, the lack of theory has also resulted in highly inconsistent research methodologies and definitions (Bringle, 2003; Eyler, 2002; McLellan & Youniss, 2003). Clearly, researchers need to create and/or test theories from various disciplines that relate to learning and development (Bringle, 2003).

In addition to theoretical problems in the service-learning research, there are a number of methodological problems. Perhaps the most troublesome problem is that of self-selection. In many studies, students in service-learning courses have better outcomes than those not involved in service-learning. It is not known, however, whether differences between the groups are due to service-learning participation, characteristics of the participants, or some combination of the two. Many service-learning studies are limited by their correlational nature (Billig, 2000a, 2000b; Eyler, 2002). Many studies also rely exclusively on participant self-report. Both Larsen (1992) and Taylor (1989) found that self-reports have a number of limitations. Moreover, the reliability and validity of a number of service-learning measures remain to be established, and the field has not done a good job selecting related measures from other disciplines (Bringle & Hatcher, 2000; Furco & Billig, 2002). Overinterpretation of results and lack of recognition of methodological weaknesses serves to further undermine service-learning research (Billig, 2003a; Eyler, 2000; Eyler & Giles, 1999). It should not be surprising that there have been recent calls for increased research rigor and sophistication in the field.

The Call for More Rigorous Service-Learning Research

Eyler (2002) challenged researchers and theorists to "stretch to meet higher goals and standards for service-learning research" in her keynote address to the First Annual Conference on Service-Learning Research (p. 3). There are at least five key reasons for increasing the scientific rigor in service-learning research. While there are theoretical and empirical reasons to believe service-learning could be a powerful tool for students and communities, there is a dearth of strong inference research in the field. Before we can make conclusive statements about the impact of service-learning, more elegant research designs must be used. Second, there is some evidence that service-learning programs can have unintended iatrogenic effects (Steinke, Fitch, Johnson, & Waldstein, 2002; Wade, 2000). Jones (2002) suggested that service-learning may have a detrimental underside. To the extent to which this is true, it becomes incumbent upon researchers to be as rigorous as they can be in their work. Indeed, the authors of this chapter see this as an ethical responsibility within the service-learning field. Third, significant resources are being spent on service-learning initiatives, and this trend is likely to continue

(Ramaley, 2000). Because there are always opportunity costs associated with resource distribution, researchers must rigorously research and evaluate service-learning to understand if the cost benefit of service-learning makes sense relative to other educational initiatives. Fourth, an increased emphasis is being placed on education evaluation using elegant theory, rigorous methods, and applicability to real-world educational outcomes (Boruch, deMoya, & Snyder, 2002; W. T. Grant Foundation, 2004). Finally, service-learning will only be widely accepted and implemented on a larger scale when it has been more strenuously evaluated (Bringle, 2003; Eyler, 2002; Furco & Billig, 2002; Holland, 2001a, 2001b; Ramaley, 2000).

Indeed, researchers in service-learning are beginning to respond to the call for increased sophistication and rigor (see Billig, 2003a, for a review). For example, several studies have employed experimental designs (Markus et al., 1993; Strage, 2000), including RCFTs (Santmire, Giraud, & Grosskopf, 1999). This is a step in the right direction in service-learning research because such designs provide a rigorous test of theory-generated hypotheses and predictions.

Randomized Control Field Trials as a Powerful Research Tool

A number of researchers have argued persuasively that education research needs to come of age scientifically (e.g., Boruch et al., 2002; Brooks-Gunn, 2004; Cohen, Raudenbush, & Ball, 2002; Cook, 2002, 2004; Cook & Payne, 2002; McCall & Green, 2004). Education research will more fully mature when it recognizes that RCFTs become a primary evaluation methodology used to assess program effects (Cook, 2002, 2004).

An RCFT is an experiment that occurs outside a laboratory setting. The main components of an experiment are theory-driven hypotheses, random assignment of participants to treatments, experimenter-controlled manipulations of the independent variable, rigorously controlled conditions, and quantitative measurement and analysis (Kazdin, 1992; McCall & Green, 2004). Random assignment, therefore, is a necessary but not sufficient condition for a randomized control trail (RCT). Environmental control also needs to be established so that "all or nearly all of the possible influential independent variables not pertinent to the immediate problem of the investigation is *kept to a minimum*" (Kerlinger, 1986, p. 367). Using an RCT, the researcher can achieve "a high degree of specificity in the operational definition of his variables" (Kerlinger, 1986, p. 367). In a RCT, therefore, the researcher attempts to control or eliminate contaminating conditions so that one can strongly infer that the independent variable caused difference between experimental and control groups on the dependent variable(s).

Because of the strength of the design, Cook (2002) stated that RCTs provide the "best tool for attributing observed student change to whatever classroom or school option is under consideration as a possible cause" (p. 176). The supremacy of RCTs over other evaluation strategies has long been held in most social science disciplines primarily because it protects against self-selection bias and internal threats to validity (Campbell & Stanley, 1963; Cook, 2002, 2004; Cook & Campbell, 1979; Holland, 1986; Rubin, 1974), and provides the best assessment of intervention effects on students in a treatment group relative to those not exposed to treatment (Holland, 1986; Rubin, 1974). There is solid empirical/statistical evidence that supports the value of RCTs (Friedlander & Robbins, 1995; Heckman, Ichimura, Smith, & Todd, 1997; Wilde & Hollister, 2002). Despite the many strengths of RCTs, very few are used in service-learning research.

Why are so few RCTs undertaken in service-learning research? One possibility is that there are challenges to conducting RCTs. In the next section, the authors identify some of the main challenges to conducting this kind of research and attempt to provide information to assist researchers to overcome these challenges and difficulties. It is the author's hope that this will make the decision to use RCTs more common in the service-learning field.

Challenges Associated with RCFTs

RCFTs in service-learning are challenging to conduct on several fronts. Typically, students are not randomly assigned to their classes. Students either choose (as in college) or are placed within (as in most elementary, middle, and high schools) their classes. Therefore, true random assignment to classes is not likely. However, randomly assigning students to a service-learning and non-service-learning condition within a particular classroom provides a strong basis for an RCFT, providing that students are not in the class because they perceive it to be a service-learning class (i.e., there is no self-selection bias). In other words, equivalent groups can be formed within a classroom even though students choose or are placed into them.

RCFTs also can present thorny ethical issues (Bordens & Abbott, 1991). Specifically, RCFTs demand that experimental and control groups be treated unequally. Individuals randomly assigned to the control group do not receive what is considered to be the "active" ingredient (e.g., participating in service-learning itself) and, therefore, may be harmed. Ethical issues must always be approached cautiously and with input from colleagues and institutional review boards (IRBs). In the case of service-learning, however, there are several cogent arguments that can be used to defend the use of an RCFT. First, the evidence of a strong effect for service-learning is lacking (Eyler, 2002). Therefore, withholding service-learning may not do any harm, or at least may only do minimal harm to those in the control group. Second, the benefit to the educational and research community of strong inference investigations in service-learning may outweigh any potential harm. For example, calculation of opportunity costs, a common evaluative tool in education policy research, requires strong inference techniques of inquiry, such as that provided by RCFTs (Boruch et al., 2000). Therefore, ethical arguments against RCFTs can be overcome in a sensitive and scientifically responsible manner.

Some researchers eschew experimental studies because, while they provide a high degree of internal validity, they typically provide little in the way of external validity (Kazdin, 1992). Given the strong applied implications of service-learning research, experiments may not be seen as compelling methodological designs. However, using experiments in real classrooms or schools increases their generalizability and applicability (Boruch et al., 2000; Cook, 2002, 2004), particularly when they are replicated across heterogeneous samples and measures (Cook, 2004).

Finally, within the classroom setting, environmental control (a key component of RCTs) may be hard to establish (Bordens & Abbott, 1981; Kazdin, 1992). Therefore, internal validity can be threatened despite random assignment. In our opinion, diffusion of treatment (Aiken & West, 1990; Cook & Campbell, 1979) is one of the two most likely threats to occur in service-learning research within a classroom. In diffusion of treatment, control group members inadvertently receive components of the treatment condition. Because students interact with each other within the typical classroom, students in the experimental condition may provide students in the control group with hints or clues about service-learning and their personal experience of it. While this likely cannot be avoided completely, some protections can be put into place. As much as possible, students in the service-learning condition should be given multiple opportunities for reflection outside the classroom (e.g., journaling, feedback sessions at their community placement). This may reduce the extent to which reflection takes place within the classroom, thereby reducing the likelihood of contamination. If possible, students should be assigned to service-learning and non-service-learning recitation sections. In so doing, students in the service-learning class would have significant opportunity for reflection without diffusion of treatment. Using a debriefing questionnaire or interview, students in the control condition can be asked about the degree to which they were influenced by classroom exposure to service-learning. This information can be used as a covariate and, therefore, provide some measure of statistical control on diffusion of treatment.

While diffusion of treatment may be difficult to control within a classroom, the authors posit that it is less likely to occur in the service-learning context. Specifically, there is little a priori reason to believe that vicarious exposure to service-learning experiences would produce substantive changes within an individual. This is because service-learning's effect is due to personal out-of-the-classroom experience combined with significant reflection about those highly personal experiences. It is important to note, however, that these recommendations have yet to be tested in the field and so should be assessed in individual studies.

Another potential confounding threat to internal validity within a classroom is resentful demoralization (Aiken & West, 1990; Fetterman, 1982), which occurs when control group members discover they were not provided with the special treatment afforded members of the experimental group. As a result, control group members are thought to either become demoralized and have less positive outcomes, or they overcompensate and have better outcomes. As a result, resentful demoralization "can act to either artificially increase or decrease treatment effect estimates" (McCall & Green, 2004, p. 7). Because there have been so few experimental designs in service-learning research to date, it is difficult to predict a priori the direction or strength of this bias. Therefore, we suggest that researchers use pilot data to determine how students would feel about being in a control condition (e.g., writing a term paper) versus an experimental condition (e.g., volunteering in an elementary school). If pilot data suggest that students were equally content in either condition, demoralization is less likely to be present. If pilot work demonstrates that conditions may be ripe for demoralization, classroom assignment for the control group should be chosen in a manner to reduce these feelings.

Diffusion of treatment and resentful demoralization are more likely to occur when the control and experimental groups come in contact with each other. One way to lessen these problems is to randomly assign units larger than the individual to treatment versus comparison groups (McCall, Ryan, & Plemons, 2003). For example, entire schools or classrooms can be randomly assigned. Successful examples of this kind of approach can be found in various research disciplines (Boruch & Foley, 2000). Indeed, some service-learning studies have used experimental approaches of this nature (Billig, 2003a).

Experimental Studies in Service-Learning

A few service-learning studies have used RCFT designs. In one seminal study, two discussion sections of an undergraduate political science course were randomly assigned to contain a service-learning component including 20 hours of service (e.g., working with homeless people, women in crisis, tutoring), while the other sections had no such service-learning component (Markus et al., 1993). The design of this study ensured students in the treatment and control groups "attended the same lectures, were assigned the same course readings, and took the same midterm and final examinations, graded according to the same set of standards" (Markus et al., 1993, p. 413). Several interesting results emerged. Students in the service-learning sections received significantly higher course grades. They also reported higher levels of civic awareness and intentions for future civic engagement. Although this study was soundly designed, there were several weaknesses. First, the study lacked a theoretical formulation. Second, it is not clear whether or not graduate students teaching the various sections of the course were blind to the purposes and/or hypotheses of the study. Therefore, it becomes difficult to rule out experimenter effects. Finally, to analyze the data, the researchers conducted multiple t tests increasing the likelihood of a Type 1 error. The failure to control for Type 1 error increases the likelihood for spurious findings.

In another experimental study, Santmire and colleagues (1999) randomly assigned seventh-grade students to either an "exploratory" curriculum that included a service-learning component (i.e., two periods each day for the entire academic year) or a traditional "core" curriculum. Students in the service-learning curriculum achieved higher total and math scores on Metropolitan Achievement Tests (MAT). There were no between-group differences on any of the language-based subtests of the MAT. While the study is a good example of using random assignment to conditions, the interpretation of results is clouded by important limitations in the degree of experimental control that was established. Teachers of the service-learning curriculum all volunteered to teach the service-learning curriculum due to their interest in service-learning, while teachers in the core curriculum were assigned to teaching assignments using normal school procedures. This raises the issue of potential experimenter effects in the service-learning condition. Specifically, it may be that students in the service-learning condition were exposed to more enthusiastic, caring, and invested teachers. Students in the service-learning curriculum also received shortened periods of academic content to accommodate their service-learning projects. One might argue that this difference makes the finding of group differences more impressive. However, shortened academic periods may have affected service-learning students' motivation, mood, and the like.

In a large study of 25 sites, high school students were randomly assigned to either a service-learning or non-service-learning condition (Allen, Philliber, Herrling, & Kuperminc, 1997). Students in the service-learning condition engaged in community volunteer service and once-per-week classroom-based discussions of service experiences. At the end of the school year, female students in the service-learning condition were less likely to have been suspended, fail a course, or become pregnant. The strength of this study lies in its size. However, service-learning experiences varied widely in content, time requirement, and quality across locations. Aggregating across intervention sites does not allow for examination of what happened at specific sites, and it is possible for large disparities of effect across sites depending on aspects of the service learning experience. Moreover, students in the service-learning condition also engaged in small peer group discussions focused on self-understanding, life skills, family stress, and social and emotional challenges common to adolescents. These small group discussions were not connected to the service-learning experience. Therefore, it is difficult to disentangle the relative contribution of the service-learning and peer group experience.

While experimental studies such as those just described represent an important step in the right direction for service-learning research, each of these studies had significant limitations. Therefore, even the more rigorous attempts at service-learning research leave the field with many unanswered questions. In the near future, we will begin an RCFT of service-learning. We designed the study to address a number of the weaknesses in prior service-learning research. In the next section, the theoretical model to be examined in the study is described.

A CONCEPTUAL MODEL OF SERVICE-LEARNING

As shown in Figure 8.1, we have outlined a conceptual model of service-learning gleaned from the service-learning literature and informed by developments in cognitive psychology and the neurosciences. As can be seen, this model specifies several moderators, a mediator, and both proximal and distal outcomes. By stipulating a well-articulated model, we will be able to examine the relative contribution of various components of service-learning on pertinent outcomes so that researchers can better understand why service-learning works, for whom, and under what conditions. The conceptual model is outlined in some detail below.

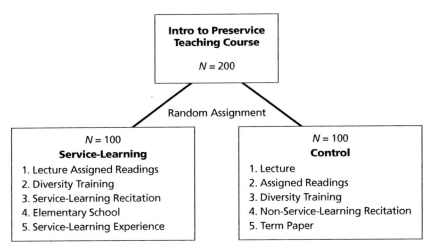

Figure 8.1.   Proposed study design.

Moderator Variables in Service-Learning

Moderators are variables that affect the direction and/or strength of the relation between an independent variable and a dependent variable (Baron & Kenny, 1986). In essence, moderators specify when an effect will hold. Oftentimes, moderators are characteristics of individuals such as age, sex, race, and socioeconomic status. In terms of correlations, a moderator is a third variable that affects the zero-order correlation between two variables. In analysis of variance (ANOVA), moderation is seen when there is a significant interaction effect.

In the service-learning literature, there are several variables that appear to moderate the relationship between service-learning and various outcomes. For example, students with prior community service experience evidence greater benefit from service-learning than do those with no such prior experience (Astin & Sax, 1998). The effects of service-learning appear to be stronger for females than for males (Astin & Sax, 1998; Eyler & Giles, 1999; McLellan & Youniss, 2003). Studies with university students have shown that students who achieved better grades in high school are more strongly influenced by service-learning interventions than students with lower high school grades (Astin & Sax, 1998). The more students view the social issue addressed by the service-learning project as interesting and important, the greater their response to service-learning interventions (Eyler & Giles, 1999). Students from families with greater educational attainment respond more strongly to service-learning interventions than students whose families have less formal education (B. Holland, personal communication, October 11, 2004).

Predictors of Service-Learning's Effect

Several key predictors of service-learning have been identified. These predictors are the elements of service-learning that are believed to influence pertinent outcomes. *Direct community experience* is one of the key components of service-learning. Exposure to the complexities and intricacies of the real world provide the key experiences of service-learning. Perhaps the most important predictor in service-learning is reflection (Eyler, Giles, & Gray, 1999). *Reflection* is the process of students making their own salient connections to the subject matter via the integration of service and learning. This is typically accomplished through discussions, writing assignments, and journaling (Eyler & Giles, 1999; Eyler et al., 1996). Reflection should be continuous, connect service experience to classroom instruction, and be challenging and befitting of the context (Eyler et al., 1996). Reflection should also be done by the student alone, with classmates, and with community partners (Eyler, 2001). Moreover, it is critical that the reflection be applied in a way in which the classroom and service experiences are integrated (Eyler & Giles, 1999). In other words, the more integrated service and learning is, the more powerful the service-learning effect. *Quality of placement* is believed to be another important component of an effective service-learning program (Eyler & Giles, 1997). Indeed, students who express satisfaction with their service experience report and demonstrate a stronger response to service-learning (Eyler & Giles, 1999). Finally, the more *prepared* students feel for their service experience, the more positive is service-learning's effect (Battistoni, 2001; Eyler & Giles, 1999). These four predictors can be thought of as aspects of a service-learning intervention that must be present if service-learning is to have outcome effects. In our model, each of these predictors serves to increase cognitive complexity, which we hypothesize as a key mediating variable in service-learning.

Cognitive Complexity as a Key Mediator in Service-Learning

A mediating variable accounts for the relationship between independent and dependent variables (Baron & Kenny, 1986). Mediating variables specify and explain how or why effects occur. After reviewing the literature, we believe a strong argument can be made that service-learning impacts proximal and distal outcomes because it improves the capacity of students to think in complex ways. The notion of cognitive complexity is not new to service-learning. Indeed, thought on service-learning has been heavily influenced by the thinking of educational theorists (e.g., Boyer, 1990; Dewey, 1938; Perry, 1970) who posited that active, hands-on, and real-world learning environments increase students' ability to think in increasingly flexible and adaptive ways. Today, service-learning researchers theorize that service-learning improves students' ability to grasp complex and nuanced information, think more critically about phenomena, apply concepts across disparate topics, integrate information in new ways, and think at more advanced levels (Billig, 2000a, 2000b; Eyler & Giles, 1999; Eyler, Root, & Giles, 1998; Slavkin, 2002; Steinke & Buresh, 2002; Steinke et al, 2002; Steinke, Klaassen, & Vos, 2003). Indeed, students themselves report that service-learning helps them think better (Astin & Sax, 1998; Eyler & Giles, 1999; Fitch, 2004).

The case for cognitive complexity as a key mediating variable in service-learning is bolstered by recent work in cognitive psychology and neuroscience. For example, cognitive complexity learning theory (CCLT; Breuer & Tennyson, 1995) views thinking as a multitiered, fluid-dynamic phenomenon that is highly interactive with the environment, is influenced by affective states, and is often nonlinear in structure (i.e., information is not processed neatly from working to short-term and then to long-term memory). The theory suggests that there are several key subsystems of cognition that provide the framework for awareness, information evaluation, storage and access to previously acquired information (e.g., concepts, domains, schemas), and the use of acquired information (including how, why, when, and where to use selected concepts, rules, and principles with newly encountered situations). Moreover, CCLT embeds an affective component to learning, recognizing that feelings, attitudes, emotions, and values interact with the key cognitive subsystems and thereby influence the acquisition, storage, retrieval, use, and interpretation of information (Goleman, 1995; Labouvie-Vief & Diehl, 2000).

CCLT posits three primary cognitive abilities.

1. *Differentiation* is the ability to understand a situation by applying appropriate contextual criteria (i.e., standards, situational appropriateness, values) and selectively retrieving specific knowledge of use in that situation;

2. *Integration* is the ability to elaborate or restructure existing knowledge in the face of new experiences or problem situations;

3. *Construction* is the ability to both discover and create new knowledge in novel or unique situations. Individuals are cognitively complex to the extent to which they differentiate, integrate, and construct

information for "optimal adaptive functioning" (Breuer & Tennyson, 1995, p. 171).

Cognitive complexity theory, and related theories, have implications for instructional design and practice (Breuer & Tennyson, 1995; Bransford, 1993; Larson, 2000; Resnick, 1987; Schon, 1995). Because cognition is nonlinear, active, influenced by affect and values, and responds in self-correcting ways in its reciprocal relationship with the environment, learning occurs best through multitiered levels and channels. Moreover, cognitive complexity theory suggests that instructional approaches that accommodate the processing of affect, beliefs, and values may be particularly effective. Indeed, traces of the kind of thinking embedded in CCLT and related cognitive theories of learning are increasingly seen in educational instruction and practice (Brandt, 1997; D'Arcangelo, 1998, 2000; Goleman, 1995; Wolfe & Brandt, 1998). Instructional approaches using rich and varied learning environments are being promulgated because it is believed they place increased demand on the cognitive subsystems, thereby creating more synapses or connections between nerve cells (Breuer & Tennyson, 1995; Diamond & Hopson, 1999; Slavkin, 2003). In other words, it is believed that well-designed learning environments, such as those provided by well-designed service-learning, actually change the morphology of the brain and hence its capacity to think complexly. Some researchers theorize that enriched learning environments increase and strengthen neural connections, thereby enhancing retrieval of needed information and the better application of that information to new situations (Cardellichio & Field, 1997; Pool, 1997; Reeves, 1996; Sternberg, 1999). It is important to note that this work is in the embryonic stages and has yet to be applied to service-learning. Nonetheless, enough work has been done to suggest that service-learning works because it provides an environment for neural branching and cognitive complexity.

A Proposed RCT in Service-Learning to Address Previous Experimental Shortcomings

In our proposed study, students in an introduction to preservice teacher education course will be randomly assigned to either a service-learning or a non-service-learning condition (see Figure 8.2). Students in the service-learning condition will attend the same recitation/ discussion section, while the control students will attend their own recitation section. During the semester, students in the service-learning condition will spend 20 hours working in rural elementary school classrooms in central Pennsylvania providing youngsters with a

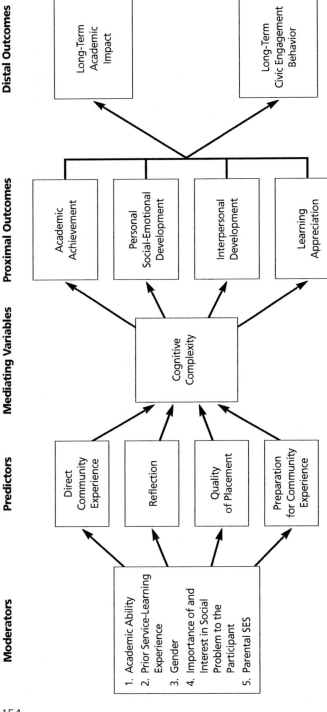

Moderators **Predictors** **Mediating Variables** **Proximal Outcomes** **Distal Outcomes**

Figure 8.2. Process model of service-learning versus non-service-learning conditions (pre/post intervention).

curriculum designed to increase the school children's awareness of and appreciation for multiculturalism and diversity.

Following Markus and colleagues (1993), students in the service-learning and non-service-learning condition will receive identical in-class lectures and assigned reading materials. Students in both conditions will also participate in a six-session diversity training program that has been designed to prepare the students in the service-learning condition to work with elementary schools in an effective way. The training program will use didactics, readings, class discussion, and experiential exercises. Training will focus on self-awareness, the many forms of diversity, and strategies to use to help students talk to elementary students about diversity. This training program was recently pilot tested (Aronson, Webster, Reason, & Ingram, 2005), although similar approaches to diversity training have been used elsewhere (Aronson, Venable, Sieveking, & Miller, 2005; Richard, 1996; Tatum, 1994). After these training sessions, students in the service-learning condition will co-facilitate with preservice teachers the presentation of a multisession multicultural curriculum to fourth- and fifth-grade students that is integrated into history and art appreciation lessons within the elementary school. The multicultural curriculum was designed by two of us, who are elementary school teachers from central Pennsylvania and who have been recognized with various teaching awards for their multicultural curriculum.

Course material will be tied to the service-learning experience (Eyler & Giles, 1999), and students in the service-learning condition will have reflection assignments given to them in recitation. Students in the control condition will receive this material in a more traditional, static fashion. All students will complete a number of pre- and post-intervention assessments related to their ethnic identity development, racial and cultural beliefs, depth of thinking, grasp of class material, and career aspirations.

Hypotheses

It is hypothesized that the effects of service-learning will be influenced by several moderating variables that have already been established in prior research (i.e., GPA, prior service-learning experience, gender, belief in the importance of the issue being addressed by the service-learning intervention, interest in the issue being addressed, parental socioeconomic status [SES]). Furthermore, we predict that cognitive complexity will at least partially mediate (see Baron & Kenny, 1986, for a discussion of partial and full mediation) the relationship between key predictors of service-learning (i.e., direct community experience, reflection, quality of placement, and preparation for community experience) and the outcome variables. Students exposed to service-learning, controlling for moderating effects, will exhibit greater academic achievement, social emotional development, intention to become more civically engaged, and appreciation for learning. We also predict that students in the service-learning condition will report greater feelings of teaching self-efficacy and more confidence in their career aspirations and goals as teachers. It is important to note that in this study, we will only be able to assess proximal outcomes.

Participants

Participants will be undergraduate students, many of whom will not have declared a major, in an introductory curriculum and instruction course that will be adding a service-learning component for the first time. Therefore, although students self-select to take the class, they will not enroll in the class because it includes a service-learning component. However, we will also track who drops the class and ascertain why they did via an anonymous survey sent to all students at the end of the semester.

Planned Measures

Moderators. Hypothesized moderators will be measured using extensive demographic and background questionnaires used in other studies of service-learning within the university context (e.g., Eyler & Giles, 1999; Fitch, 2004).

Predictors. *Direct community experience* will be measured by student self-report on the following dimensions of (a) amount of direct community contact with elementary students, teachers, and administrators, and (b) satisfaction with the amount of direct contact. In addition to student self-report, elementary classroom teachers and students will be asked to rate the amount of direct contact they had with university students and their satisfaction with that contact. *Reflection* will be measured by student self-report in terms of (a) the amount of time they engaged in reflection, (b) the depth of their reflection, (c) the quality of their reflection, and (d) the extent to which they felt their reflection was tied to course material and recitation section discussions. This will allow measurement of several dimensions of reflection, including the frequency with which students and instructors allude to integration of material, the quality of integration provided by instructors, and the extent to which students demonstrate meaningful integration. An objective index of reflection based solely on the number of reflection and journal entries completed will also be used. *Quality of placement* will be assessed via student report of

1. The extent to which they felt the elementary school teachers and administrators were involved in the service-learning project;
2. The level of cooperation they felt was offered by the elementary school;
3. The degree to which they had a voice in how the service-learning project was implemented and carried out in the elementary school; and
4. The extent to which they felt their presence made an impact on the elementary school.

Preparedness for community service will be measured by the students themselves, preservice teacher co-leaders, and the elementary classroom teacher. Students will complete a self-report measure, while co-leaders and classroom teachers will complete an independent assessment of each student's preparedness (e.g., grasp of multicultural material, control of classroom, delivery of curriculum). It is important to note that information collected will not rely exclusively on student self-report.

Cognitive Complexity. Cognitive complexity will be measured in several ways. The Learning Environment Preferences (LEP; Moore, 1989) is an objective measure of intellectual development using Perry's theory of intellectual development, which describes how college students come to reason more complexly about knowledge, truth, learning, and commitment. We will also use the Scale of Intellectual Development (SID; DeMars & Erwin, 2003; Erwin, 1983), which also assesses Perry's scheme, but demonstrates a slightly different factor structure and allows for "unfolding" statistical analyses (Roberts, Donoghue, & Laughlin, 1998). Unfolding recognizes and accounts for the fact that some scores decline and some scores increase as students' cognitive complexity develops.

Proximal Outcomes. *Academic achievement* will be measured by course grade, using the total number of points earned on examinations only. By using examination grades only, problems inherent in comparing grades across the differing assignments between service-learning and control students (Markus et al., 1993) are avoided. Academic achievement will also be assessed via problem-solving interviews and content analysis of written course assignments (Eyler & Giles, 1999; Fredericksen, 2001). *Personal social emotional development* will be evaluated by asking students to indicate the extent to which they gained self-understanding, developed spiritually, felt rewarded by their service-learning experience, and the extent to which the service-learning experience contributed to their thinking about future career/internship choices (Billig, 2000b; Eyler & Giles, 1999; Warchal &

Ruiz, 2004). *Openness to diversity* will be assessed via the Oklahoma Racial Attitudes Scale (ORAS; LaFleur, Leach, & Rowe, 2002), which assesses racial self-awareness. Openness to diverse others will be measured via the Brigham Attitude Survey (Brigham, 1993), the Quick Discrimination Index (QDI; Ponterotto et al., 1995), and the Color Blind Racial Attitudes Scale (Neville, Lilly, Duran, Lee, & Browne, 2000), which all assess attitudes toward diverse others.

Interpersonal development will be measured using the Communicative Adaptability Scale (Duran, 1992), which indicates the extent to which respondents are skillful in various dimensions of interpersonal skill. Students will also be asked to rate the extent to which they felt connected to classmates, the elementary school students, and the elementary school teachers. Cooperation will be measured by the students themselves, the trainers, the preservice teachers, and the classroom teacher on two dimensions (i.e., cooperation among the university students themselves and cooperation among the university students and preservice teacher co-leaders). *Learning appreciation* will be assessed via the Academic Locus of Control Scale (Trice, 1985), which assesses the extent to which respondents feel agentic with respect to their academic performance. Finally, course attendance will be used as an objective index of learning appreciation.

Data Analysis Plan

The data analysis plan includes two components. To analyze the fit of our conceptual model, we will use hierarchical linear modeling (HLM; Bryk & Raudenbush, 1992) to determine moderation and mediation effects (Baron & Kenny, 1986). HLM will be used to analyze scores on within-subject measurements (e.g., content analysis of written work), which are measured on multiple occasions, and between-subject measures (moderators and predictors), which are measured on a single occasion. Using HLM to analyze moderation and mediation is preferred to standard regression analysis because it allows for a more sensitive estimation of effects (Kenny, Kashy, & Boger, 1998). To analyze differences between service-learning and controls on outcomes of interest, we will use multiple {AU: MANOVA is 'multivariate'...)analysis of variance (MANOVA), which allows one to determine if group differences exist on multiple dependent measures while controlling for Type 1 error (Pedhazur & Schmelkin, 1991).

CONCLUSION

Research conducted to date suggests that service-learning has promise as a pedagogical approach. However, strong inference studies have been lacking in the field. RCFTs provide a very rigorous approach to study service-learning. RCFTs not only control for self-selection bias, they also protect against threats to internal validity (e.g., history, maturation). Moreover, because they take place in a real-world context, RCFTs add a measure of external validity that is lacking in laboratory experiments, particularly when they are replicated across heterogeneous samples. It is important to note, however, that RCFTs present service-learning researchers with some challenges (e.g., ethical issues, diffusion of treatment, resentful demoralization). We have attempted to provide service-learning researchers with information they can use to overcome these challenges. Therefore, RCFTs should be used more frequently in service-learning studies. The theoretical model presented in this chapter, which will be assessed using a RCFT design, posits that cognitive complexity, which has heretofore been viewed solely as an outcome of service-learning, actually mediates the effect of service-learning on a wide variety of outcomes. The body of work emanating from cognitive psychology and neuroscience suggest that enriched learning environments, such as that provided by service-learning, may change both the morphology and functioning of the learner's brain. The hands-on learning opportunities, reflection, processing of feelings and values, and exposure to complex problems provided by service-learning may contribute to the development of enhanced cognitive processing skills. These skills can then be used across multiple domains (e.g., academic, social, personal) to enhance the person's functioning and adaptation. While the developments in cognitive psychology and the neurosciences are quite new (and rapidly evolving), they represent an exciting area for future investigation in service-learning.

REFERENCES

Aiken, L. S., & West, S. G. (1990). Invalidity of true experiments: Self-report pretest biases. *Evaluation Review, 14,* 374–390.

Allen, J. P., Philliber, S., Herrling, S., & Kuperminc, G. P. (1997). Preventing teen pregnancy and academic failure: Experimental evaluation of a developmentally based approach. *Child Development, 4,* 729–742.

Aronson, K. R., Venable, R., Sieveking, N., & Miller, B. (2005). Teaching intercultural awareness to first-year medical students via experiential exercises. *Intercultural Education, 16,* 15–24.

Aronson, K. R., Webster, N., Reason, R., & Ingram, P. (2005). *Cultural diversity training with undergraduates at a large rural university.* Unpublished manuscript, Pennsylvania State University.

Astin, A.W., & Sax, L.J. (1998). How undergraduates are affected by service participation. *Journal of College Student Development, 39,* 251–263.

Baron, R. M., & Kenny, D. A. (1986). The moderator-mediator variable distinction in social psychological research: Conceptual, strategic, and statistical considerations. *Journal of Personality and Social Psychology, 51,* 1173–1182.

Battistoni, R. M. (2001). Service-learning and civic education. *Campus Compact Reader, 2,* 6–14.

Berkas, T. (1997). *Strategic review of the W. K. Kellogg Foundation's service-learning projects, 1990–1996.* Battle Creek, MI: W. K. Kellogg Foundation.

Billig, S. H. (2000a). The effects of service-learning. *School Administrator, 57,* 14–18.

Billig, S. H. (2000b). Research on K–12 school-based service-learning: The evidence builds. *Phi Delta Kappan, 81*(9), 658–664.

Billig, S. H. (2003a). *The Michigan Educational Assessment Program.* Retrieved from http//service-learningpartnership.org/admin/uploadfiles/MEAP_evaluation_sb.ppt

Billig, S. H. (2003b). *The quality of K–12 service-learning research.* Retrieved October 1, 2005, from http://servicelearningpartnership.org/admin/uploadfiles/quality_K12_slsearch-sb.ppt

Bordens, K. S., & Abbott, B. B. (1991). *Research, design, and methods: A process approach.* Mountain View, CA: Mayfield Publishing

Boruch, R., de Moya, D., & Snyder, B. (2002). The importance of randomized field trials in education and related areas. In F. Mosteller & R. Boruch (Eds.), *Evidence matters: Randomized trials in education research* (pp. 50–79). Washington, DC: Brookings Institution Press.

Boruch, R. F., & Foley, E. (2000). The honestly experimenting society: sites and other entities as the units of allocation and analysis in randomized trials. In L. Bickman (Ed.), *Validity and social experimentation* (pp. 3–44). Thousand Oaks, CA: Sage.

Boyer, E. L. (1990). *Scholarship reconsidered: Priorities of the professorate.* Princeton, NJ: Carnegie Foundation for the Advancement of Teaching.

Brandt, R. S. (1997). On using knowledge about the brain. *Educational Leadership, 54,* 16–19.

Bransford, J. D. (1993). Who ya gonna call? Thoughts about teaching problem solving. In P. Hallinger, K. Leithwood, & J. Murphy (Eds.), *Cognitive perspectives on educational leadership* (pp. 171–191). New York: Teachers College Press.

Breuer, K., & Tennyson, R. D. (1995). Psychological foundations for instructional design theory: Cognitive complexity theory. *Journal of Structural Learning, 12,* 165–173.

Brigham, J. C. (1993). College students' racial attitudes. *Journal of Applied Social Psychology, 23,* 1933–1967.

Bringle, R. G. (2003). Enhancing theory-based research in service-learning. In S. H, Billig & J. Eyler (Eds.), *Advances in service-learning research: Vol. 3. Deconstructing service-learning: Research exploring context, participation, and impacts* (pp. 3–24). Greenwich, CT: Information Age Publishing.

Bringle, R. G., & Hatcher, J. A. (2000, Fall). Meaningful measurement of theory-based service-learning outcomes: Making the case with quantitative research. *Michigan Journal of Community Service Learning* [Special issue], 68–75.

Brooks-Gunn, J. (2004). Don't throw the baby out with the bathwater: Incorporating behavioral research into evaluations. *Social Policy Report, 18,* 14–15.

Bryk, A. S., & Raudenbush, S. W. (1992). *Hierarchical linear models: Applications and data analysis methods.* Newbury Park, CA: Sage.

Campbell, D. T., & Stanley, J. C. (1963). *Experimental and quasi-experimental designs for research.* Chicago: Rand-McNally.

Cardellichio, T., & Field, W. (1997). Seven strategies that encourage neural branching. *Education Leadership, 54,* 33–36.

Cohen, D. K., Raudenbush, S. W., & Ball, D. L. (2002). Resources, instruction, and research. In F. Mosteller & R. Boruch (Eds.), *Evidence matters: Randomized trials in education research* (pp. 80–119). Washington, DC: Brookings Institution Press.

Cook, T. D. (2002). Randomized experiments in educational policy and research: A critical examination of the reasons the educational evaluation community has offered for not doing them. *Educational Evaluation and Policy Analysis, 24,* 175–199.

Cook, T. D. (2004). Beyond advocacy: Putting history and research on research into databases about the merits of social experiments. *Social Policy Report, 18,* 5–6.

Cook, T. D., & Campbell, D. T. (1979). *Quasi-experimentation: Design and analysis issues for field settings.* Boston: Houghton Mifflin.

Cook, T. D., & Payne, M. R. (2002). Objecting to the objections to using random assignment in educational research. In F. Mosteller & R. Boruch (Eds.), *Evidence matters: Randomized trials in education research* (pp. 150–178). Washington, DC: Brookings Institution Press.

D'Arcangelo, M. (1998). The brains behind the brain. *Education Leadership, 56,* 20–25.

D'Arcangelo, M. (2000). How does the brain develop? A conversation with Steven Petersen, *Education Leadership, 58,* 68–71.

DeMars, C. E., & Erwin, T. D. (2003). Revising the Scale of Intellectual Development: Application of an unfolding model. *Journal of College Student Development, 44,* 168–184.

Dewey, J. (1938). *Experience and education.* New York: Collier Books.

Diamond, M., & Hopson, J. (1999). *Magic trees of the mind.* New York: Plume.

Duran, R. (1992). Communicative adaptability: A review of conceptualization and measurement. *Communication Quarterly,* 40, 253–268.

Erwin, T. D. (1983). The Scale of Intellectual Development: Measuring Perry's scheme. *Journal of College Student Personnel,* 24, 6–12.

Eyler, J. (2000, Fall). What do we need to know about the impact of service-learning on student learning? *Michigan Journal of Community Service Learning,* pp. 11–17.

Eyler, J. (2001). Creating your reflection map. *New Directions for Higher Education, 114,* 35–43.

Eyler, J. (2002). Stretching to meet the challenge: Improving the quality of research to improve the quality of service-learning. In S. H. Billig & A. Furco (Eds.),

Advances in service-learning research: Vol. 2. Service-learning through a multidisciplinary lens (pp. 3–14). Greenwich, CT: Information Age Publishing.

Eyler, J., & Giles, D. E., Jr. (1997). The importance of program quality in service-learning. In A. Waterman (Ed.), *Service-learning: Applications from the research* (pp. 57–76). Hillsdale, NJ: Lawrence Erlbaum Associates.

Eyler, J., & Giles, D. E., Jr. (1999). *Where's the learning in service-learning.* San Francisco: Jossey-Bass.

Eyler, J., Giles, D. E., Jr., & Gray, C. (1999). *At a glance: Summary and annotated bibliography of recent service-learning in higher education.* Minneapolis, MN: National Service-Learning Clearinghouse.

Eyler, J., Giles, D. E., Jr., & Schmiede, A. (1996). *A practitioner's guide to reflection in service-learning: Student voices in reflection.* Nashville, TN: Corporation for National Service.

Eyler, J., Root, S., & Giles, D. E., Jr. (1998). Service-learning and the development of expert citizens: Service-learning and cognitive science. In R. Bringle & D. Duffy (Eds.), *With service in mind.* Washington, DC: American Association for Higher Education.

Fetterman, D. M. (1982). Ibsen's baths: Reactivity and insensitivity (A misapplication of the treatment-control design in a national evaluation). *Educational Evaluation and Policy Analysis, 3,* 261–279.

Fitch, P. (2004). Effects of intercultural service-learning experiences on intellectual development and intercultural sensitivity. In M. Welch & S. H. Billig (Eds.), *New perspectives in service-learning: Research to advance the field* (pp. 107–126). Greenwich, CT: Information Age Publishing.

Fredericksen, P. J. (2001). Does service learning make a difference in student performance. *The Journal of Experiential Education, 23,* 64–74.

Friedlander, D., & Robbins, P. (1995). Evaluating program evaluations: New evidence on commonly used nonexperimental methods. *American Economic Review,* 85, 923–937.

Furco, A., & Billig, S. H. (2002). Establishing norms for scientific inquiry in service-learning. In S. H. Billig & A. Furco (Eds.), *Advances in service-learning research: Vol. 2. Service-learning through a multidisciplinary lens* (pp. 3–14). Greenwich, CT: Information Age Publishing.

Giles, D. E., Jr., & Eyler, J. (1998). A service-learning research agenda for the next five years. *New Directions in Teaching and Learning, 73,* 65–72.

Goleman, D. (1995). *Emotional intelligence.* New York: Bantam Books.

Heckman, J. J., Ichimura, H., Smith, J. C., & Todd, P. (1997). Characterizing selection bias. *Econometrica, 66,* 1017–1098.

Holland, P. W. (1986). Statistics and causal inference. *Journal of the American Statistical Society, 81,* 945–970.

Holland, B. A. (2001a, May). *Exploring the challenge of documenting and measuring civic engagement endeavors of colleges and universities: Purposes, issues, ideas.* Paper presented at the Campus Compact Advanced Institute on Classifications for Civic Engagement.

Holland, B. A. (2001b). Progress toward strategies to evaluate civic engagement. *Campus Compact Reader, 2,* 21–27.

Jacoby, B. (1996). Service-learning in today's higher education. In B. Jacoby & Associates (Eds.), *Service-learning in higher education: Concepts and practices* (pp. 3–25). San Francisco: Jossey-Bass.

Jones, S. R. (2002). The underside of service learning. *About Campus, 7,* 10–15.

Jones, S. R., & Abes, E. S. (2004). Enduring influences of service-learning on college students' development. *Journal of College Student Development, 45,* 149–166.

Kazdin, A. E. (1992). *Research design in clinical psychology.* Boston: Allyn & Bacon.

Kenny, D. A., Kashy, D. A., & Bolger, N. (1998). Data analysis in social psychology. In D. Gilbert, S. Fiske, & G. Lindzey (Eds.), *Handbook of social psychology* (4th ed., pp. 233–265). New York: McGraw-Hill.

Kerlinger, F. N. (1986). *Foundations of behavioral research* (3rd ed.). Orlando, FL: Holt, Rinehart & Winston.

Labouvie-Vief, G., & Diehl, M. (2000). Cognitive complexity and cognitive-affective integration: Related or separate domains of adult development. *Psychology and Aging, 15,* 490–504.

LaFleur, N. K., Leach, M. M., & Rowe, W. (2002). *Manual: Oklahoma racial attitudes scale.* Unpublished manual.

Larsen, R. J. (1992). Neuroticism and selective encoding and recall of symptoms: Evidence from a combined concurrent-retrospective study. *Journal of Personality and Social Psychology, 62,* 480–488.

Larson, R. W. (2000). Toward a psychology of positive youth development. *American Psychologist, 55,* 170–183.

Markus, G. B., Howard, J. P. F., & King, D. C. (1993). Integrating community service and classroom instruction enhances learning: Results from an experiment. *Educational Evaluation and Policy Analysis, 15,* 410–419.

McCall, R. B., & Green, B. L. (2004). Beyond the methodological gold standards of behavioral research: Considerations for practice and policy. *Social Policy Report, 18,* 3–12.

McCall, R. B., Ryan, C. S., & Plemons, B. W. (2003). Some lessons learned on evaluating community-based, two-generation service programs: The case of the Comprehensive Child Development Program (CCDP). *Journal of Applied Developmental Psychology, 24,* 125–141.

McLellan, J. A., & Youniss, J. (2003). Two systems of youth service: Determinants of voluntary and required youth community service. *Journal of Youth and Adolescence, 32,* 47–58.

Melchior, A. (1998). *National evaluation of Learn and Serve America school and community-based programs: Final report.* Waltham, MA: Brandeis University, Center for Human Resources.

Moore, W. S. (1989). The learning environment preferences: Exploring the construct validity of an objective measure of the Perry scheme of intellectual and ethical development. *Journal of College Student Development, 30,* 504–515.

Neville, H. A., Lilly, R. L., Duran, G, Lee, R. M., & Browne, L. (2000). Construction and initial validation of the Color-Blind Racial Attitudes Scale (CoBRAS). *Journal of Counseling Psychology, 47,* 59–70.

O'Bannon, F. (1999). Service-learning benefits our schools. *State Education Leader, 17,* 3.

Perry, W. H. (1970). *Forms of intellectual and ethical development in the college years.* Austin, TX: Holt, Rinehart and Winston.

Ponterotto, J. G., Burkard, A., Rieger, B. P., Grieger, I., D'Onofrio, A., Dubuisson, A., et al. (1995). Development and initial validation of the Quick Discrimination Index (QDI). *Educational and Psychological Measurement, 55,* 1016–1031.

Pool, C. R. (1997). Maximizing learning: A conversation with Renate Nummela Caine. *Educational Leadership, 54,* 11–15.

Ramaley, J. (2000). Embracing civic responsibility. *Campus Compact Reader, 1,* 1–5.

Reeves, W. W. (1996). *Cognition and complexity: The cognitive science of managing complexity.* Lanham, MD: Scarecrow Press.

Resnick, L. (1987). *Education and learning to think.* Washington, DC: National Academies Press.

Richard, H. W. (1996). Filmed in black and white: Teaching the concept of racial identity at a predominantly white university. *Teaching of Psychology, 23,* 159–161.

Roberts, J. S., Donoghue, J. R., & Laughlin, J. E. (1998). *The generalized graded unfolding model: A general parametric item response model for unfolding graded responses (RR-98–32).* Princeton, NJ: Educational Testing Service.

Rubin, D. B. (1974). Estimating causal effects of treatments in randomized and non-randomized studies. *Journal of Educational Psychology, 66,* 688–701.

Santmire, T. E., Giraud, G., & Grosskopf, K. (1999, April). *Furthering attainment of academic standards through service-learning.* Paper presented at the National Service Learning Conference, San Jose, CA.

Scales, P., & Blyth, D. (1997, Winter). Effects of service-learning on youth: What we know and what we need to know. *The Generator,* 6–9.

Schon, D. (1995). Knowing in action: The new scholarship requires a new epistemology. *Change, 27,* 27–34.

Shaffer, B. (1993). *Service-learning: An academic methodology.* Stanford, CA: Stanford University.

Slavkin, M. E. (2002). The importance of brain functioning on cognition and teacher practice. *The Journal of Teaching and Learning, 6,* 21–34.

Slavkin, M. E. (2003). Engaging the heart, hand, and brain. *Principal Leadership, 3*(9), 20–25.

Steinke, P., & Buresh, S. (2002). Cognitive outcomes of service-learning: Reviewing the past and glimpsing the future. *Michigan Journal of Community Service Learning, 8,* 5–14.

Steinke, P., Fitch, P., Johnson, C., & Waldstein, F. (2002). An interdisciplinary study of service-learning outcomes. In A. Furco & S. H. Billig (Eds.), *Advances in service-learning research, Vol. 2. Service-learning through a multidisciplinary lens.* Greenwich, CT: Information Age Publishing.

Steinke, P., Klaassen, J., & Vos, T. (2003, November). *Impact of academic service-learning and goal based characteristics on cognitive learning: Outcomes of college students.* Paper presented at the 3rd Annual International K–H Service-Learning Research Conference, Salt Lake City, UT.

Stephens, L. (1995). *The complete guide to learning through community service, grades K–9.* Boston: Allyn & Bacon.

Sternberg, R. J. (1999). *The nature of cognition.* Cambridge, MA: MIT Press.

Strage, A. (2004). Long-term academic benefits of service-learning: When and where do they manifest themselves? *College Student Journal, 38,* 257–260.

Strage, A. A. (2000). Service-learning: Enhancing student learning outcomes in a college-level lecture course. *Michigan Journal of Community Service Learning, 7,* 5–13.

Tatum, B. D. (1994). Teaching White students about racism: The search for white allies and the restoration of hope. *Teachers College Record, 95,* 462–476.

Taylor, S. E. (1989). *Positive illusions: Creative self-deception and the healthy mind.* New York: Basic Books.

Trice, A. D. (1985). An academic locus of control scale for college students. *Perceptual and Motor Skills, 61,* 1043–1046.

Wade, R. C. (2000). Service-learning for multicultural teaching competency: Insights from the literature for teacher educators. *Equity & Excellence in Education, 33,* 21–29.

Warchal, J., & Ruiz, A. (2004). The long-term effects of service-learning programs on postgraduate employment choices, community engagement, and civic leadership. In M. Welch & S. H. Billig (Eds.), *New perspectives in service-learning: Research to advance the field* (pp. 87–106). Greenwich, CT: Information Age Publishing.

Wilde, E. T., & Hollister, R. (2002). *How close is close enough? Testing nonexperimental estimates of impact against experimental estimates of impact with education test scores as outcomes* (Discussion Paper No. 1242–02). Madison, WI: Institute for Research on Poverty.

Wolfe, P., & Brandt, R. (1998). What do we know now from brain research. *Educational Leadership, 56,* 8–13.

W. T. Grant Foundation. (2004). *Report and resource guide 2003–2004.* New York: Author.

Ziegert, A. L., & McGoldrick, K. (2004). Adding rigor to service-learning research: An armchair economists' approach. In M. Welch & S. H. Billig (Eds.), *New perspectives in service-learning: Research to advance the field* (pp. 23–36). Greenwich, CT: Information Age Publishing.

CHAPTER 9

USING PRINCIPLES OF RESEARCH TO DISCOVER MULTIPLE LEVELS OF CONNECTION AND ENGAGEMENT

A Civic Engagement Audit

Robert Shumer and Susan Spring Shumer

ABSTRACT

The goal of a civic engagement audit is to define the civic landscape of higher education. The audit reported in this study focuses on both formal and informal connections with the community to produce a process by which a university vision, mission, and educational goals statement become the measure of civic engagement. Constructs of institutional penetration of courses and baseline data provide a system that has broad implications for standardizing the measurement of civic connections. This audit breaks new ground for better reporting of the relationships between an institution of higher education and its faculty, staff, and students, and the community it serves.

Improving Service-Learning Practice: Research on Models to Enhance Impacts, pages 167–185
Copyright © 2005 by Information Age Publishing

Civic engagement is a popular topic in higher education. Much has been written about the reasons for engagement, and several efforts have been undertaken to describe the nature and function of engaged campuses (Beaumont, Colby, Ehrlich, & Stephens, 2003; Bowley, 2003; Campus Compact, 2003; Driscoll, Gelmon, Holland, Kerrigan, & Spring, 2000; Holland, 1997; O'Meara & Kilmer, 1999). While the discussion is important, few initiatives have been conducted to measure and define basic levels of engagement. The focus of this chapter describes the creation of a civic engagement audit as a system to conceptualize and measure civic connections at Metropolitan State University in Minneapolis–St. Paul, Minnesota.

O'Meara and Kilmer (1999) noted that there is not just one definition of civic engagement. Civic engagement is broadly defined as activities that reinvigorate the public purposes and civic mission of higher education. Others, such as Patrick (2000), suggested civic engagement, at its core, is the interaction of citizens with their society and their government to acquire knowledge, cognitive skills, participatory skills, and dispositions. Citizens must use this knowledge and skill to affect issues and policies. The key term is "use." Engagement requires action and change.

O'Meara and Kilmer (1999) described efforts that demonstrate various forms of measurement, not just of community programs, but of civic purposes and civic missions. Some, such as the Urban Universities Portfolio Project, a collaboration among six urban public universities to develop prototypes of electronic institutional portfolios, use approaches where faculty and others present specific information about their engagement. Additional institutions use profiles and different descriptive processes to categorize types of engagement.

Hollander, Saltmarsh, and Zlotkowski (2002) identified 13 areas important to engaged campuses and engaged learning. The goal of this effort was to identify exemplars of engaged practice to help colleges and universities expand their understanding and practice of civic engagement. However, the project was focused on identifying basic areas of engagement, such as civic mission, administrative leadership, faculty development, and student voice, not on actually grounding the process for individual campuses. The effort also focused on community and tribal colleges, not on institutions such as Metropolitan State University.

The above-mentioned efforts tended to capture trends and the intents of civic engagement. However, they appear to understate the simple connection between people, organizations, and institutions as the basic building blocks of civic engagement. The focus of this civic engagement audit is to present a different approach—to use the language and concepts of the university's administration, students, faculty, and staff—to frame a basic, systematic investigation of community connections. Such connections become the foundation of more sophisticated measures of civic engagement and civic intent.

Measuring civic engagement is the act of determining how a university community connects to its citizens, cities, and civil affairs. This connection assumes the word engagement means producing movement, such as in engaging a gear. As gears mesh, so too do people mesh to produce movement or change in a community. The goal of the study was to understand how members of the university community engaged with citizens and organizations in the surrounding areas to produce movement and/or change. The purpose of Metropolitan State's audit was to *hear* about civic engagement by conducting a formal, methodical examination of every aspect of the university's connection to the community.

The Metropolitan State University vision statement includes a direct reference to civic engagement:

> Metropolitan State University, a member of the Minnesota State College and University System, will be the premier urban, public, comprehensive system university in the Twin Cities metropolitan area and will focus on providing high-quality, affordable, educational programs and services in a student-centered environment. The faculty, staff and students *will reflect the area's rich diversity and will demonstrate an unwavering commitment to civic engagement.*

This "unwavering commitment" sets a high standard for the institution and suggests that most courses/programs should have an interest in community connections.

The mission statement and educational goals include a similarly strong stand on service to the community and a focus on improving the quality of life for residents and the institution. The mission statement concludes: *The University is committed to academic excellence and community partnerships through curriculum, teaching, scholarship, and services designed to support an urban mission.*

This statement helps us to begin to think about the focus on civic engagement in vital areas such as curriculum, teaching, scholarship, and service. Thus, community partnerships must contain activities and purposes that embrace the civic mission and goals of the institution. These four areas actually became part of the framework for developing the institutional instrument to measure civic engagement.

RESEARCH METHODS

This research was conducted in response to Metropolitan State University's desire to create a process to measure the ongoing commitment to civic engagement. Metropolitan State University has two unique features that make the study of civic engagement more complex. As a nontraditional, urban institution, it educates students from a much broader age range than a traditional university. The average age of the student body is 33, with over 85% working while attending classes. These students serve in many important roles in their communities and bring vast experience to community connections.

The faculty composition also differs from traditional institutions. With approximately 100 resident faculty members, whose primary roles are teaching and research, Metropolitan State also has more than 500 community faculty members who teach at the university part time and work full time in other capacities. Their occupations range from being members of the state legislature to operating businesses and social service agencies in the community. Community faculty members bring an additional dimension to the notion of civic engagement because their expertise and contribution to the university is derived from the natural connection with the world outside the institution.

The audit began with an attempt to determine formal connections between Metropolitan State and its community. Draft surveys, along with a feedback form, were sent to 45 randomly selected individuals representing all 10 university units, including financial and administrative affairs, academic affairs, student affairs, equal opportunity and diversity, department chairs, faculty, the President's office, students, general university units, and university advancement. Of the 17 responses received, there was at least one response from each of the 10 units. Surveys and feedback forms were analyzed for both content (response to the questions) and process information (ease of filling out forms, clarity of questions, etc).

Based on the survey responses and the feedback forms, questions were developed for focus group meetings to determine how the surveys might be modified. Individuals who completed the forms were invited to participate in refining and improving the instruments. The university units surveyed were collapsed into three focus groups based on their positions and responsibilities: (1) administration, (2) students and staff, and (3) faculty.

It was discovered through the focus groups that every person within the institution could be part of the civic engagement process through formal and informal connections. For example, while student affairs was being surveyed to identify all the student organizations, the authors found many students were engaged informally with the community on a personal level, such as tutoring in a church program, outside the formal academic areas of the university.

Based on feedback from the focus groups, the following modifications were made:

- The surveys were distributed through a Web-based format;
- Each survey included common questions that focused on personal connections encouraging participants to answer full questionnaires; and
- University advancement, administrative and financial affairs, and equal opportunity and diversity units were combined into the General Category.

DATA

Electronic surveys were sent to 1,008 faculty members, staff, and administrators. Paper surveys were made available to more than 500 students. Within 3 weeks, completed surveys were received from:

- 23% of faculty, staff, and administrators (234 respondents);
- 100% of academic affairs and the President's office;
- 35% of resident faculty and 19% of community faculty;
- 55% of department chairs; and
- 64% of administrative affairs.

Other administrative staff, making up the General Category, returned 51% of the forms. Approximately 10% of the students returned their hard copy surveys.

Each survey began by asking participants the same generic questions. The goal of the first series of questions was to determine the number and nature of formal and informal connections, as shown in Exhibit 9.1. Student responses are separated from the total to give a clearer picture of the university's staff and faculty engagement, but necessary to provide an inclusive profile.

Exhibit 9.1. Do You Currently Connect with the Community in Any Particular Way in Either Your Personal or Professional Life?

Groups	Percent Yes	Percent No
General	55	45
Academic Affairs	86	14
Student Affairs	78	22
Faculty	84	15
Department Chairs	71	29
President's Office	100	0
Total	75	25
Students	65	35

These data demonstrate that 75% of administration, faculty, and staff connect with the community in a variety of ways. According to Independent Sector (2001), the national average of adults volunteering in their communities is 44%; therefore, Metropolitan State University personnel serve at rates substantially higher than the national average.

Exhibit 9.2.   How Are You Connected with the Community?

	Percent				
Groups	Personally Volunteer	Community Organization/ Agency Volunteer	Volunteer in Professional Capacity	As part of Professional Service for University	Other
General	24	43	8	23	3
Academic Affairs	43	57	29	29	14
Student Affairs	22	44	22	33	22
Faculty	27	63	38	28	13
Department Chairs	7	50	36	21	14
President's Office	0	33	0	33	0
Column Average	**21**	**48**	**22**	**28**	**11**
Students	28	48	13	18	0

The responses in Exhibit 9.2 provided important information about the nature of the connections. The greatest percentage of people connected to the community through organizations or agencies. A large percentage of university faculty members and staff connect through professional roles either individually or as a representative of the university. Only with academic affairs is personal volunteering found to exceed the other three major categories.

Survey responses provided 325 examples of the kinds of connections between staff, students, and the community. The connections reported ranged from typical examples such as tutoring, mentoring, and serving on local, state, and/or national boards, to more unique notions, including "shopping in the local community to help the economy and to learn from residents what was going on in the community." Clearly, the notion of civic connection was quite varied.

The responses to the question in Exhibit 9.3 indicate that a high percentage of people involved in the community are those in general administrative roles, academic affairs, department chairs, and faculty members—the people who have a tendency to be involved with the institution over a long period of time. When compared with students,

Exhibit 9.3.   How Long Have You Been Engaged with the Community (While Enrolled or Employed at Metropolitan State)?

	Percent of Time						
Groups	*More than 1 month*	*Less than 1 month*	*More than 6 months*	*More than 1 year*	*More than 2 years*	*More than 5 years*	*More than 10 years*
General	1	5	3	8	20	9	13
Academic Affairs	14	0	14	0	14	14	29
Student Affairs	11	0	11	11	22	22	0
Faculty	0	2	5	12	19	14	32
Department Chairs	7	0	7	14	7	7	29
President's Office	0	0	0	0	33	0	0
Column Average	7	4	8	9	23	13	21
Students	9	27	21	18	18	3	3

professional staff members have longer periods of connection with the community, suggesting that perhaps longevity at the institution appears to increase the length of community connection.

Besides the same initial questions on each survey, the seven units responded to a series of queries pertaining to their areas of community involvement and connection. The questions covered issues related to policy, practice, support, research, and the nature and quality of the community-based educational programs.

Data were analyzed for trends and patterns. For example, in academic affairs a majority of respondents believed the university supports community-connected programs: developing courses, regulating grades and credits, and linking community connections to tenure and promotion.

A second pattern indicated that, depending on the issue, 14% to 34% of respondents simply do not know about community-based programs. This pattern is repeated throughout the other surveys and indicates that no one person or unit seems to have full knowledge of total community connections/civic engagement within the institution.

Data also revealed conflicting trends. Department chairs, on one hand, said they plan to expand community programs and clearly had a policy that connected community-based learning with tenure and promotion. Yet, they also acknowledged that

- The majority of the faculty did not require such courses;
- The departments did not provide much training;

- The faculty members did not meet regularly with community members;
- Faculty members were not engaged predominantly in community-based research;
- Departments did not have a grading policy for community-based learning; and
- The institution was not sure how many faculty members were involved in community-based learning strategies.

These data are a bit confusing when compared with faculty members' input and suggest there is a communication gap in the departments around the topics/issues of community-based learning.

Faculty member responses also provided a mixed message. Although there were many less supportive comments and responses than expected, a majority said they included community service-learning in elective courses. However, almost every other answer was less inclusive of such learning. The majority of faculty members did not include community service-learning in required courses, did not use independent study for such approaches, did not conduct as much community-based research, nor did they do any other type of community service-learning.

The inconsistencies in these data bear investigation. Department chairs believe community-based research is valued for tenure and promotion. Yet, faculty say less than a third are involved in such research. Department chairs do not believe there are grading policies for community service-learning; yet a majority of faculty members who include community-based learning use reflective practices and other known techniques that lead to good learning and academically appropriate grading.

In any event, it is important to explore these inconsistencies between groups to improve university understanding and communication. Through dialogue it is possible to get the various groups to discuss these issues and to work toward resolving the differences in what they say they want and what they actually do.

COURSES AND FORMAL PROGRAMS THAT CONNECT WITH COMMUNITY

Part of the audit process required that the study determine how many courses and programs had community connections. These courses, when compared to the total number of courses offered at the university, provided a statistic, a percent that measures a *level of course penetration*. All units involved in the academic endeavor, including faculty, academic affairs, department chairs, and members of the Center for

Community-Based Learning (the administrative point on campus for these activities) were asked to list courses and programs that contained a community component.

One hundred and fifty separate course titles and 161 sections of courses that included a community connection were identified. Thirty-seven courses were identified by the Center for Community-Based Learning staff, with an additional 134 courses noted by faculty. This information is certainly underreported because it came from less than half of the resident faculty and roughly 20% of the community faculty.

Information obtained from the Registrar's Office indicated that the university offered 941 separate course titles during the 2002–2003 academic year. Based on the number of regular courses offered, the following institutional facts were:

- 1,513 total sections of regular courses were offered during the academic year;
- 150 separate courses were identified as having a community connection; and
- 161 sections were identified as having a community connection.

These data allowed us to present a numerical picture of the level of institutional penetration for courses that have a community connection. Based on this evidence, 16% of all courses offered (150/941) have a community connection, and 11% of all sections offered of regular courses (161/1513) have a community connection.

These are simple, yet important statistics. These numbers tell us how the university is doing relative to the percentage of courses that include community connections. They provide a factual construct that says this university has 16% of its courses that claim a community connection. There is a baseline number that can be compared with future studies, providing a concrete notion of whether the university is adding or losing community-connected courses. Thus, the issue of one component of institutionalization can be based on simple course counts to determine whether a university is moving forward or backward on its course offerings that are community based. This baseline also sets the mark for determining changes in civic engagement over time, indicating the change in number of courses and other elements that determine direction, force, and speed of movement.

These data may greatly underestimate the total number of community-connected courses at Metropolitan State because only a portion of the faculty reported. The potential number of courses could more than double, to over 300, when all information is completed. However, we only report here what actually was reflected in the faculty and administration responses in the initial surveys.

INDEPTH DATA COLLECTION

While information about courses was helpful in determining the level of community course penetration, it did little to provide information about the quality of those connections. Faculty members provided some information about the connections, such as how they involved the community and the nature of assignments. However, many of the details about the quality of the community interactions and the impact of the connections were missing. There was a strong need to find out how courses and programs were conceived and how they led to real community change and student acquisition of citizenship knowledge, skills, and dispositions.

To get a better understanding, one department/program was selected for indepth interviews regarding components that contributed to the quality of community connections. The Department of Social Work was selected specifically because it had a course/program sequence that was continuously connected to their community partner, La Familia Guidance Center. It would seem that social work departments nationwide are generally better connected to the community because of the heavy clinical emphasis of most social work programs. Yet, this investigation was conducted to highlight what civically engaged departments look like and how they function.

Interviewing the chair of the department, we discovered important information about the social work–community connections that were not reported or did not come cross clearly in the survey data. It was found that social work had 11 courses that supported their community work and La Familia. In return, agency personnel sat on the social work department board and provided important feedback on the needs of the community. Both financial and human resources were shared between the two organizations, and specific courses were focused on community-based research and advocacy. Almost every facet of the program met the university's civic mission: truly connecting with the surrounding populations for service, education, and research. It was clear that the connections were about both education and community change, two important components of engaged campuses. Students and community members were armed with the knowledge and skills to improve the quality of life for inhabitants of the community.

The interview was instructive because it demonstrated that the survey alone did not provide the information necessary to determine the quality and extent of the community connections. The conversation, the materials collected, and the observation of the actual community setting helped to explain the richness and completeness of the civic engagement. It appears that only through portfolios, interviews, and other forms of indepth data collection will an institution be able to ascertain the quality level of civic engagement for individual faculty members, the courses taught, and the departmental commitment.

INSTITUTIONAL ASSESSMENT INSTRUMENT

Using the vision, mission, and educational goal statements from the institution as a guide, we developed an assessment instrument for the seven university units and an overall assessment instrument for the entire institution, shown in Exhibit 9.4. The goal was to develop tools to help the institution begin to measure and interpret the results of the survey and interview data by constructing a device based on institutional criteria.

Thirteen items, which were selected from the educational goals and institutional statements, became the benchmarks by which to measure the community connections and civic engagement of the university. Each item was developed around the notion of engagement as a "geared" system, where direction, force, and speed explain the nature of connection and movement. The items on the instrument were designed to measure how fast an institution was moving toward civic engagement, how widespread the initiative (force), and the direction of the change (either positively or negatively).

Using data from the audit surveys provides the information necessary to rate each section. For example, the first category, Vision and Mission, would rate a "3" in categories dealing with Engagement and Speed, because civic engagement is a prominent part of both documents. One cannot ask for a stronger vision and mission statement than one that highlights civic engagement as a goal of the institution. Direction certainly would rate a "1," because the two statements are very positive. Force, in this rating, would be "NA," since it does not relate to the statement.

Similarly, the university rating for the President's involvement receives the highest marks because the responses to the survey by the President and his staff demonstrated their strong commitment to the civic mission of the institution. Also, the section dealing with Personal Engagement of faculty, staff, and students would rate the highest marks ("3") in Engagement, Force, and Speed because survey data demonstrated that more than 50% of all people in the institution claimed to have community connections. It would rate a "1" for Direction because certainly there is evidence that the institution is moving forward in its connection to community.

Exhibit 9.4. Institutional Civic Engagement Instrument

	Nature of Connection and Movement		
	Engagement / *Direction*	*Force*	*Speed*
Gear 1 Starting	1 Positive progress	1 Weak: involves few people or programs	1 Slow: making minimal progress in development
Gear 2 Moving	0 Stopped, not going anywhere	2 Medium: up to half institution engaged	2 Normal: making normal development
Gear 3 Moving well	−1 Reverse, backward	3 Strong: broad-based, more than half institution engaged	3 Strong: Top: doing extremely well in all areas
Benchmarks			
1. Vision and Mission	3 1	N/A	3
2. President's Involvement	3 1	3	3
3. Administrative Influence			
4. Student Involvement			
5. Community Partnerships Through: Curriculum			
6. Community Partnerships Through: Teaching			
7. Community Partnerships Through: Scholarship			

Exhibit 9.4. Institutional Civic Engagement Instrument (Cont.)

Nature of Connection and Movement

	Engagement	Direction		Force		Speed	
Gear 1	Starting	1	Positive progress	1	Weak: involves few people or programs	1	Slow: making minimal progress in development
Gear 2	Moving	0	Stopped, not going anywhere	2	Medium: up to half institution engaged	2	Normal: making normal development
Gear 3	Moving well	−1	Reverse, backward	3	Strong: broad-based, more than half institution engaged	3	Strong: Top: doing extremely well in all areas
Benchmarks							
8. Community Partnerships Through: Service							
9. Integrates Theory and Practice							
10. Prep for Careers and Service to Community							
11. Assessment System in Place							
12. Personal Engagement of Faculty, Staff, and Students	3	1		3		3	
13. Partnerships with Public and Private Organizations							

The institutional instrument includes many of the elements determined by other studies of civic engagement (Holland, 1997; O'Meara & Kilmer, 1999) and include institutional values and goals as expressed through the mission statement, President's role, institutional vision and goals, administrative support, faculty engagement through instruction, personal service, assessment systems, engaged departments, and student roles and contributions. Each one of these categories needs to be addressed in order to determine the final "level of engagement" represented collectively by the aggregate responses.

The instrument has value, not as much for its actual form and substance, but rather for the process of developing it for the individual institution. Selecting the benchmarks is as important as the audit itself, for it lays out the criteria for evaluation. Each institution needs to establish definitions for the categories of Direction, Force, and Speed that pertain to their setting and situation.

CIRCLE OF ENGAGED LEARNING

In addition to developing the surveys and the instruments for measuring community connections and civic engagement, the audit also involved faculty members and staff of the Center for Community-Based Learning in developing a list of concepts/terms that described the various components of civic connections at Metropolitan State. Gathering this information helped us better understand the connection between courses and the prevalence of community-based learning instructional strategies, such as service-learning, internships, field studies, and the like, at the university. The list of terms with definitions was created through a process that included input from faculty, administration, community members, and students. Once the categories and definitions were carefully selected they were presented to the university community at a university-wide dialogue on civic engagement. The items included were:

- **Community Connection.** Relationship with one or more community organization(s) and one or more department(s) or program(s) within the university to accomplish a shared nonacademic objective on a short-term basis.
- **Service to Community.** One or more university department(s) or program(s) are committed to regular opportunities for students and faculty to assist community organizations with *their* (organizational) objectives, which may or may not include academic learning.
- **University–Community Service**. A university department or program and a community partner are committed to the mutual sharing of

objectives in this reciprocal relationship, which may or may not include an academic component.

- **Community-Based Learning.** A method of teaching, research, or experiential learning that combines authentic community or public service experience with academic instruction, focusing on critical, reflective thinking as well as development of civic responsibility and/or personal growth.
- **Community–University Partnership.** A mutually defined relationship between at least one university department or program and one or more community-based organization(s), of sufficient scale and duration to significantly benefit the community organization(s) while providing important learning opportunities for university students.
- **Civic Engagement Partnership.** University-wide involvement with community partner(s)/organization(s) that mutually commit to working together in areas that go beyond each partner's capacities to achieve civic objectives alone.
- **Social Transformation Engagement.** A long-term unified commitment by the university and the larger community to alter social disparities by working toward social change and social justice.

Once the seven original categories were shared with the university community, they were configured to appear in a circular pattern, as shown in Figure 9.1, suggesting that there is not necessarily a hierarchical ordering of these items but rather an integrative pattern where various categories could be achieved without moving through an ontologically constructed system. At the same time, the university president requested that Social Transformation Engagement be placed at the outside of the *Circle of Engaged Learning*, indicating that all categories and efforts strive for this long-term ideal of actually bringing about change that would benefit both the institution and the community. By request of faculty, one addition was made to the original categories:

Community Immersion. A university course or program that involves significant student immersion in a community or public service that includes academic instruction, focusing on critical, reflective thinking as well as on the development of civic responsibility and/or personal growth of students.

What is important is the notion that there are multiple levels of engagement described in their basic form as simple, short-term connections, to ones that are long-term, engaged relationships where social change and social justice outcomes are expected and measured. These constructs parallel some of the ideas outlined by Kahne and Westheimer (1996), who describe individual movement from charity to social action.

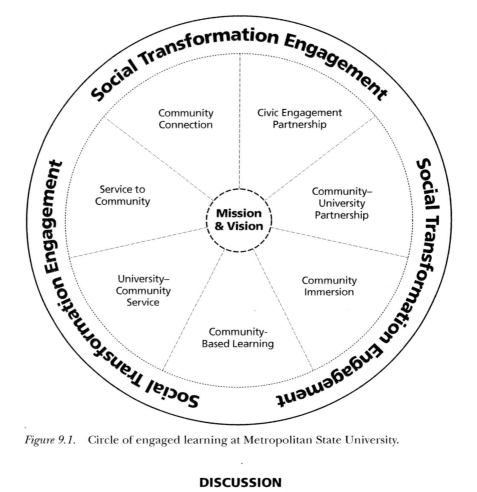

Figure 9.1.   Circle of engaged learning at Metropolitan State University.

DISCUSSION

What has been the value of the Metropolitan State University civic engagement audit to the field of service-learning and the civic role of higher education? Perhaps the most important contribution is that it reminds readers that the basic unit of civic engagement is simple, informal and formal human connections. These connections are the building blocks of any discussion of civic engagement or civic movement. Rather than dwell on some of the abstract and theoretical notions of civic engagement found in the current literature (Colby, Ehrlich, Beaumont, & Stephens, 2003; Hollander et al., 2002), the audit has demonstrated that concepts of "institutional penetration"—the indicator of just how many courses in an institution have community connections compared with the total course offerings—provides a quantifiable way of representing civic engagement as a function of courses. Similarly, the representation of departments involved in community work provides a benchmark number in the percentage of departmental units that connect with the community in some measurable way.

The audit also demonstrated that everyone at an institution can be involved in the civic process, from the president to first-year students. Everyone potentially can connect with the community, and in fact, many of the connections by faculty, students, and staff are at highly professional levels and at rates above the national average for volunteerism and community engagement.

The civic engagement audit also had some sobering discoveries from the survey data. While many of the indicators were positive or represented forward movement on the part of the institution, the relatively high percentage of "no-response" or "do not know" answers suggest that previous efforts to determine levels of engagement by interviewing only a few people on campus (Bowley, 2003) may not provide the entire picture. While not generalizing to a large sample of campuses, these data suggest that no one—from the Center for Community-Based Learning staff, to the department chairs, to the personnel in academic and student affairs, to the alumni/foundations personnel—had a comprehensive understanding of all the civic connections existing at the institution. Practitioners need to engage in a more thorough data-gathering and analysis process, similar to the one held at Metropolitan State, to get a much more accurate picture of what actually exists.

While using a framework similar to the *Circle of Engaged Learning*, practitioners also need to gather much more information about the quality of the engagement and the outcomes associated with their efforts. It makes little sense to discuss the number and kind of connections with the community without having some indication of the nature of institutional, faculty, student, and community impact. Embedding a process similar to the social work example, interviewing and describing the details of a particular course or program, can determine the kind of overall impact on the institution and its personnel, as well as what changes are occurring in the community. Without this knowledge, concern for civic engagement seems incomplete, focused more on effort than on process and impact.

CONCLUSION

Measuring civic engagement is perhaps one of the most important issues facing higher education today. Returning colleges and universities to their public purpose and public service through engaged scholarship is an important goal. While important, our knowledge of the process for ascertaining measurable benchmarks and systems of connection is limited. We know how to survey and interview people and document the processes, but we have less experience describing the measurement of actual people, courses, programs, and outcomes of such engaged efforts.

The audit at Metropolitan State University provided some new dimensions of measurement that will hopefully help to standardize approaches to engagement across institutions. Using online survey instruments to determine the number and kind of civic connections, the number of actual courses that have civic connections, and the actual number of departments that include civic engagement as part of their mode of operation, can now be documented in a uniform manner. Developing systems to measure penetration of civic connections into courses provides a gross indicator of civic engagement. So, too, does the measure of departmental penetration.

Developing instruments to measure the force, speed, and direction of institutional movement is another important product of the audit. Without faculty, administration, and student input into the nature of engagement, it will be hard to develop a process that has practical value, where data are applied through a continuous improvement model. Also, using mission, vision, and educational goal statements to construct the instruments for the audit forces the institution to conduct its own self-assessment, where the criteria used are all internal to the institution and its constituents. It is this latter construct that makes the audit valuable and makes the process one that every institution of higher learning can undertake.

There is much to be done to connect colleges and universities across the country with their communities for purposes of civic engagement. Participating in self-evaluative audits can be one approach to document the quantity and quality of the effort and to showcase the many successes that currently exist. It is a long and complicated process, but one that is necessary for the continued development of higher education as a true partner with the communities they serve.

NOTE

Funding for this project was provided by the State of Minnesota through the Higher Education Services Office awarded by Minnesota Campus Compact's Post Secondary Service-Learning and Campus Community Collaboration grant program.

REFERENCES

Bowley, E. (2003). *The Minnesota Campus Civic Engagement Study: Defining engagement in a new century*. St. Paul: Minnesota Higher Education Services Office and Minnesota Campus Compact.

Campus Compact. (2003, June). *Campus compact survey reveals record numbers of students involved in service* [News release]. Retrieved March 28, 2005, from http://www.compact.org/newscc/news-detail.php?viewstory=3414

Colby, A., Ehrlich, T., Beaumont, E., & Stephens, J. (2003). *Educating citizens: Preparing America's undergraduates for lives of moral and civic responsibility*. San Francisco: Jossey-Bass.

Holland, B. (1997). Analyzing institutional commitment to service: A model of key organizational factors. *Michigan Journal of Community Service Learning, 4*, 30–41.

Hollander, E., Saltmarsh, J., & Zlotkowski, E. (2002). Indicators of engagement. In M. E. Kenny, L. A. K. Simon, K. Kiley-Brabeck, & R. M. Lerner (Eds.), *International series in outreach scholarship: Vol. 7. Learning to serve: Promoting civil society through service-learning* (pp. 31–49). Norwell. MA: Kluwer Academic.

Independent Sector. (2001). *Independent sector survey measures the everyday generosity of Americans*. Retrieved May 9, 2004, from http://www.independentsector/programs/research/GVO/main.html

Kahne, J., & Westheimer, J. (1996). In the service of what? The politics of service-learning. *Phi Delta Kappan, 77*(9), 592–599.

O'Meara, K., & Kilmer, H. (1999). *Mapping civic engagement in higher education: National initiatives*. Providence, RI: Campus Compact.

Patrick, J. (2000). Introduction to education for civic engagement in democracy. In S. Mann & J. Patrick (Eds.), *Education for civic engagement and democracy: Service-learning and other promising practices* (pp. 1–8). Bloomington, IN: ERIC Clearinghouse for Social Studies/Social Sciences.

CHAPTER 10

IN THEIR OWN VOICES

A Mixed Methods Approach to Studying Outcomes of Intercultural Service-Learning With College Students

Peggy Fitch

ABSTRACT

Three studies are reported in this chapter. Sample sizes range from 10 to 14. Each study uses a combination of quantitative measures (e.g., Hammer & Bennett's Intercultural Development Inventory, 2001; McConahay's Modern Racism Scale, 1986; and self-reporting scales) and qualitative measures (open-ended responses and interviews) to assess outcomes of intercultural service-learning experiences on college students at two small liberal arts colleges and to identify some best practices for designing and implementing such experiences. Results indicate that an intensive short-term experience (Study 1) can be as effective as a semester-long experience (Study 3) and that reflection and training to prepare students for the intercultural experience play essential roles.

Improving Service-Learning Practice: Research on Models to Enhance Impacts, pages 187–211
Copyright © 2005 by Information Age Publishing

INTRODUCTION

Chatterji (2004) contended that while quantitative experimental studies are considered the gold standard for valid assessment of educational programs, when used exclusively they can result in "poorly conceptualized 'black box' evaluation(s)" (p. 4) that do not examine the impact of variables specific to educational contexts. Like others (Burke Johnson & Onwuegbuzie, 2004; Gelmon, Furco, Holland, & Bringle, 2004), she advocated for the use of carefully designed mixed methods research that uses both quantitative and qualitative measures. Shumer (2002) argued that high-quality service-learning, by its nature, is a form of qualitative inquiry and calls for the inclusion of more qualitative approaches to studying its effects. A particular advantage of qualitative methods is the richness that can be gained from reporting students' reflections in their own words, as illustrated in Tilstra and Van Scheik's (1999) report of one college student's international service-learning experience.

The studies reported in this chapter build on prior quantitative (e.g., Fitch, 2004; Frazier, 1997; Myers-Lipton, 1996; O'Grady, 2000), qualitative (e.g., Boyle-Baise, 2002; O'Grady, 2000), and mixed methods (Rice & Brown, 1998) empirical research on the effects of service-learning on intercultural sensitivity and racial attitudes. In principle, well-designed intercultural service-learning experiences have the potential to promote intercultural development and improve racial understanding. Several scholars (Coles, 1999; O'Grady, 2000; Wade, 2000; Warren, 1998), however, offered cautions about the potential risks involved in such experiences, as well as proposed recommendations for designing them effectively.

THEORETICAL FOUNDATIONS

The line of research described in this chapter is grounded in two primary areas of theory: Allport's (1954) contact theory and Bennett's (1993) developmental model of intercultural sensitivity. Contact theory has implications for the design of intercultural service-learning experiences and the analysis of their outcomes. Bennett's model provides a way of describing and explaining the changes individuals experience during the course of intercultural encounters.

Contact Theory

Allport (1954) proposed certain conditions under which direct contact with others whose ethnic or racial group differed from one's own was most likely to reduce prejudice and negative stereotypes and to promote intercultural understanding. The theoretical basis for these conditions was derived from research in social psychology and learning, such as in-group/ out-group theory and conditioning, and was supported by empirical studies of the effects of integration in housing and the armed services. The most important conditions were that individuals should have equal status within the group and that group members should not compete, but should work cooperatively to achieve common goals. Moreover, the contact should be intimate rather than merely casual, permitting the formation of deeper acquaintances and providing opportunities to counteract stereotypes. Finally, contact should be sanctioned by institutions and cultural norms. Amir (1969) reviewed this research and explored the possibility of applying contact theory to guide changes that were being proposed in the Israeli educational system. On the basis of later research with college students in job training studies, Cook (1985) added a fifth condition: that contact should occur over a period of time rather than being a short-term or one-time experience.

Erickson and O'Connor (2000) applied contact theory as a theoretical framework to the analysis of service-learning experiences that are designed to reduce prejudice. They suggested that whether intercultural service-learning meets each condition posited by contact theory depends greatly on the particular context in which the experience occurs. For example, in a service-learning project that involves tutoring, the pursuit of a common goals condition may be met if the tutor's goals are inextricably tied to the successful achievement of the tutee's goals in a way that makes the two individuals interdependent. Moreover, the authors maintained that the tendency for individuals to engage in ego-defensive strategies that preserve their current attitudes makes it particularly difficult to meet the condition that contact challenges stereotypes. They asserted that service-learning experiences that do not meet all five conditions "may actually *increase* prejudice as individuals engage in more and more frequent ego-defensive strategies (the cognitive equivalent of digging in one's heels)" (p. 68).

O'Grady (2000) offered several caveats for careful attention to the design of multicultural service-learning experiences so they do not inadvertently reinforce stereotypes and cultural superiority. She listed McPherson and Kinsley's (cited in O'Grady, 2000) five challenges to educators wishing to integrate service-learning and multicultural education, some of which parallel those for contact theory (e.g., collaboration with community, not reinforcing stereotypes). O'Grady acknowledged that initially she was not favorable toward using service-learning in her multicultural education courses, which comprised predominantly white students, citing concerns that it "can too easily reinforce oppressive outcomes" and "perpetuate racist, sexist, or classist assumptions about others and reinforce a colonialist mentality of superiority" (p. 12). Eventually, however, she came to view the integration of service-learning and multicultural education as an essential vehicle for social justice and social change: "Without this context [multicultural education], programs may foster an attitude of paternalism on the part of the server and one of dependence on the part of those being served" (p. 12).

Development of Intercultural Sensitivity

A second major theory that forms the basis for this chapter comes from Bennett's (1993) six-stage model of intercultural sensitivity development that describes how an individual interprets and responds to cultural differences. As Fitch (2004) described in greater detail, the first three stages are ethnocentric (Denial, Defense, Minimization), while the last three are ethnorelative (Acceptance, Adaptation, Integration). Initially, individuals deny that cultural differences even exist. Then they defend their own culture as superior, though occasionally the dualism of defense results in a rejection of one's own culture. Next, cultural differences are minimized ("After all, we're all human"). Eventually they are accepted as legitimate through different frames of reference, and the individual learns how to adapt readily to them when crossing cultural boundaries. Finally, some internalize a truly bicultural or multicultural identity, though Bennett acknowledged that this stage is rare.

PURPOSE

The purpose of this chapter is to compare and contrast the results from three mixed methods, small-sample studies of the effects of service-learning experiences that provide intercultural contact on the development of college students' intercultural sensitivity. The primary research question is: What factors, such as length of contact, quality of contact, preparation for contact, and depth of reflection, contribute to the effectiveness of intercultural service-learning experiences? Specifically, under the right conditions can an intensive short-term experience be as effective as a long-term one? An explicit goal of this research was to examine the specific contexts in which intercultural service-learning occurred to identify some best practices and explore the implications of contact theory for the development of such experiences. As each study is discussed, the reader may benefit from referring to Exhibit 10.1 where certain features of the method for each are summarized.

Exhibit 10.1. Comparison of Course(s), Time Frame, and Measures

	Study 1 (N = 14)	Study 2 (N = 10)	Study 3 (N = 10)
Time Frame	3 weeks	3 weeks	15 weeks
Course	MLK Legacy of Servant Leadership	Cultural Awareness Experiential Module	Ethnic Encounters Child Development Intermediate Spanish
Measures			
Learning Objectives	post		
Service-Learning Project Survey	post		
Racism	pre and post		
Intercultural Development Inventory (IDI)	post	pre and post	pre and post
Interviews	post	post	post

STUDY 1: METHOD

Participants

Study 1 included 14 students at a private, liberal arts college located in a small town in Iowa who were enrolled in a January-term course on servant-leadership and the legacy of Dr. Martin Luther King, Jr. The group was divided equally by gender. One student was from Africa and the remainder identified themselves as European American. The age range was 18 to 28 years and the mean age was 21.36 (SD = 2.65). There were more upper-level than lower-level students (1 first-year, 3 sophomores, 4 juniors, 5 seniors).

The Course

"Dream the Dream: Servant-Leadership and the Legacy of Dr. Martin Luther King, Jr." was a 3-week course offered during January 2001. A team of four individuals designed and facilitated the course:

- An assistant professor of religion/director of service-learning;
- The director of community service and internships;
- The director of student activities; and
- The director of intercultural programs.

The course included readings about King and about service, as well as a service-learning project with the local schools and an extended field trip to the King Center in Atlanta. The development of cultural awareness was explicitly integrated into the course as reflected in specific objectives in the syllabus: "developing your familiarity with... diversity" and "appreciation of difference and 'otherness,'" including racial/ethnic and economic otherness.

Service-Learning

Both local and national service-learning projects were integrated into the course. Students who were enrolled in an extended-day school program attended the middle school in Storm Lake. They were mentored by the college students. Their primary goal was to work together to develop educational programs that were performed in all the elementary schools to celebrate the Martin Luther King holiday. A program handbook was printed in both Spanish and English, a fact that reflected the growing population of primarily Latino/a and Hispanic families who had joined the community.

Beyond the community, the students enrolled in the course took a 5-day trip to Atlanta to participate in the Martin Luther King, Jr. (MLK) Service Summit, a 3-day conference including workshops, speakers, an art festival, and faith-based events that culminated in a national day of service. On this day students participated in at least one of two projects: seven students joined the East Point Community Action Team to clean up and paint a community center, and all of the students except one served food and distributed clothing at a local shelter.

Reflection Opportunities

Students reflected daily on the readings and their experiences through group discussions and journaling. Their daily journals, according to the syllabus, were "more than just a summary" and were included in a portfolio that included scrapbook-type artifacts, accompanied by explanations about why the artifacts were important, and creative expressions such as poetry and drawings. Portfolios concluded with a written manifesto that integrated their experiences, feelings, and insights with reflections about the course material, their vision of servant-leadership, and their understanding of Dr. King's legacy.

Training/Preparation for Intercultural Service-Learning

Approximately 7 hours of structured training time was integrated into the course to prepare students for mentoring the children, for intercultural service-learning both in Storm Lake and Atlanta, and for the challenges they were likely to experience from the course material and discussions. A majority of the training was led by the director of intercultural programs and included a variety of strategies such as role-plays, decision-making situations, listening exercises, resources on white identity development, examination of power/dominance issues, and audio-visual presentations. In his interview he reported that training became an ongoing dialogue, extending well beyond the formal sessions into class discussions and informal interactions. He acknowledged that presenting a balance of images is extremely important and difficult to do at times. When students were in Atlanta for the MLK Service Summit, he arranged for them to see both Morehouse and Spelman Colleges, as well as poverty areas in the city.

Measures

Questionnaire

At the beginning and end of the course, students completed written questionnaires. The pre-test included three open-ended questions about why they enrolled in the course, what they expected or hoped to learn, and which aspects of the course they thought would be most challenging for them, as well as forced-choice items about demographics (age, sex, year in school, racial/ethnic background, major) and prior service experience. The questionnaire required 20–30 minutes to complete. A Learning Objectives scale assessed students' perceptions of how well the college courses they had taken to date had achieved a series of 35 objectives. For example, students rated their agreement on a 6-point scale (1 = strongly disagree, 6 = strongly agree) with learning objectives such as "experience the cultural diversity that exists in the United States," and "develop a richer understanding of the community in which I live." These 35 items were collapsed into five subscales based on conceptual relatedness and intercorrelations among the items: diversity (8 items), social responsibility (5 items), civic awareness/engagement (7 items), self-awareness (8 items), and connections between classroom and life (7 items).

The pre-test also included McConahay's (1986) Modern Racism Scale, which was labeled "Social Attitudes Scale" on the questionnaires. Participants rated their level of agreement with seven statements on a 5-point scale where 1 = strongly disagree and 5 = strongly agree (e.g., "Discrimination against Blacks is no longer a problem in the United States"); and two statements on a 4-point scale where 1 = none and 4 = many (e.g., "How many Black people in Iowa do you think miss out on jobs or promotions because of racial discrimination?"). Scores ranged from 9 to 43. Higher scores indicated more racist attitudes.

The post-test included open-ended questions parallel to those on the pre-test for students to discuss what they learned in the course and what was most challenging, as well as post-test versions of the Learning Objectives scale, to rate the course they had just completed, and the Modern Racism Scale. The Service-Learning Project Survey assessed the amount of time spent in the service-learning project (how many weeks and how many hours per week) and asked students to identify the primary focus of their role in the service-learning project by checking all that applied from the following five options:

1. Direct involvement with people served by the agency (e.g., tutor, coach, visit);
2. Special project for group (e.g., brochure or fundraiser);
3. Indirect service (e.g., clerical, physical labor, transport);
4. Supervise other volunteers/manage program; and
5. Create/plan/organize new program.

The service-learning project survey also included 32 items adapted from prior studies (Eyler & Giles, 1999; Steinke, Fitch, Johnson, & Waldstein, 2002) to assess students' perceptions of their service-learning experiences. Students rated either their agreement (1 = strongly disagree, 5 = strongly agree) with a particular statement such as "the experience challenged my previous opinions"; or how frequently (1 = never, 5 = very often) a particular activity took place, for example, "related the project to what we were learning in class." The items were combined into subscales to assess five specific aspects that had been previously identified as predictors of effective service-learning experiences in prior research (Eyler & Giles, 1999; Steinke et al., 2002):

1. Quality of placement (7 items);
2. Student voice (4 items);
3. Diversity (5 items);
4. Community engagement (5 items); and
5. Reflection (11 items).

The post-test also included Hammer and Bennett's (2001) Intercultural Development Inventory (IDI), which measured the development of an individual's perceptions about, and responses to, people from other cultures and was based on Bennett's (1993) Developmental Model of Intercultural Sensitivity. It comprised six subscales of 10 items each (60 items total). Participants rated their level of agreement with each item on a 7-point scale (1 = strongly disagree to 7 = strongly agree). Ratings were averaged for each subscale, thus scores ranged from 1 to 7. The subscales were combined into three broad stages: Denial/Defense, Minimization, and Acceptance/Adaptation (Cognitive and Behavioral). Sample items are shown in Exhibit 10.2.

Exhibit 10.2. Intercultural Development Inventory Sample Items

Stage	Items
Denial	I do not like to be around people who look like they are from other cultures.
Defense	My culture is closer to being perfect than most other cultures in the world.
Minimization	All people are basically the same.
Acceptance	People should not describe culture as superior or inferior.
Cognitive Adaptation	I use different cultural criteria for interpreting and evaluating situations.
Behavioral Adaptation	Although I feel I am a member of my own culture, I am nearly as comfortable in one or more other cultures.

As reported in the IDI manual (Hammer & Bennett, 2001), the subscales demonstrate high internal reliability (coefficient alpha range = .80 to .91) and good construct validity as measured by significant correlations in predicted directions with the Worldmindedness Scale (i.e., negative with Denial, Defense, and Minimization; positive with Acceptance and both Adaptation subscales) and the Intercultural Anxiety Scale (i.e., positive with Denial and Defense; negative with Minimization, Acceptance, and both Adaptation subscales).

Interviews

One-on-one interviews were conducted with each of the four facilitators, as well as the community partner who coordinated the extended-day school program for middle school students in the town. Time constraints did not permit individual interviews with students. Instead the investigator attended the final class period, listened, and took notes as students reflected on their experiences over the last 3 weeks.

Interviews were semi-structured and audiotaped, with permission from the interviewees. Time for each interview ranged from 20–45 minutes and was determined by the interviewee's schedule and amount of elaboration. The purpose of the interviews was to garner a richer description of the course than could be gleaned from paper-and-pencil measures and to hear reflections about the experience from the facilitators and community partners in their own words.

Procedure

In compliance with the American Psychological Association's ethical standards, students signed an informed consent agreement. As an incentive to participate, individual students had a chance to win $25 if they completed both the pre-test and the post-test. In addition, the class was awarded $50 and asked to decide together how to use this money to benefit their community partner.

The investigator traveled to Storm Lake twice during the study. On the first day of the course she met the students, invited them to participate, and administered the consent agreement and pre-test. Following this class session, the investigator went with the students and co-facilitators to their local service-learning site and observed as the college and middle school students met and got acquainted. Subsequently, the students met together on four occasions for a total of about 8 hours to collaborate on the development of educational outreach assemblies for the elementary schools to celebrate the birthday of Martin Luther King, Jr.

Nineteen days later the investigator returned to Storm Lake for the last 2 days of the course. The first day she attended four of the five school assemblies. The next day she collected the written post-test data, conducted interviews with the co-facilitators and community partner representative, and listened to students' final processing of their experiences in the course.

STUDY 1: RESULTS

Quantitative Analyses

Quantitative outcomes were assessed by comparing students' pre-test and post-test responses on the Modern Racism Scale (McConahay, 1986) and Learning Objectives subscales, as well as examining their self-report of items on the Service-Learning Project Survey and the pattern of responses on Hammer and Bennett's (2001) Intercultural Development Inventory (IDI). The latter two measures were assessed at post-test only. Because the sample size was small, pre/post difference scores on the Modern Racism Scale and Learning Objectives subscales were examined for normality using stem-and-leaf plots and histograms, and descriptive statistics were calculated. The Learning Objectives subscale pre/post differences were generally normally distributed. Pre- and post-racism scores were fairly normally distributed, though the distribution of difference scores on this measure showed two outliers. Given that the skewness-to-standard error ratios were less than 2.0, the data were continuous measures rather than simple change scores, and the sample size was too small to use the nonparametric Sign Test reliably (Gravetter & Wallnau, 2004), a decision was made to use a one-tailed paired *t*-test with an alpha of .05.

Racism

One participant was excluded from this analysis because of incomplete answers on the pre-test. Of the 13 remaining students, eight decreased in racism, three increased, and two demonstrated no change. The mean difference overall was statistically significant, $t(12) = -1.79$, $p < .05$ (one-tailed), $d = .50$, (pre-test $M = 13.85$, $SD = 4.10$; post-test $M = 16.08$, $SD = 4.97$).

Learning Objectives

One-tailed paired *t* tests using an alpha level of .01 after applying Bonferroni's correction (.05/5 tests) were used to analyze pre/post differences in the learning objective subscales. Three of the five subscales (Diversity, Civic Awareness/Engagement, and Social Responsibility) indicated changes in the predicted direction that exceeded the .01 alpha level (see Exhibit 10.3).

Exhibit 10.3. Study 1: Pre/Post Differences on Learning Objectives (N = 14)

Subscale	Pre-Test		Post-Test		*t* (one-tailed)	*d*
	M	*SD*	*M*	*SD*	*df = 13*	
Diversity	3.61	1.19	5.45	.36	5.56***	1.48
Civic Awareness/Engagement	3.97	.86	5.03	.64	4.45***	1.19
Social Responsibility	4.06	1.04	5.13	.75	3.78**	1.01
Self-Awareness	4.64	.99	5.21	.40	2.39	.64
Connection between Classroom and Life	4.61	.91	4.95	.80	1.37	.37

** $p < .01$, *** $p < .001$

Service-Learning Project Survey

Administered at post-test only, this measure elicited students' ratings of themselves, the service-learning projects, and the course on 5-point scales. Items with means greater than 4 (agree or fairly often) are shown in Exhibit 10.4. In general, students reported that the service-learning project and course contributed to their cultural awareness and community engagement and gave them opportunities to work with people who are different from themselves and to reflect on their experience.

Exhibit 10.4.   Study 1

Service-Learning Project Survey Items Rated "Agree/Fairly Often" or "Strongly Agree/Very Often" on the Post-test

Reflection:

- Discussed the project with other students in class.
- Kept a journal about my project.
- Discussed the project with other students outside of class.
- Discussions focused on sharing feelings and reactions.
- Related the project to what we were learning in class.
- Faculty responded to my writing about the project.

Quality of Placement:

- Did things myself instead of just observing.

Community Engagement:

- I feel I made a real contribution.
- The project met needs identified by members of the community.
- I believe I did *not* make a positive impact on the community. (reverse coded)

Diversity:

- The project served people from diverse racial/ethnic backgrounds.
- I learned to appreciate different cultures more.
- By the end, I felt comfortable working with this community.
- Interacted with people from diverse backgrounds.

Student Voice:

- I was *not* free to develop or use my own ideas. (reverse coded)
- I was *not* very interested in doing this project. (reverse coded)

Note. Items included in the table had mean ratings 4 or higher (Agree/Fairly Often or Strongly Agree/Very Often), except for reverse-coded items, which had mean ratings of 2 or lower (Disagree/Once in a Great While or Strongly Disagree/Never).

Intercultural Development Inventory (IDI)

The IDI was given at post-test only. Mean scores on each subscale can range from 1 to 7. The profile of participants' responses on this measure indicated that by the end of the course they demonstrated relatively low levels of Denial/Defensiveness ($M = 1.88$, $SD = .62$) and relatively high levels of Minimization ($M = 4.58$, $SD = .81$) and Acceptance/Adaptation ($M = 4.84$, $SD = .62$), consistent with what was expected.

Qualitative Analyses

Interviews in Study 1 were used primarily as a rich source of description about the course and to verify patterns found in the quantitative analyses. This was the second time the faculty member had taught the course, and he said the retreat was essential for team-building. He considered the retreat and the planning time for the school assemblies major aspects of the course's success. The addition of the trip to Atlanta also contributed immensely to students' experience, although he wished they could have had more time there. Next time he would offer more specific guidelines about how to write the daily journal and might consider using other texts that go beyond stories to pose more substantive questions. The concluding manifesto worked extremely well, and he said he would use this assignment again.

The director of intercultural programs who conducted the training was generally satisfied with the quality of the dialogue that was created throughout the course. He saw substantial openness in some students, which supports the findings from the Modern Racism Scale, but realized that he was unable to reach other students. He believed his effectiveness as a trainer came from the variety of methods he used, his attempts to balance the positive and negative exposures they received in Atlanta (though he was not entirely satisfied that he had achieved this objective), and his inclusion of material about issues of power, privilege, and dominance. His personal stories became a powerful tool for challenging some students' perspectives.

The community partner reported that the service-learning project to develop school outreach assemblies for MLK Day definitely met the organization's needs. She worked collaboratively with the other course facilitators to match children with mentors and was very satisfied with the outcomes. A few students had been in the program the prior year and had demonstrated greater leadership and engagement this year. She saw better behavior and responsibility from many of them and valued the opportunities for children to be exposed to higher education as a potential goal.

Nearly all of the college students reported substantial positive changes in their perspective as a result of the course (e.g., "life-changing"; "more aware of myself"; "what I have learned will show up in the legacy I leave behind"), and several cited the service-learning components in particular (e.g., "the mentoring experience ... got into it"; "learning about my mentee and her family"; "realized they [middle school students] have some of the same problems as us"). The trip to Atlanta was "a big eye-opener" for most, as were the discussions with the director of intercultural programs and "being open to what he had to say." The student from Africa said this was the first time at college that she "really felt part of a class." A few students were more cautious in their self-assessments. One said she was focusing on her awareness of diversity and realized she does not "really know much, but it's a place to start." Another reported that the course provided a reality check because "we're secluded here in northwest Iowa and can live in ignorance thinking everything is fine." She said she is somewhat bitter in her manifesto; she realizes she needs to do something, but she is not sure what: "Can't someone else do this?" Overall, much gained had to do with the quality and intensity of the relationships they developed, even over this short period of time.

STUDY 2: METHOD

Participants

Study 2 included 10 students (6 female, 4 male) from a second private liberal arts college located in a different small town in Iowa who participated in a January-term service-learning module in Tucson, Arizona. All were European American except one, who had come to the United States from Vietnam at age 12. All reported that their current hometown was in Iowa. All were traditional college age (18 to 22 years); there were two first-year students, three sophomores, and five juniors.

The Course

The Experiential Module (CRCL 383) is a two-semester-hour course offered through the cross-cultural division and designed to meet the college's liberal arts core requirement of experiential learning for cultural awareness. To receive credit for this core requirement, students must have at least 15 hours of intercultural contact and engage in some type of formal reflection opportunity such as a paper, presentation, journal, or project as well as ongoing discussion with the module supervisor. The module is flexible and may be taken during a semester or during a time outside of the semester such as January, fall or spring break, or summer. The content varies depending on how the student and faculty design the experience; thus, the module functions as an independent study in intercultural learning.

This particular module was offered in Tucson, Arizona, for 3 weeks in January 2002. It was developed by the director of community-based learning (the administrator responsible for working with faculty to coordinate service-learning experiences), who worked with one of the college's trustees to arrange a variety of opportunities for students to have intercultural contact in Tucson. A professor in the English department also accompanied the group. No readings were required before the students went to Tucson. Opportunities for intercultural contact came from service-learning activities (described below), interacting with community members at a meeting to discuss a "livable wage" proposal, and a day trip to Nogales, Mexico.

Service-Learning

Two of the four opportunities for intercultural contact can legitimately be defined as service-learning because the students worked collaboratively with people in the community to accomplish goals that had been identified by the agency. All students helped daily in an after-school program for exceptional children from diverse ethnic backgrounds (non-Hispanic White, Hispanic American, Mexican, African American). In addition, six of the ten assisted at a local soup kitchen by packaging and distributing bags of food.

The other two opportunities for intercultural contact did not involve service-learning. The four students who did not help at the soup kitchen instead attended a city council meeting where a "livable wage" proposal was considered for adoption, and they interacted with community members after the meeting. All students went on the day trip to Nogales where they shopped and dined at the downtown market. While it could be argued that these were valuable learning experiences for students, they were still simply observational.

Reflection Opportunities

Eight of the ten students were enrolled in the service-learning module to earn their experiential credit and wrote a daily journal. All but two reported using the journal primarily to describe or document what they did; the other two students explicitly reported using the journal for deeper reflection. Two students were required by their on-campus faculty supervisors to write a chapter after they returned. One student wrote poetry while on the trip and put it together in a book after he returned. All students reported participating in a limited amount of informal discussion with peers about their experiences. Five who were taking the module for credit also participated in a few group discussions with the staff and/or faculty who accompanied them; three reported these discussions as extensive and valuable. The two students who were not enrolled in the module participated in the service-learning projects, although they did not engage in the written reflection activities or in any of the group reflection sessions.

Training/Preparation for Intercultural Service-Learning

No formal training was offered to prepare students for their intercultural service-learning experiences. In preparation for the shopping trip to Nogales, the trustee who facilitated some of their activities told students what to expect and offered them some advice about safety and how to bargain with merchants.

Measures

Questionnaire

Participants completed the IDI before and after their trip to Tucson.

Interviews

After the students returned to campus, they were interviewed individually. These interviews lasted 45 minutes to one hour and, with participants' permission, were audiotaped for later transcription. Interview topics are listed in Exhibit 10.5. Because the interview was semi-structured, not all questions were asked in exactly the way or in the order that appears in the table.

Exhibit 10.5.   Interview Questions

- What did you do in your intercultural experience and with whom? How connected did you feel to this community? How comfortable do you feel now?

- What training did you receive to prepare you for this experience? What was most helpful?

- What were the most valuable assignments or learning experiences?

- What written and oral reflection activities were included in the course?

- What were some important cultural similarities and differences you encountered during your experience? How did you respond to these similarities and/or differences? In particular, did you encounter any beliefs and values that differed significantly from your own?

- How have you changed as a result of this intercultural experience? What have you learned about yourself? About others?

Procedure

Students read and signed an informed consent agreement and were compensated $20 for their time and effort ($5 for the pre-IDI; $15 for the post-IDI and interview). Students were also asked to share some of their written assignments. Pre-test IDIs were collected the day before students left for Tucson. Within a month or so after returning from Tucson, students completed post-test IDIs and were interviewed. Interviews were transcribed by an undergraduate research assistant who was instructed about maintaining confidentiality of participants' responses.

STUDY 2: RESULTS

Quantitative Analyses

Examinations of stem-and-leaf plots, histograms, and descriptive statistics for pre/post difference scores on the three IDI stages revealed normal distributions and skewness ratios well below 2, so one-tailed paired t tests were used to assess changes in intercultural sensitivity. Bonferroni's correction was applied ($.05/3$), which reduced the alpha level to .017. As shown in Exhibit 10.6, none of these t tests were significant at $p < .017$, though means were in the expected directions (i.e., decrease in Denial/Defense; increases in Minimization and Acceptance/Adaptation).

Exhibit 10.6. Pre/Post Differences in Intercultural Sensitivity (IDI Scores)

Study	Subscale	Pre-Test		Post-Test		t (one-tailed)	
		M	SD	M	SD	$df = 9$	d
Study 1 ($N = 14$)	Denial/Defense			1.88	.62		
	Minimization			4.58	.81		
	Acceptance/Adaptation			4.84	.62		
Study 2 ($N = 10$)	Denial/Defense	2.27	.90	2.15	.61	-.77	.24
	Minimization	4.74	.81	5.04	.77	.89	.28
	Acceptance/Adaptation	4.70	.79	5.03	.69	2.23	.70
Study 3 ($N = 10$)	Denial/Defense	2.21	1.00	1.81	.63	-2.47[**]	.78
	Minimization	4.42	.62	4.90	.98	2.11	.66
	Acceptance/Adaptation	5.08	.64	5.64	.45	2.94[**]	.93

[**] $p < .01$

Qualitative Analyses

Interviews were coded by the author for themes related to the major questions and were used for rich description and to corroborate the quantitative analyses. With a few exceptions, Study 2 participants' reflections on their experience were fairly simplistic. Connections with the community were rarely mentioned, with the exception of those who had attended the "livable wage" hearing who emphasized the importance of hearing people's stories firsthand. Most did not report finding very many significant cultural differences except during the shopping trip to Nogales. In general, those who attended the after-school program for exceptional children perceived these kids as "a lot like kids we know at home," though they were surprised at how smart, polite, and respectful they were. Most commonly students reported intellectual, spiritual, or ethical insights such as having their "savior" self-image challenged:

> You have this impression in your mind that you're going there to help these people, like you're going to change their lives. But I don't think that's what they really need and I don't think that's what they want. It kind of strikes you that they don't really need you in that way. They just want you to be there and be friends or help out a little bit. It's not that you are dramatically changing their lives.

STUDY 3: METHOD

Participants

Study 3 included 10 students (8 females, 2 males) from the same institution as Study 2. All were European American, from hometowns in Iowa, and of traditional age (5 first-year students, 2 sophomores, 2 juniors, 1 senior).

The Courses

Participants were enrolled in 2002 spring semester courses in anthropology (ANTH 366, Ethnographic Field Methods), intermediate Spanish (SPAN 222), or psychology (PSYC 382, Child and Adolescent Development). All 10 were enrolled in these courses in part to fulfill their cultural awareness experiential core requirement.

Service-Learning

All service-learning experiences for Study 3 took place in Iowa. For the anthropology course, two students interviewed residents of Perry, Iowa, for the Hometown Oral History Project to document perceptions of changes in the community as a result of increased immigration; one conducted these interviews in Spanish, and the other conducted them in English. Six students in intermediate Spanish were involved with the Latino/a community, either through St. Mary's Catholic Church in Ottumwa; Hispanic Educational Resources (HER) in Des Moines; or three public schools: one elementary, one middle, and one high school. At St. Mary's and the schools, the students' role was to help the individuals learn English and to assist children with their schoolwork. At HER, students either assisted in the preschool or helped clients with limited English prepare to file their tax returns. The two psychology students helped in the after-school program offered at the Willkie House in Des Moines, which serves primarily African-American children from the local area. They had actually begun this experience during the fall 2001 semester as part of the requirements for the child and adolescent development course and elected to continue their involvement through an experiential module in the spring.

Reflection Opportunities

Students in Ethnographic Field Methods transcribed and "cleaned up" their interviews and wrote a final chapter where they reflected on the process of collaborating in the oral history project. They also had frequent discussions with each other both in class and outside of class, as well as with the professor who advised them closely throughout the project. For students in intermediate Spanish, integration with course material included five chapters written in Spanish and an oral proposal conducted in Spanish and delivered to the class members who functioned as a hypothetical council with funds to dispense to the agency or community with whom the student worked. The psychology students wrote biweekly journals where they connected their service-learning experience to the course material and reflected on the implications of what they were learning. They also met biweekly with the professor to discuss their service-learning experiences. Reflection through informal discussion occurred between the students as they traveled together to their site each week.

Training/Preparation for Intercultural Service-Learning

Most of the preparation for service-learning experiences came though the course content, although some sites offered a brief orientation. Anthropology students read books about conducting ethnographic research using an emic approach. They also took a tour of Perry and read articles about the town. Faculty in charge of the project modeled how to conduct an interview. Students in the Spanish class learned the language, studied aspects of Latino culture, and read about immigration issues. Besides the course content about child development and specific topics related to culture, the psychology students were asked to read books and articles that would help them to learn more about African American children and families and to journal about them.

Procedure

The procedure was identical to that in Study 2, except that interviews were held during the last week of classes and final exam week.

STUDY 3: RESULTS

Quantitative Analyses

Analyses of the IDI subscale scores were identical to those conducted in Study 2. As shown in Exhibit 10.6, over the semester students decreased in Denial/Defense subscale score and increased subscale score in Acceptance/Adaptation, both p-values < .01.

Qualitative Analyses

Analyses of interviews were conducted in the same manner as those for Study 2. As predicted, participants' responses were generally richer and analysis more complex than was the case for those who went on the short-term service-learning experience in Tucson. Many more reported feeling connected to the community, as illustrated by the following quote.

> I'm ten times more comfortable now than I was at the beginning. I was extremely uncomfortable when I first went just for the fact that I hadn't had any contact with the African American community. I was really nervous and unsure of myself, but I think now I feel like I have a lot of bonds built with the children and the adults. They are as close to me as most of my nieces and nephews are.

More of their prior expectations and stereotypes were challenged. For example, the African American children at Willkie House were more affectionate and caring than they expected, and Latino/a immigrants in Ottumwa and Perry were middle class, whereas they expected them to be poor. They also typically assumed that people from other countries want to live in the United States.

> You think America is the land of opportunity, but it's not for everybody. . . . A lot of people look at immigrants as coming in and taking their jobs and

trying to take all of the American resources, but this woman didn't want to be here and that was interesting for me.... I never think about people not wanting to be in America, so I think I learned a lot from her and I would like to spend more time with her because I think I could learn a lot more.

Finally, they identified more significant things they had learned about themselves or ways they had changed. They developed more patience for immigrants and for people whose first language is not English. They learned not to judge people by their appearances. They anticipated changing not just their attitudes, but their behavior as well.

I really realized the importance of mixing with other cultures, and I wish more people would get to.... I think in the future, even as I go home there are a lot of Latino families that come to the place where I work and I think I'm going to be more open to say if you need any help, just call.

Several students also said that the experience had confirmed a career focus for them such as using their Spanish to work with people and entering a service profession.

DISCUSSION

This chapter reports on the results of two short-term service-learning experiences, one intensive (Study 1) and one considerably less so (Study 2), as well as semester-long service-learning courses (Study 3). Both quantitative and qualitative measures showed positive changes in student outcomes as a function of intercultural service-learning experiences; however, these changes were greatest for students in either the short-term intensive (Study 1) or semester-long (Study 3) service-learning experiences. As predicted, students in Study 1 decreased in racism, and students in Study 3 decreased in Denial/Defense and increased in Acceptance/Adaptation. The courses examined for both of these studies incorporated more reflection and preparation for the intercultural aspects of the service-learning experiences than did the course in Study 2, where students demonstrated minimal changes in predicted directions.

These results are also consistent with what contact theory would predict. It is useful initially to control the length of contact time by comparing Studies 1 and 2, both of which were short-term courses. For the most part, Study 1 met three or four of the five conditions proposed, whereas Study 2 met only one. For example, the intimacy of the intercultural contact for students in Study 1 (with the director of intercultural programs, as well as the Latino/a children they mentored) was significantly greater than that for students in Study 2 where the contact (a few days at the food shelter or attendance at a city council meeting, and a shopping trip to a border town) was largely superficial. The quality of contact experienced in Study 1 was also more likely to challenge stereotypes, whereas the contact in Study 2 was more likely to reinforce them. The pursuit of common goals was much greater in Study 1 where the college students worked together with the middle school children to develop MLK programs for the elementary schools. The intercultural service-learning projects in Study 2 involved contact with groups of lower status individuals (children, people who were homeless) than the participants, whereas intercultural contact in Study 1 was with one group of lower status (children) and with other adults of equal or higher status than the participants (director of intercultural programs, college and community leaders in Atlanta). Both studies met the condition that intercultural contact was sanctioned by authorities and social norms.

The semester-long service-learning projects in Study 3 often met all five contact theory conditions. With respect to the equal status condition, though the psychology students were working with children most of the time, they reported in their interviews that the most valuable experience was when they spent time with the adults. Both anthropology and Spanish students reported that the Latino/a immigrants with whom they worked were middle class, like them.

The mixed methods, small sample approach used for the three studies was both a strength and a limitation. It enabled the author to examine the context of the service-learning experiences and their potential impacts in greater depth than would be allowed with larger samples and added richness beyond the mean scores reflected in the quantitative measures. Given that students were not randomly assigned to courses or service-learning experiences, however, the usual cautions about selection bias apply. In this particular set of studies the author was willing to trade off the ability to make clear causal inferences for the opportunity to hear in students' own words the meaning they made from their intercultural service-learning experiences.

Implications for best practices for designing intercultural service-learning experiences are suggested by contact theory and were confirmed through the interviews. Among these were the variety of reflection activities used in Studies 1 and 3 that required students' analysis of these relationships in ways that countered stereotypes, and the power of stories to transform cultural awareness and sensitivity. Also the confirmation that intercultural service-learning experiences with children are easier for white middle-class students than those with adults, but the gain is limited by their inherently higher status due to age. Knowing this, it would be important to design such service-learning experiences so students have opportunities to interact regularly and collaboratively with adults in the setting as well.

Central to the focus of this chapter is the need for optimal training before and during intercultural contact, alhough as one student suggested, perhaps they cannot be completely prepared for these intercultural experiences: "I don't think you can prepare yourself for it. I think you just have to go enmesh yourself with the culture and see what you see.... Just by reading you can't understand ... I mean, you can learn a lot from a book, but you're not going to learn the same thing."

To attempt to do so might actually detract from the power of the experience and the student's own meaning-making. That said, however, it seems that more could be done to prepare students to get the most from service-learning experiences in particular by challenging their prior expectations about being a "savior" and helping them understand the collaborative nature of the service-learning relationship, which is precisely O'Grady's (2000) concern. Indeed, the students did not tend to see that a primary goal of these experiences was to help them develop intercultural sensitivity and competence. More explicit integration of principles of multicultural education as O'Grady suggested may help bridge this gap, for example, by developing specific reflection strategies that focus on issues of power and privilege.

Erickson and O'Connor (2000) contended that for intercultural service-learning experiences to reduce rather than reinforce prejudice, all five conditions proposed by contact theory must be present. At the same time, Pettigrew (2004) argued that intercultural contact by itself can have positive effects and that the minimal conditions proposed by contact theory "facilitate the reduction of prejudice but are not essential" (p. 525). He based this conclusion on the results of a meta-analysis that has been submitted for publication (cited in Pettigrew, 2004). The opposing assertions of these authors suggest that a valuable area for future research would be to analyze a variety of intercultural service-learning experiences for how well they meet contact theory's five conditions and how well each condition predicts the development of intercultural sensitivity, among other outcomes.

ACKNOWLEDGMENTS

The author wishes to acknowledge the contributions of the following groups and individuals: Iowa College Foundation and Carver Trust Fund for financial support for this project; research assistant Samantha Smith; statistical consultant Jim Schulze; library staff member Jane Friedman; facilitators of the MLK, Jr. course: Maggie Baker, Chris Johnson, Nichol

Kleespies, and Leon Williams, and their students at Buena Vista University; the faculty and students at Central College who gave generously of their time.

REFERENCES

Allport, G. (1954). *The nature of prejudice.* Cambridge, MA: Addison-Wesley.

Amir, Y. (1969). Contact hypothesis in ethnic relations. *Psychological Bulletin, 106,* 74–106.

Bennett, M. J. (1993). Towards ethnorelativism: A developmental model of intercultural sensitivity. In R. M. Paige (Ed.), *Education for the intercultural experience* (2nd ed., pp. 21–71), Yarmouth, ME: Intercultural Press.

Boyle-Baise, M. (2002). *Multicultural service learning: Educating teachers in diverse communities.* New York: Teachers College Press.

Burke Johnson, R., & Onwuegbuzie, A. J. (2004). Mixed methods research: A research paradigm whose time has come. *Educational Researcher, 33*(7), 14–26.

Chatterji, M. (2004). Evidence on "what works": An argument for extended-term mixed-method (ETMM) evaluation designs. *Educational Researcher, 33*(9), 3–13.

Coles, R. (1993). *The call of service: A witness to idealism.* Boston: Houghton Mifflin.

Coles, R. (1999). Race focused service-learning courses: Issues and recommendations. *Michigan Journal of Community Service Learning, 6,* 97–105.

Cook, S. (1985). Experimenting on social issues: The case of social desegregation. *American Psychologist, 40,* 452–460.

Erickson, J. A., & O'Connor, S. E. (2000). Service-learning: Does it promote or reduce prejudice? In C. R. O'Grady (Ed.), *Integrating service-learning and multicultural education in colleges and universities* (pp. 59–70). Mahwah, NJ: Lawrence Erlbaum Associates.

Eyler, J., & Giles, D. E. (1999). *Where's the learning in service-learning?* San Francisco: Jossey-Bass.

Fitch, P. (2004). Effects of intercultural service-learning experiences on intellectual development and intercultural sensitivity. In S. Billig & M. Welch (Eds.), *Advances in service-learning research: Vol. 4. New perspectives in service-learning: Research to advance the field* (pp. 107–126). Greenwich, CT: Information Age Publishing.

Frazier, D. (1997, Fall). A multicultural reading and writing experience: Read aloud as service-learning in English class. *Michigan Journal of Community Service Learning,* pp. 98–103.

Gelmon, S., Furco, A., Holland, B., & Bringle, R. (2004, October). *Beyond anecdote: Challenges in bringing rigor to service-learning research.* Presentation at the 4th Annual International Conference on Service-Learning Research, Greenville, SC.

Gravetter, F. J., & Wallnau, L. B. (2004). *Statistics for the behavioral sciences* (6th ed.). Belmont, CA: Wadsworth.

Hammer, M. R., & Bennett, M. J. (2001). *Intercultural Development Inventory (IDI) manual.* Portland, OR: Intercultural Communication Institute.

McConahay, J. B. (1986). Modern racism, ambivalence, and the Modern Racism Scale. In J. F. Dovidio & S. L. Gaertner (Eds.), *Prejudice, discrimination and racism* (pp. 91–125). San Diego, CA: Academic Press.

Myers-Lipton, S. J. (1996, Fall). Effect of a comprehensive service-learning program on college students' level of modern racism. *Michigan Journal of Community Service Learning*, pp. 44–54.

O'Grady, C. R. (2000). Integrating service-learning and multicultural education: An overview. In C. R. O'Grady (Ed.), *Integrating service-learning and multicultural education in colleges and universities* (pp. 1–19). Mahwah, NJ: Lawrence Erlbaum Associates.

Pettigrew, T. F. (2004). Justice deferred: A half-century after *Brown v. Board of Education. American Psychologist, 59*(6), 521–529.

Rice, K. L., & Brown, J. R. (1998). Transforming educational curriculum and service learning. *The Journal of Experiential Education, 21*(3), 140–146.

Shumer, R. (2002). Service-learning as qualitative research: Creating curriculum from inquiry. In A. Furco & S. H. Billig (Eds.), *Advances in service-learning research: Vol. 1. Service-learning: The essence of the pedagogy* (pp. 183–197). Greenwich, CT: Information Age Publishing.

Steinke, P., Fitch, P., Johnson, C., & Waldstein, F. (2002). An interdisciplinary study of service-learning predictors and outcomes among college students. In S. H. Billig & A. Furco (Eds.), *Advances in service-learning research: Vol. 2. Service-learning through a multidisciplinary lens* (pp. 171–194). Greenwich, CT: Information Age Publishing.

Tilstra, T., & Van Scheik, W. (1999). Coupling experiential education with practical service involvement. *Journal of Experiential Education, 22*(1), 54–56.

Wade, R. C. (2000). Service-learning for multicultural teaching competency: Insights from the literature for teacher educators. *Equity and Excellence in Education, 33*(3), 21–29.

Warren, K. (1998). Educating students for social justice in service learning. *The Journal of Experiential Education, 21*(3), 134–139.

Section IV

FUTURE DIRECTIONS

CHAPTER 11

THE INTERNATIONAL K–H SERVICE-LEARNING RESEARCH ASSOCIATION

A Call to Action

Shelley H. Billig

ABSTRACT

This chapter addresses the prospect of forming a professional association for the service-learning research community. The etiology of the idea, benefits of forming an association, the need for incorporation into a nonprofit organization, ways to get started, a board composition and regeneration plan, bylaws and a code of ethics, and a strategic plan for growth and sustainability are discussed. The chapter concludes with a call to action.

INTRODUCTION

In 2004, a group of service-learning researchers and supporters met to discuss the future of the Annual International K–H Service-Learning

Improving Service-Learning Practice: Research on Models to Enhance Impacts, pages 215–224
Copyright © 2005 by Information Age Publishing

Research Conference. This group was specifically comprised of those individuals who have served or have pledged to serve as conference cohosts, organizations that have served as sponsors in the past, and those who have been involved in conference logistics. The question before the group was whether and how the conference and its accompanying book series should be sustained, given that a primary funder was no longer going to underwrite the costs for the conference.

The conference was launched initially by the University of California, Berkeley, and RMC Research Corporation. A group of advisors was formed to facilitate initial decision making, with the idea that the conference and book series would provide an important venue for presentation and publication of studies that related to service-learning, including research that addressed service-learning in K–12 and higher education venues.

The principles on which the conference and book series were formed acknowledged the need to raise the credibility of the field, provide a place where people could learn about and comment on each other's research, initiate another peer-reviewed forum for publication, and promote research agendas that nurtured more and better research in service-learning. Over the years, the conference has been cohosted by RMC Research Corporation and the University of California, Berkeley (2001), Vanderbilt University (2002), the University of Utah (2003), Clemson University (2004), and Michigan State University (2005). Conference attendance has ranged from about 325 to 400. The conference features keynote speakers during luncheons and dinners, featured forums with experts who have recently published important work in the field, and sessions with peer-reviewed presenters that include interactive forums, paper presentations, roundtables, and poster sessions. About 50–60 submissions are accepted for presentation each year.

The conference has also traditionally funded graduate student scholarships and a graduate student forum. Sponsored by Campus Compact and the Spencer Foundation, these activities have served to bring more young researchers to the field and connect them with others who can serve as mentors and sources of information about employment.

The cohost idea was meant to help the university that served as cohost to bring greater visibility and credibility to service-learning on its campus. Cohosting required the university to sponsor a Presidential reception, designate an individual to serve as chief programmer and co-editor of the book series, establish a Web site for advertising and paper submission and a fund for tax-deductible donations, and recruit individuals to help with logistics on the day of the conference. RMC Research provided most of the conference logistics in the form of organizing paper reviews, conducting the preregistration and registration, collecting registration fees, recruiting featured forum and keynote speakers and arranging logistics for invited speakers, organizing the reviews for the book series, co-editing the book, providing feedback for the book chapters, and technical editing for the chapters of the book.

The book series that accompanies the conference is called *Advances in Service-Learning Research*. The co-editors of the book series each year are the individuals that cohosted the past year's conference. The first two books were co-edited by Furco and Billig, the third by Billig and Eyler, the fourth by Welch and Billig, and now this volume by Root, Callahan, and Billig. The books are comprised of papers that are selected by a peer-review process from those research studies presented at the conference. The acceptance rate ranges from 15% to 22%. Cohosts also contribute chapters to the book in the form of the introduction and final chapter.

When the group convened to consider the future of the conference and book series, several issues arose that influenced the recommendations that were made. First, the group acknowledged that there were many benefits, both for the field and for its individual researchers, to having an annual conference and publication venue. Both helped researchers from higher education settings with tenure and promotion and both served an important function of information dissemination, sharing of research tools, increasing the rigor of the research, identifying important issues within the field, encouraging young researchers, and improving service-learning practice.

The group also acknowledged difficulties associated with the conference and book series. Too often the quality of submissions was low and too many were program descriptions. Too few people were involved with operations, and the conference relied on a lot of volunteer time and good will. The group felt, however, that the conference served an important function and should be continued and enhanced. To that end, several options were considered, the most popular of which was to develop a professional association.

BENEFITS OF PROFESSIONAL ASSOCIATIONS

Professional associations can perform a variety of functions. As delineated by the University of Melbourne (2005), these functions may include:

- Establishing and monitoring standards for practice;
- Advising educational institutions on curriculum development or practice;
- Producing regular publications, including books, journals, and newsletters;
- Creating and maintaining a professional library for members;

- Providing professional and/or career development activities;
- Maintaining a forum for member networking;
- Promoting the profession in the community;
- Providing career information for those seeking to enter the field; and/or
- Assisting members with career planning or job seeking.

The association can help members increase their knowledge and build on the work of others in the field, network with colleagues, and learn about new developments that may impact the work being conducted in the field. Opportunities for leadership could be provided and, with the conduct of both more rigorous and more interrelated research, establish greater credibility for the field and enhance the reputation of the field and its members. Finally, the professional association helps its members identify the potential leaders of the field, helping its members decide with whom they would like to work, and provides important opportunities for professional development and employment.

In addition, Robinson (2005) wrote that members provide the support necessary to fulfill the association's mission and goals. Members lend credibility to the profession, can exert political influence, provide important expertise, assist with outreach and validation, donate time, and promote financial stability.

To attract members, Robinson (2005) suggests that the professional association must somehow meet a perceived need and share the organization's core mission. The association should appeal to "people like me" and resonate with the member as one that has similar values and credibility.

CREATING A NONPROFIT ORGANIZATION

The process of creating a nonprofit organization can be very confusing. Fortunately, several guides are available so that many decisions can be made before needing the advice of an attorney. In the case of the International Service-Learning Research Association, it would be necessary to incorporate into a 501(c)(3) organization because the conference and book series that have already been created generate a surplus that is used to fund the next year's conference. The current initiative also tries to attract tax-deductible contributions from private and public donors and requires protection from legal liabilities.

The costs of incorporation include legal incorporation documents, annual tax returns, and other recordkeeping and reporting requirements. Filing fees and related expenses tend to cost several hundred dollars and it is wise to retain an attorney, whose incorporation fees tend to be about $1,000. With incorporation, the term "member" has a legal definition that must be followed. Members have the right to vote for election of directors and have a say in the sale of corporate assets, should any accrue. They can also decide whether the association can dissolve or can be acquired. Rights must be specified in the incorporation documents. Also, the name of the association must be approved by the Secretary of State in the state in which incorporation occurs.

The professional association, of course, would incorporate as a nonprofit, meaning it has no shareholders, pays no dividends, and uses all of its earnings to operate the organization and further its purposes.

HOW TO GET STARTED

To get started, experts recommend that the field define its membership base, develop an organizational structure, specify logistics, file for legal status and establish a financial structure, and develop strategies for attracting members and maintaining a membership base.

Membership

Membership is important to define so that the professional association can track progress, identify problems, and capitalize on opportunities. In the case of the K–H International Service-Learning Research Association (or whatever the name of the professional association may be), membership would most likely be defined as individuals who conduct or who are interested in service-learning research. This type of definition says the professional association concerns without being restrictive and thus may represent a good choice.

Decisions about membership levels will also need to be made. Robinson (2003) noted that about 80% to 90% of members will fall at some basic membership level, but the group needs to consider those who fall outside the norm. For example, should there be special membership levels for graduate students? Should undergraduate students or even K–12 students be allowed to join, and if so, at what levels? What should be done if an individual wants to present at the conference but does not want to join the association? Should there be special new member rates? Should there be rates for those who receive publications that differ from those who do not?

What are the benefits and costs of membership? Several of the advisors to the conference mentioned that they believed there should be an electronic journal and/or newsletter. Others suggested that there be opportunities for professional development or other training events.

A communications structure will need to be established, along with a campaign for recruitment and retention. Since this organization initially has very little operating capital, it will need to rely on volunteers for much of this work, and some sort of incentive or recognition program will need to be developed. In addition, it will need to establish a Web site, membership directory, and communications plan along with a budget to create and maintain the structure.

Executive Director and Board

The group that establishes the professional association will need to determine its structure. Two early decisions that must be made are the composition and function of the governing board and how leadership, most likely in the form of the board Chairperson and/or Executive Director, will be established and regenerated each year. Recruiting individuals for particular positions within the professional association should not be too difficult since the benefits are relatively obvious and the field has a tradition of "citizen volunteers."

The advisors for the conference have proposed that the initial board be comprised of those who have served as cohosts for the conference, those who have volunteered to cohost the conference in the future, representatives of major national or international service-learning research organizations or supporters, chief funders, and a graduate student representative. The board would have about 11 members, with one or two rotating off each year. The new board member would be the next person to pledge to host the conference and the "retiring" board member would be one who had already served as cohost. In addition, the graduate student would rotate each year so that many would have the chance to serve.

The group proposed that the board chairperson be the person who hosted the conference during the prior year and the chair-elect would be the person who is hosting the conference in the current year. The term of chair would be for one year. The role of the chair would be to run the board and lead the board decision-making process, edit or co-edit the book attached to the conference for that year, lead the process for identifying who will win the recognition award to be given during the next conference, and serve as one of the conference moderators. The chair-elect would undertake most of the traditional cohost roles, including selecting the papers that will comprise the program (based on the peer reviews), developing the program, inviting special speakers, hosting a Presidential reception and perhaps tours of the campus, and serving as host for the conference by welcoming participants, introducing speakers, and so forth.

The role of the board can vary and ultimately needs to be decided by the board-elect. Most likely, the board will undertake at least the following roles:

- Developing the mission and vision for the professional association;
- Creating operating principles;
- Making decisions about strategic plans, products, and services, including whether there should be a journal and, if affirmed, making decisions about how the journal can be created, who will serve as editor, processes for article selection, fundraising, and ways in which the journal can be used to advance practice in the field;
- Planning for future conferences, including selection of the venue and negotiation of contracts and costs;
- Engaging in fundraising to support the conference;
- Establishing and amending the bylaws and policies;
- Deliberating avenues for action;
- Making decisions about keynote and featured forum speakers;
- Conducting the conference evaluations; and
- Dealing proactively with emerging issues.

Decisionmakers must also decide if the professional association needs (and can afford) an Executive Director. The Executive Director can oversee and ensure smooth operations of the association and can undertake several of the roles necessary for operations, including membership recruitment, communications, journal editing, review processes, and other tasks that may be designated by the board.

If there is an Executive Director, the board will need to develop a job description, performance appraisal system, reporting plan, and contract. The board will need to identify procedures for recruitment and selection. Initially, however, it is unlikely that the International K–H Service-Learning Research Association will be able to fund this position, and thus for several years, may need to rely on volunteers to fulfill these functions.

One task the board and association must undertake is to consider how to fund and contract with a group for conference logistics. The operation of the conference and the work needed to produce the accompanying book series is labor intensive and cannot rely solely on volunteers. There are many good conference logistics organizations that can be contracted, but the group will need to plan for the contract, specify all of the actions needed, ensure that there are sufficient funds to cover costs, and develop quality assurance mechanisms. The conference logistics group most likely will be the ones to conduct the preregistration and registration processes, meet the audiovisual needs of presenters, print the programs, assemble the conference materials, and generally serve as conference troubleshooters.

Funding will need to be procured for this group. The conference profits are intended to be used for this purpose. Current profits come in the form of registration fees and royalties from book sales. Conference participants have suggested that the conference regularly sponsor preconference sessions that include indepth professional development for quantitative and qualitative research activities, information on grant writing, and opportunities for various interest groups to form research agendas, build common instruments, or develop topics that may be investigated by those considering dissertations in the field.

The board may also want to consider the formation of committees to aid in the accomplishment of the work and to gain greater buy-in from the larger membership constituency. Potential committees could include a membership committee, resource development committee, or program committee.

State laws impose certain "standards of care" for boards of nonprofits and professional associations (Duca, 1996) that include provisions such as conducting activities "in good faith" and in the best interest of the organization. As such, the board is obligated to "carefully review and evaluate information (e.g., financial statements) before making decisions; prudently manage the organization's resources; ensure the safety of the corporation's legal documents; and act in a professional manner" (Duca, 1996, p. 22). Certain actions, such as conflicts of interest, are to be strictly scrutinized. It is recommended that the association procure insurance to protect it and its board in case of any sort of issue with liability or errors in judgment.

BYLAWS AND A CODE OF ETHICS

Bylaws must be created to delineate the governing structure of the organization. As a nonprofit organization, certain bylaws will need to be established. These include, for example, bylaws about lobbying, unrelated business income that would include any income not directly related to the association's tax-exempt purpose, and fundraising activities, including what to do with non-cash donations. Bylaws should be linked to the association's core mission and be posted on the association's website. Most experts recommend that an attorney review the bylaws to ensure that they comply with federal and state laws for nonprofit organizations and with the Internal Revenue Service.

Professional associations benefit from a Code of Ethics that specifies the principles for maintaining appropriate professional conduct. In general, the code of professional ethics addresses commitments to individuals, society, and the profession. For example, as a commitment to individuals, the professional association may pledge to encourage individuals' pursuits of learning and protect the rights of access to materials of varying points of view. As a commitment to society, the professional association may establish rules that address how members should distinguish between personal and institutional or organizational points of view and engage in fair and equitable practices. As a commitment to the profession, the association might discuss ways to avoid commercial exploitation of its members, strive to improve professional skill, and/or pledge to conduct business through appropriate channels (see, for example, the Code of Professional Ethics, Association for Educational Communications and Technology, 2001).

STRATEGIC PLAN FOR GROWTH AND SUSTAINABILITY

Once the K–H International Service-Learning Research Association is established and viable, it will be important for leaders to develop a strategic plan for growth and sustainability. The plan should focus on critical issues related to prioritized goals and provide explicit direction for action. Typically these documents underscore the assumption that the future is uncertain so environmental scanning, contingency planning, and analysis of leverage points are needed. The plan should address what will happen in the next 3, 5, and 10 years and be oriented toward helping the association sustain over time. Among other issues, the strategic plan should consider how to recruit and maintain growing numbers of members, how to ascertain needs of the members and execute tactics and strategies oriented to meeting needs, and how to engage in continuous improvement. Typically the board develops the strategic plan and presents it to the membership during an annual meeting, in this case, the annual conference.

As part of the strategic plan, the board will also need to consider the formation of strategic alliances. Currently, there are many strong and growing associations and organizations in the field of service-learning. The K–H International Service-Learning Research Association may wish to consider some form of collaboration or alliance with the National Service-Learning Partnership, Campus Compact, the National Service-Learning Clearinghouse, the Corporation for National and Community Service, Youth Service America, the *Michigan Journal for Service-Learning Research*, and other organizations dedicated to service-learning or related fields.

CALL TO ACTION

The decisions about the formation of a professional association are urgently needed because the current structure can no longer be supported through the Research Network formation initiative sponsored by RMC Research. The initiative will end with the 2005 conference. While RMC Research has pledged to help for one more year, action is needed if the conference and book series are to be continued.

The conference has a strong base of participation, about 275 stable participants who have attended for at least 2 years and a total participation rate of about 350 per year. Leadership over the first 5 years of the conference has been relatively stable, and a plan for short-term viability for that period of time was developed and executed without disruption. The conference is relatively popular and clearly serves an important purpose. Both the conference and the book series are profitable.

During the 2005 conference, a Call to Action will be issued. The Call to Action will include a proposition for a professional association and an appeal for participants to volunteer for various leadership positions. The field of service-learning research needs champions and leadership, visibility, a stable revenue source, an infrastructure of support, policies to enhance sustainability and practice, and tangible evidence of its success to survive. A strong foundation has been created, but help is needed now if the conference and book series are to be sustained.

REFERENCES

Duca, D. J. (1996). *Nonprofit boards: Roles and responsibilities and performance.* New York: John Wiley & Sons, Inc.

Robinson, E, M. M. (2003). *The nonprofit membership toolkit.* San Francisco: Jossey-Bass.

University of Melbourne. (2005). Available at unimelb.edu.au.

Welliver, P. W. (Ed.). (2001). *A code of professional ethics: A guide to professional conduct n the field of Educational Communications and Technology.* Bloomington, IN: Association for Educational Communications and Technology.

ABOUT THE CONTRIBUTORS

Jeffrey B. Anderson, Ph.D., is a Professor in the Master in Teaching program at Seattle University where he teaches "Service Leadership for Social Justice," a required course for all teacher candidates. He also is the Director of the Seattle University Academic Service-Learning Faculty Fellows Program and a member of the Board of the International Center for Service-Learning in Teacher Education.

Keith Aronson is the Assistant Director of the Social Science Research Institute and Children, Youth, and Families Consortium at The Pennsylvania State University. He is interested in the methodological approaches used in service-learning research.

Shelley H. Billig, Ph.D., is Vice President of RMC Research Corporation. She directs the Carnegie Corporation of New York national study of the impact on service-learning on civic engagement as well as several other research studies involving service-learning, citizenship, and educational reform. She is Series Editor of *Advances in Service-Learning* and co-edited the first four volumes in the series. She has authored numerous articles.

Jane Callahan, Ph.D., is a Professor in the Education Department at Providence College. Her research is in the areas of service-learning and teacher education and the institutionalization process necessary for the integration of service-learning into schools and teacher education programs. She has authored a number of articles and chapters on service-learning and has presented at numerous conferences on service-learning pedagogy and the effects of service-learning on preservice and inservice

Improving Service-Learning Practice: Research on Models to Enhance Impacts, pages 225–228
Copyright © 2005 by Information Age Publishing
All rights of reproduction in any form reserved.

teachers. She is a founding member of the International Center for Service-Learning in Teacher Education at Clemson University.

Kirsten Davies is a senior majoring in Health Promotion at the University of Utah in Education and a student leader in the Bennion Center.

Peggy Fitch, Ph.D., is a Professor of Psychology at Central College in Pella, Iowa, whose research interests include service-learning, student intellectual development, and the development of intercultural competence. She has been using service-learning in her developmental psychology courses for several years.

Jean Gonsier-Gerdin, Ph.D., is an Assistant Professor in the Department of Special Education, Rehabilitation, and School Psychology in the College of Education at California State University, Sacramento. Her teaching and research interests include use of service-learning in special education teacher preparation to promote advocacy and leadership skills, inclusive education policies and practices, interprofessional collaboration, and family support.

Patreese D. Ingram is an Associate Professor of Agricultural and Extension Education at The Pennsylvania State University. Her major focus area is university–community partnerships around diversity education.

Dan Jesse, Ph.D., is a Senior Research Associate at RMC Research Corporation, Denver. His research interests include turning around low-performing schools, teacher quality, data-based decision making, school climate, and character education.

Peter Miller is an Assistant Professor in the Department of Educational Leadership and Foundations at Duquesne University in Pittsburgh. His research interests include university–community partnerships, leadership theory, and critical theory.

Devi Miron is a doctoral student in School Psychology at Tulane University. She is currently working on her dissertation project investigating college student preferences for engaging in community service.

Kimber Hershberger Mitchell has been a teacher in the State College Area School District (Pennsylvania) for 16 years. She supervises student interns from Penn State and has written curriculum that helps students understand diversity and multiculturalism.

Barbara E. Moely is Professor Emerita of Psychology at Tulane University, where she served as Director of the Office of Service Learning from 1998 to 2004 and taught numerous service-learning courses in psychology. Currently, she is Principal Investigator of a Learn and Serve America Consortium grant involving a collaboration of seven colleges and universities throughout the United States, all involved in enhancing their capacity and expertise in service-learning.

James Nolan is Professor of Curriculum and Instruction and Supervision. His research focuses on school-based supervision, coaching, and staff development intended to promote reflection, self-direction, and problem solving.

Robert D. Reason is an Assistant Professor of Education, a Research Associate in the Center for the Study of Higher Education, and Professor in Charge of the College Student Affairs Program at The Pennsylvania State University.

Diane Reed teaches elementary school in the State College Area School District (Pennsylvania). She has a special interest in teaching students about diversity.

Susan Root, Ph.D., is a Research Associate at RMC Research Corporation with extensive experience in teacher education and service-learning. She recently retired from the Education Department at Alma College in Michigan where she taught for 16 years. She was a regional director of the American Association for College Teachers of Education's National Service-Learning in Teacher Education Partnership and has conducted research on the effects of service-learning on undergraduates, prospective teachers, and K–12 students. She is currently a project manager for a national study of service-learning and civic engagement, funded by the Carnegie Corporation.

Joanna Royce-Davis currently serves as Associate Vice President for Student Life and Coordinator of the graduate program in Student Affairs located in the department of Educational Administration and Leadership at the University of the Pacific. During her tenure at Pacific, she has taught and co-taught multiple service-learning courses at both graduate and undergraduate levels. Recently, Royce-Davis and her colleagues taught a service-learning senior capstone course focusing on ethical decision making and leadership and are conducting a study to assess the effect of service-learning on students' moral development.

Marcy Schnitzer is a doctoral student in the Governance and International Affairs program at Virginia Tech, in Blacksburg, Virginia. She served as Special Programs Assistant and Assistant Director of the Service-Learning

Center at Virginia Tech and was an evaluation consultant until 2005. She is co-author of a case study in *Intergenerational Service-Learning in Gerontology: A Compendium* (1999).

Robert Shumer, Ph.D., former director of the National Service-Learning Clearinghouse at the University of Minnesota, is currently assessing higher education/K–12 partnerships in four states. Dr. Shumer teaches courses on experiential learning and service-learning, as well as on the qualitative research process, youth development, and school-to-work issues.

Susan Shumer, M.S., is the co-founder and director of the Center for Community-Based Learning at Metropolitan State University.

Nicole S. Webster is an Assistant Professor in the Department of Agricultural and Extension Education at The Pennsylvania State University. Her area of research is on service-learning and outreach in youth populations.

Marshall Welch is the Director of the Lowell Bennion Community Service Center and a faculty member at the University of Utah. He teaches an undergraduate honors course using service-learning to promote service politics and civic engagement as well as a graduate-level course on the pedagogy of service-learning.

INDEX

A

C